THE GOOD, THE BAD, AND THE

BEAUTIFUL

THE GOOD, THE BAD, AND THE
BEAUTIFUL

DISCOURSE ABOUT VALUES IN
YORUBA CULTURE

BARRY HALLEN

INDIANA UNIVERSITY PRESS
Bloomington and Indianapolis

Publication of this book is made possible in part with the
assistance of a Challenge Grant from the National Endowment for
the Humanities, a federal agency that supports research, education, and public programming in the humanities.

This book is a publication of
Indiana University Press
601 North Morton Street
Bloomington, IN 47404-3797 USA

http://www.indiana.edu/~iupress

Telephone orders 800-842-6796
Fax orders 812-855-7931
Orders by e-mail iuporder@indiana.edu

The paper used in this publication meets the minimum
requirements of American National Standard for Information
Sciences—Permanence of Paper for Printed Library Materials, ANSI
Z39.48-1984.

Manufactured in the United States of America

Library of Congress Cataloging-in-Publication Data
Hallen, Barry
The good, the bad, and the beautiful : discourse about values in
Yoruba culture / Barry Hallen.
p. cm.
Includes bibliographical references and index.
ISBN 0-253-33806-9 (cl : alk. paper) — ISBN 0-253-21416-5
(pa : alk. paper)
1. Yoruba (African people)—Intellectual life. 2. Philosophy, Yoruba.
3. Yoruba (African people)—Social life and customs. 4. Social
values—Nigeria. 5. Yoruba language.   I. Title.

DT515.45.Y67 H36 2000
305.896'333—dc21   00-039644
1 2 3 4 5 05 04 03 02 01 00

FOR
CARLA

CONTENTS

ACKNOWLEDGMENTS

Since the origins of this book date back to 1973, the list of individuals and institutions that have made it possible is a long one. But they all deserve mention here, because without their contributions and support it would never, and could never, have been written. I begin by expressing my enduring gratitude to the Central Research Committees of the University of Lagos and the Obafemi Awolowo University (formerly University of Ife), Nigeria, for affirming the credibility of the original research projects on Yoruba thought and philosophy, and for providing funding that was indispensable to their completion. Throughout the more than a decade that these projects involved, the commitment, communications skills, and scholarship demonstrated by my student, colleague, and friend Olufemi Osatuyi, the Chief Research Assistant on the project, was remarkable. He deserves the highest of accolades for his love of his native Yoruba culture and for the objectivity with which he was able to approach and to interpolate that culture on scholarly grounds. My friend, colleague, and coauthor of my previous volume on Yoruba philosophy, the late J. Olubi Sodipo, also deserves a very special mention for both supporting and participating in the project from the very first day I took up the position of Lecturer in Philosophy at the then University of Ife.

In the town of Ijan-Èkìtì, where my arm of the overall project was sited, there would of course have been no research done without the cooperation and support of Oba J. A. Obarinde, the Onijan of Ijan-Èkìtì. And most importantly I am profoundly indebted to the fifteen gentlemen, herein referred to generally as *onísègùn,* masters of medicine, herbalists, or traditional doctors, who at various points summoned up the patience, knowledge, and insight required while participating in the numerous discussions that produced the corpus of materials that I have drawn upon in order to construct this text. The days, weekends, and months spent in Ijan in their company constitute a truly memorable period of my life, when I was afforded the luxury of being taught by people in another culture how they perceived themselves, one another, and the world in which they lived.

This second book would never have been undertaken, much less finished, without my initial year (1995–96) as a resident Fellow of the W. E. B. Du Bois Institute at Harvard University, and for these succeeding four years as a nonresident Fellow of the same institution. The generous, consistent support of its director, Henry Louis Gates Jr., and of my colleague in the Department of Afro-American Studies at Harvard, Anthony Appiah, provided me with the freedom, incomparable resources, and intellectual stimulation that are the marks of truly first-rate scholars in a first-rate academic institution.

Among my fellow Fellows at the Du Bois, one who must be singled out is Mary Hamer. Mary took the time not only to read, but also to ponder and constructively criticize elements of the manuscript's form and content. Among the administrative staff of the Du Bois Institute, Richard Newman, the Fellows Officer and a serious scholar in his own right, deserves my most sincere thanks—not just for welcoming my very persistent presence, but for the friendship, warmth, and wit which he seems able to dispense in limitless quantities. Gay Mekhissi and Lisa Thompson offered comprehensive secretarial counsel and support. I cannot thank enough the two Harvard students who at one point acted simultaneously as my research assistants, Alison Moore and Ike Gbadegesin, for the hard work and serious commitments they made toward completion of my project.

Among the many colleagues who were kind enough to peruse the manuscript in draft form, several deserve very special mention. Kwasi Wiredu toiled for months to come to terms with it as a comprehensive whole, and the literally hundreds of constructive comments and suggestions he made have definitely made a significant difference to the overall quality of the 'finished' product. My friend and colleague from those Ife years, Karin Barber, also read through the manuscript with a thoroughness I did not expect and cannot recompense, except to thank her for the constructive comments that also led to significant revisions in the original text. Another old friend from the Ife days, Rowland Abiodun, took pains to make sure the Yoruba translated passages cohered with the adjoining textual commentary.

W. V. O. Quine was once again kind enough to read through portions of the text and to make several important suggestions relevant to the chapters on moral epistemology and on ethics. Mark Risjord took the time to write me several long letters by means of which he introduced me to the idea of a 'thin' notion of truth. Suzanne Blier made several interesting suggestions as to how the epistemology might be related to the aesthetics.

Others who were subjected to the manuscript, in whole or part, and were kind enough to share their reactions to it with me are 'Wande Abimbola, Monni Adams, Akinsola Akiwowo, Anthony Appiah, Eli Bentor, Hans Guggenheim, Paulin Hountondji, Sidney Kasfir, Babatunde Lawal, Nancy Neaher Maas, Wyatt MacGaffey, Valentin Mudimbe, Nkiru Nzegwu, Moses Oke, Lucius Outlaw, Tsenay Serequeberhan, Steve Stich, Zoe Strother, 'Femi Taiwo, and Olabiyi Yai. In Atlanta I am grateful to Esi Nicholl, who put me in touch with Chief Adebolu Fatunmise, who in turn introduced me to 'Femi Opaaje, a scholar of Yoruba literature and language who helped immeasurably with the collation of the Yoruba-language passages in the appendix.

Last but far from least, I offer my most sincere thanks to my editor at Indiana University Press, Dee Mortensen; to Janet Rabinowitch, Assistant Managing Director, who I know was somehow "there" for me throughout and who encouraged me to submit the manuscript in the first place; and to Jane Lyle, the Managing Editor, and Kendra Boileau Stokes, Assistant Managing Editor, who helped guide me through the final revisions. David E. Anderson, my copyeditor, made numerous suggestions that resulted in a final text that is both rhetorically and orthographically refined.

A NOTE ON TRANSLATION

A text such as this, which purports to discuss the abstract ideas of one culture (Yoruba) with the language of another (English), is well advised to say something explicit about the issues involved in translations between potentially radically different language cultures. Many of these theoretical and methodological questions, and the more practical problems that follow from them, are discussed in detail in my previous book on Yoruba thought/philosophy, coauthored with J. Olubi Sodipo, *Knowledge, Belief, and Witchcraft: Analytic Experiments in African Philosophy* (see especially chapter 1, "Indeterminacy and the Translation of Alien Behavior," and the afterword to the 1997 edition, "Indeterminacy, Ethnophilosophy, Linguistic Philosophy, African Philosophy").

In this text I have relied upon that most venerable of Yoruba-language dictionaries, R. C. Abraham's *Dictionary of Modern Yoruba,* as my standard source for the English-language meanings of Yoruba-language terms. Whenever readers encounter the acronym "etm" (borrowed from the work of W. V. O. Quine and used as an abbreviation for "established translation manual") followed by a page reference, this is the source from which the English-language equivalent has been derived. Readers who do not have access to a copy of Abraham and who would like to obtain a copy of a Yoruba-English/English-Yoruba dictionary that is in print are referred to Yai (1994).

The Yoruba term which occurs most frequently in my text is "*oníṣè-gùn,*"* and since it is a professional title of the members of that culture with whom I worked most closely while doing my research and I could

---

*Its phonetic pronunciation may be rendered as "oh-knee-shay-gune" (this last syllable to rhyme with the English-language "dune").

find no easy equivalent for it in any dictionary, I have retained the Yoruba original throughout. But these do happen to be the same gentlemen who were stigmatized, long ago, with the title of "witch doctors" and have since been variously dubbed "herbalists," "traditional doctors," "native doctors," "sorcerers," "medicine men," and so forth.

A glossary of basic and important Yoruba terminology is included, as well as an appendix of the numbered translated passages in the original Yoruba. Finally, since pronouns in Yoruba are *not* gendered, I have used gender-neutral terminology in all instances where context did not render it inappropriate.

THE GOOD, THE BAD, AND THE

BEAUTIFUL

1

ORDINARY LANGUAGE AND AFRICAN PHILOSOPHY

One of the convictions underlying much of this book is that the systematic analysis of ordinary, everyday language usage in non-Western, particularly African, cultures can prove to be of fundamental philosophical value. The methodological inspiration for this kind of analysis derives, most obviously, from ordinary language philosophy as enunciated by anglophone philosophers during the mid–twentieth century. In my own case, how this inspiration came to be transferred to sub-Saharan West Africa is a story that perhaps deserves telling in some detail.

In 1970 when I first arrived in Nigeria, of the six federal universities three had departments of philosophy (sometimes paired with religion and religious studies). The existent philosophy syllabi were for the most part explicitly articulated in the British analytic tradition. This was understandable in a country that until recently had been a British colony for roughly sixty years, where universities as components of a 'modern' educational system had been inaugurated under colonial auspices, and in an internationally academic discipline in which, apart from phenomenology, the anglophone analytic tradition was, even if beginning to ebb, still supreme.

For African students the consequences of such a teaching program were not felicitous. De facto philosophy was presented as an enterprise that was one of the more exclusive domains of Western culture. Its topics and problems were therefore of non-African inspiration, even if another message of the teaching program was that they were things which should have been and should be of interest and concern to all "rational" human beings, wherever they happened to be. Consequently the discipline was perceived and received by students as something that was culturally alien. It became just one more odd subject in which they had to pass examinations in order to obtain the "paper qualifications" that marked successful acquisition of a 'modern' education. Even more worrisome was the tacit implication, most obvious by the absence of African course content, that Africa's indigenous cultural heritage was philosophically insignificant. In other words, there had been no philosophers or philosophy in precolonial Africa because its modest intellectual priorities had not encouraged a sufficient level of intellectual development. In fact, in some teaching programs the preferred pedagogical use of Africa's supposed indigenous patterns of reasoning was to employ them as illustrations of how *not* to reason.

Fortunately I had no disciplinary background in African studies. At the time I was a graduate student in the United States, I doubt that there was a mainstream philosophy department in which it would have been possible to obtain one. If I had such a background, it most probably would have been obtained via training in one of the social sciences (ethnography, anthropology), in which case I could have ended up a social scientist in philosopher's clothes. So I use the word "fortunately" to acknowledge explicitly my initial professional incompetence for intercultural studies and to indicate how it happened that I had no choice but to be thrown back upon the methodological resources of my mother discipline.

What it meant to behave in a rational manner, and to have an intellect that could reason in a rational manner, had long been issues of concern to Western philosophy. When I expressed an interest in reading comparative studies about African cultures, I was referred to a wide variety of primarily anthropological monographs and to comparative, analytically synoptic studies based upon such monographs (Abraham 1962; Banton 1966; Beattie 1966a; Evans-Pritchard 1937; Forde 1954; Jahn 1961; Mbiti 1970; Radin 1927; Tempels 1959; Turner 1967). From these I soon discovered that anthropology itself was anything but a unanimous discipline when it came to discussions of the African intellect and of rationality in the African context. It offered a diverse spectrum of views on these subjects, ranging from those who argued that African conceptual systems were best interpreted as genuinely rational attempts to explain, predict, and control human experience (Evans-Pritchard 1937; Horton 1967), to those who continued to defend a relatively 'primitive' view of the African mentality (Beattie 1966a). According to the latter, neither the rational nor the intellectual had reached a noteworthy level of development in such cultures. Their beliefs about the world were therefore formulated primarily on an emotive or symbolic (ritualistic, preverbal) basis—mythical stories or patently false causal explanations (even if devoutly believed) that could be turned to for reassurance in important or difficult situations (Beattie 1966a, chap. 5).

One conclusion almost all such studies shared was that the indigenous African intellect was somehow qualitatively different from its generalized Western counterpart. The variety of adjectives used to type or to distinguish it in this regard themselves seemed to share something in common: uncritical or precritical, unreflective or pre-reflective, proto-rational, and proto-scientific. I appreciate that it can be both difficult and dangerous to hazard generalizations about these terms' meanings as used by a fairly wide variety of fieldworkers. Nevertheless that "common" element to which I refer seemed to involve a claim to the effect that, while the beliefs of such cultures could be appreciated as the product of rudimentary reason employed by people to explain, predict, and control their environment, it was not reason that had identified objective "truth" as an end, an aim, to be sought in its own right. Hence beliefs formulated at a certain point in time did come to be regarded as "true," but this meant that they were then taught and enforced as a form of dogma, as absolutes that were to be preserved and defended *against* criticism rather than to be refined, revised, or even rejected when and if proven false by further experience.

What both intrigued and challenged me, as a student of philosophy, about these characterizations of African rationality was that they were being made by nonphilosophers. Few evidenced familiarity with the innumerable resources on the subject provided by my discipline, resources that I had been made to understand were fundamental to serious discussion of this comparatively rarified topic. I therefore wanted to find a way to communicate with this 'different' form of rationality, to experience it directly as a philosopher. When it appeared that might involve going outside of my university classrooms (in order to encounter African "thought" firsthand), I was cautioned by well-meaning academic colleagues that I had no professional training or qualifications to undertake this kind of (comparatively empirical and intercultural) research. On that point, at least, it was difficult not to agree with them.

It was the timid inquiry of a student about whether there ever could or would be a course on African philosophy in our department that provided me with the opportunity that eventually produced a solution to my predicament. If I could not reach indigenous African society outside the classroom directly on my own, I at least could try to communicate with it indirectly via my students. Many, I already knew, came from small towns (or 'villages') with families (nuclear and extended) that they described as "traditional." Internal departmental policies and politics at that time made even the idea of a philosophy course having to do with indige-

nous African "thought" a problematic undertaking. But I was able to secure permission to organize a voluntary, noncredit study group that met
in my office one evening a week. I did this by posting a notice on the
departmental bulletin board outlining very generally the study group's
aims and asking students who might be interested to write their names
below. Through very informal individual interviews with those who had
expressed interest, a core group of nine participants (mostly second- and
third-year students) was established.

Our first few meetings were purely organizational: to determine how
much effort full-time students were willing to expend for an undertaking
that could offer them no credit toward their degree; how university students should go about collecting reliable information about their native
cultures; and to select a topic that could be relevant both to academic
philosophy and to the cultural heritages of the various ethnic groups with
which they would be concerned. The consensus reached with regards to
each of these concerns was the following: (1) students would use the
longer holiday periods (Christmas, semester break), when they had the
opportunity to travel home, to 'interview' select elders; (2) each student
would produce one essay per semester inclusive of such interviews, and
at each meeting of the study group a student would present the results of
his research; and (3) the topic would be the equivalent of the English-
language "person." Their enquiries were to target what the components
or elements of the "person" were thought to be (as in the English-language
"body," "soul," "mind").

From the beginning the students' enthusiasm was remarkable, and my
memories of that study-group experience are still very positive. All of the
participants presented credible essays, and its Yoruba, Ibgo, Edo, and Tiv[1]
members were genuinely intrigued by both the common and divergent
opinions their various cultures had to offer on the subject. The material
provided by one student, in particular, which appeared more acute, intelligent, and systematic than that of the others, first drew my special attention to my then and future student, graduate student, research assistant,
colleague, and friend—Olufemi L. Osatuyi. 'Femi, as he prefers to be
called, had as great an intellectual interest in and respect for the heritage
of his native Yoruba culture as he did for the contents of the university
curriculum. I began to discuss with him my 'dream' of doing some form
of intellectual 'fieldwork' from a philosophical perspective. I asked
whether it might be possible for me to undertake such an enterprise in his

---

1. Four of the original participants whom I particularly remember were C. E. Achor-
Odoemene, Innocent Modo, C. O. L. Osatuyi, and W. I. Uttah.

home town, using sources comparable to those he had been consulting for the study group. The aim, I emphasized, was to introduce some of this material into the Nigerian university curriculum so that the "problems" and "topics" of academic philosophy could become more relevant to a Nigerian student body. 'Femi said he would make the appropriate enquiries on his next trip home.

It was almost precisely at this point that I had the very good fortune to make the acquaintance and gain the counsel of Professor Dorothy Emmet. A former student of Whitehead's, Emeritus Professor of Philosophy at the University of Manchester, England, and advisor to the University of Ibadan, Nigeria, on the feasibility of establishing a philosophy department in Nigeria's oldest university, Dorothy emphatically supported my rather vague notions of engaging in some sort of philosophical dialogue with Nigerian culture(s). I cannot emphasize enough how important it was to me at that point to receive this kind of support from a distinguished, mainstream figure in my discipline. Over the succeeding decades Dorothy's consistent advice and counsel, either through correspondence or during regular visits to Cambridge, has been a fundamental and formative influence on the research project.

In due course 'Femi informed me that I was welcome to visit his town and to discuss my interests face-to-face with the relevant people there. He agreed to accompany me, and, in effect, from that moment we both became part of a research project that had yet to be officially sanctioned as such. The town (village) involved was Ijan, approximately twenty kilometers east of Adó in the Èkìtì region of Yorubaland. When I arrived in Ijan, 'Femi introduced me to his father and then took me to the homes of several other distinguished gentlemen. Most of them, I was informed, were onísègùn—a Yoruba term which may be translated literally as "masters of medicine," herbalists, or (today) alternative medical doctors. If it was Yoruba culture in which I was primarily interested, I was informed that an informal consensus of the local population was that these gentlemen represented some of the most reliably informed. I was therefore advised to work with them, providing I could convince them that the project was worthy of their participation.

What had I come to Ijan for? What did I want? These were questions I was asked by each of the half-dozen onísègùn to whom I was then introduced. Explaining what I was already employed to do in Nigeria proved difficult enough. In university circles it is a commonplace generalization that philosophy is unusually difficult to define in summary form to undergraduate students. What was I to do with the onísègùn? I eventually worked it out so that I introduced myself as someone who taught (not gave birth to!) received 'wisdom' (ogbón, in Yoruba). I then introduced the theme that I was unhappy with the fact that most of the 'wisdom' being taught in my subject was of Western origin. I therefore hoped to introduce some Nigerian, Yoruba, "wisdom" into the department's teaching program. But I was a foreigner, an alien, largely ignorant of Nigerian culture. Would they help me to learn something about it from their informed viewpoints so that it too could then be taught as philosophy in the university?

Although most of the onísègùn at that point agreed that the project sounded like a worthy one and said they would cooperate, it was only some years later that I learned many also had a more personal, if complementary, motive for giving a positive response, one which related to their adolescent sons and daughters. Although the onísègùn had undergone no formal or "modern" education, and although none of them spoke English, despite whatever financial sacrifices were required they were determined that their children receive this kind of education. Yet children who underwent 'modern' schooling were taught that people who could not read or write and who came from a "traditional" background were comparatively uneducated and therefore ignorant. Consequently the respect they previously had for their parents (more specifically for fathers who happened to be onísègùn) diminished while domestic disciplinary problems increased. English was sometimes used deliberately by restless adolescents as a weapon of social exclusion, a 'secret' language, that excluded 'illiterate' elders from their discourse.

At least some of the onísègùn thought that if a university 'doctor' was seen to approach them "as if" a student, as someone who hoped to learn from them, who said that their knowledge was so important that it needed to be included in the university curriculum in a department that taught 'wisdom'—all of this might help to influence their children's attitudes toward a cultural heritage they were growing to disdain. But in what aspects or elements of their 'wisdom', their culture, was I particularly interested? This was a question that occupied my mind during any number of sleepless nights. And this is where I had to confront directly the issue of the nature of the African intellect. Was I there to collect mini-encyclopedias of beliefs about select, philosophically relevant topics? Beliefs presented without good reasons for them would do nothing to challenge the aforementioned unflattering stereotype of the African mentality. Coming from a philosophical background I was predisposed to think in terms of certain *fields* of enquiry, such as epistemology (or the theory of knowledge) and ethics (or morality). But, again, how was I to approach these as topics in Yoruba culture via the onísègùn?

My inadequate fluency in speaking the Yoruba language, rather than an embarrassment, became my methodological 'key'. I had completed a proficiency course in the language in Nigeria, but that had been for reading rather than for speaking. Reverting to dim memories of the founder of ordinary language philosophy, J. L. Austin (1961, 1962a), and his associates at Oxford University, I began to ask the onísègùn to help me to understand how one should speak the language correctly—why it was appropriate to use specific terms in Yoruba discourse in some circumstances and not appropriate in others—in other words, to make explicit the criteria governing the correct usage of select vocabulary.

Of course, 'Femi was with me throughout all of this. Since he was supremely fluent in the Yoruba language, these were not the sort of questions he could have asked and expected to have been taken seriously. But with me there as the persistent, dim-witted, and extraordinarily slow-learning initiator of and participant in these discussions, things seemed to go very smoothly indeed. For the onísègùn apparently enjoyed explaining and analyzing their language in detail. Needless to say, this was not something they normally spent their leisure afternoons doing. But the knowledge they extended to me so that I might appreciate their language's (and thereby culture's) viewpoints on certain subjects (via the relevant fields of discourse) demonstrated that they could be extraordinarily patient and, indeed, gifted educators.

I might add here that some commentators, perfectly understandably, have misunderstood my reasons for working with a group of onísègùn. They have assumed that the type of information I was after must have concerned professional "secrets" relating to herbal or alternative medicine in Yoruba culture, and whatever specialized knowledge or viewpoints on the human condition that might involve. Although it did prove to be the case that, as mutual trust and friendships between us grew, individual onísègùn did sometimes volunteer such information, my original and ongoing reason for soliciting their opinions was for information about correct language usage in everyday discourse. Some may question whether and why onísègùn should be regarded as specially authoritative sources for this kind of information. My response to this is twofold: the local population did regard them as more knowledgeable about the culture generally; and ordinary language *is* ordinary language—the accounts of it rendered here can always be confirmed, amended, or challenged by other researchers working with different sources. That is how scholarship should proceed.

I did channel the discussions so that, for example, the vocabulary and usage I found particularly troubling just 'happened' to correspond to the terminology with which philosophers who favored the linguistic approach were concerned when discussing epistemology ("knowledge," "belief," "truth") or ethics. But it was the work involved in putting these tape-recorded discussions into written and translated form that proved truly monumental. It's easy enough to put a tape into a machine some-where in Africa and record a conversation in an African language. I empa-thize deeply with colleagues in African studies who find they have accu-mulated whole libraries of such tapes for which there was never then adequate time, opportunity, or resources to transcribe and to translate. One of the benefits of my remaining in Africa for so many years and of having a gifted chief research assistant like 'Femi Osatuyi was that there was ample time and opportunity to devote to this aspect of the project.

As I have indicated, the issue of the character of Africa's indigenous intellectual heritage has been a vexing one. The typing of African "sys-tems of thought" as essentially "emotive," "mythic," or "symbolic"—as qualitatively distinct from those of the "rational" West—has been one source of this controversy. But what precise components or elements of such systems is it that scholars have in mind when they arrive at this con-clusion? I suspect that it is not ordinary, everyday language. For this kind of discourse *has* to be instrumental and pragmatic in cross-cultural terms (regardless of how bizarre some of its idioms may seem), or else it would lose its raison d'être and perhaps undermine the physical survival of the population concerned.

The type of discourse these scholars seem to have in mind is what is frequently referred to as the *theoretical,* what the philosopher W. V. O. Quine prefers to call the standing sentences of a natural language (Hallen and Sodipo 1986/1997; Quine 1960). Theoretical (or in some philo-sophical texts "metaphysical") discourse is what a people have recourse to when in need of an explanation or prediction that exceeds (some might say "transcends") the level of ordinary language. Whether it involves the influence of gods, (dead) ancestors, gravity, or the proverbial "germ," the kinds of *abstract* forces or entities involved and the patterns of reasoning used to justify their existence and introduction as causal factors have been treated by scholars as key indices of a culture's intellectual character.

Why is it that the nature of ordinary language has been relatively ignored by these comparative analyses? Is it because there is a general consensus on the part of all the disciplines concerned with such studies that ordinary language in Africa *is* fundamentally instrumental and prag-matic—and therefore, one might dare say, rational—in character? There-fore it becomes noncontroversial in its own right? I think this is probably the case. The question then becomes how or why a people who are lin-guistically "pragmatic" or "commonsensical" on the everyday level make such a categorically distinctive conceptual 'leap' when it comes to the theoretical? Why or how do they have recourse to talk of things like an-cestors and other spiritual forces when causal factors of a more highly abstract or theoretical character become involved? Some scholars have explained this difference as resulting from the absence of an articulated scientific tradition (including an intellectual tradition that emphasizes the importance of impartial *empirical* observation and testing) or as due to the absence of the specialized study and value of logic (deductive and inductive reasoning) as a tool of thought (Gellner 1974).

While I was putting together the ensuing text about Yoruba ethical and aesthetic discourse I found myself thinking of the expository format it was taking on as a presentation that deliberately frames and interprets this material so as to highlight dimensions to it that are pronouncedly, emphatically, empirical and rational in more or less conventionally "Western" terms. In other words, the material as presented here, whether viewed from a (supposedly) Yoruba or Western perspective, makes "good sense" when judged in terms of the reasons provided and the evidence and experience to which (empirical) appeal is made.

I suppose I could invoke the current postmodern sentiments being expressed by some contemporary intercultural scholars (Appiah 1992) and say that if this is the way I choose to tell a 'story' about Yoruba moral and aesthetic values, then I am fully entitled to do so (as long as I make such an admission). But I would prefer to avoid that kind of *deconstructive* refuge. What is important in a study such as this is to be *careful*—to try not to misrepresent African meanings and attitudes. The issue with which I was therefore compelled to come to terms is whether the undeniable emphases this narrative places upon reasoning and empirical evidence represent ways in which the *oníṣègùn* thought and spoke, or whether these elements have become disproportionately exaggerated due to selective quotation, leading remarks (during discussions with them), and my own cultural (Western) and professional (philosophical) persuasions. Perhaps I have unwittingly transformed a qualitatively different form of intellect into something I find familiar and therefore with which I can feel more comfortable.

A self-reflexive query similar to this occurs in the text of *Knowledge, Belief, and Witchcraft: Analytic Experiments in African Philosophy,* my previous book on the epistemological ramifications of ordinary-language discourse in Yoruba culture.[2] This query comes from a passage where we were anticipating postpublication critical responses to the form of that text. At that time our defense was as follows:

> Surely it is important to appreciate the perspectives the Yoruba themselves take upon what they are doing, particularly when we discover a

---

2. Hereafter referred to by the acronym *KBW.* Coauthored with J. Olubi Sodipo and published by Ethnographica Ltd., London, in 1986, and by Stanford University Press in 1997.

much greater and more explicit emphasis on elements like the hypothetical, the empirical and the critical than had heretofore been imagined.

In the quoted passages the *onísègùn* introduce numerous concrete
examples (including many that obviously did happen or are happening
in the room where the discussion is taking place). These are still in the
form of words, but they are about as close as one can get to picturing
actions with them. What is more important, however, is that they take
the accounts of the *onísègùn* well beyond the realm of [elementary]
epistemological or methodological platitudes. (*KBW*, p. 75)

To diverge, briefly but relevantly, from the discussion of whether this
text deserves to be taken as representative of the importance assigned to
the rational and the empirical in Yoruba ordinary-language discourse, the
approach that is taken to ordinary language by this project is itself rather
unusual and therefore worthy of more extensive discussion and justification. The most direct and immediate way for the philosopher of language
to observe and to record ordinary discourse in whatever culture is concerned would be to *listen* to how people who use that language talk to
one another in everyday situations. But for the most part that was not the
case in my discussions with the *onísègùn.* For I was relying upon *them*
to *explain* to *me* how people in everyday Yoruba life used the relevant
terms—or, to take it even one step further, how people *should* use the
terms if they were using the language correctly. (There are also incidents
of 'direct' or 'immediate' analysis of the *onísègùn*'s own usage of terminology as well, as evidenced by the criteria extrapolated from their remarks about firsthand-secondhand knowledge of another person's moral
character in chapter 4.)

I do not see this as introducing a controversial or even new precedent
into the philosophical canon of ordinary language.[3] The precedent was
set, long ago, by J. L. Austin and his circle of discussants when they met
on Saturday mornings at Oxford. Let me first quote their view on the point
of doing the philosophical analysis of ordinary language:

It is, at the very least, highly unlikely that a natural language should be
as it is . . . for no particular reasons; . . . where ordinary speech *does*
make a verbal distinction it is at least highly probable that there is a
distinction to be made, that the difference of expression corresponds to
some difference in the cases. . . . We have in our language, as it were
ready-made, an enormous stock of discriminations, and to take this stock

---

3. Readers who are unschooled in technical philosophy may find it helpful to read (or, at
least, to reread) this section after becoming familiar with the main body of the text.

> seriously—to examine what it contains—seems, as a precept of method, to be merely good sense. (Warnock 1969, pp. 18–19)

Then, their discussions reveal a philosophical approach to ordinary language that may engage a *plurality* of contributors:

> Philosophy could be, and should be, a co-operative pursuit . . . for many independent but co-ordinated brains. . . .
> It is relevant to mention here Austin's "Saturday mornings"—weekly meetings . . . normally lasting from two to three hours. . . . Attendance (by invitation) was formally restricted . . . to persons judged likely to be in sympathy with the matters in hand. A field of enquiry—for example, in one term [semester] the concept of a *rule*—was systematically divided into areas, and each area assigned to some one of those present for investigation (there were about ten in all). Results were to be fairly formally reported, and records kept in writing. (Warnock 1969, pp. 12–14)

It is important to note that ordinary language usage itself may not always be obviously self-explanatory of its own meanings. For example, it required Austin's elevated insights into the nature of certain forms of expression to identify and explicate the notion of "performative utterance" (Austin 1962a).

To return to the matter of rational and empirical content, and to further relate it to the relationship between ordinary or everyday discourse and theoretical discourse, one further contribution this book hopefully makes in this regard is to better illustrate the empirical concomitants to a selection of Yoruba theoretical (frequently classified as "religious") concepts and beliefs. How, for example, one reconciles the *experience* of misfortune with the *abstract notion* of an unalterable destiny (see chapter 3). Or how a belief system can accommodate feelings of being dissatisfied with one's lot in life, apparently as determined by one's destiny, and yet accept as fact that one may be able to do something about it (also in chapter 3). The point is that these issues become more than convoluted examples of cultural rationalizing, of reinterpreting empirical experience so that it can be reconciled with and to a theoretical belief. What such examples demonstrate is that the empirical dimension to the theoretical is as important a defining element of any 'abstract' belief.

As this narrative progresses another issue that must be considered is how such apparently rational and empirical elements in Yoruba culture are related to the relatively "spiritual" beliefs that Western scientism would like to characterize as superstitions. But this cannot be sufficient reason to underrate or to ignore the fact that on the level of everyday experience Yoruba discourse in its own right reveals itself to be conventionally commonsensical, rational, and empirical. In this regard, I hope the compiled remarks of the *onísègùn* will 'speak' for themselves. For the semantic and experiential networks that are about to emerge, as fundamentally interwoven, are what can make the philosophical ramifications of every natural language and language culture coherent, consistent, important, and unique.

2

MORAL
EPISTEMOLOGY

My chosen pathway into Yoruba moral discourse will be an epistemological one. If one synonym for "epistemology" is the "theory of knowledge," then the process by which people claim to "know" someone's moral character becomes an essential prerequisite to whatever moral values they thereafter attribute to that person (selfish, honorable, unreliable). *KBW* undertook the systematic study of Yoruba epistemological discourse. Appreciating the concerns of philosophical epistemology is facilitated if we begin from a typically everyday perspective. During the course of a lifetime an enormous amount of information is put at the disposal of the average person—via family and friends, education, the media. The task of distinguishing between information that is more or less reliable, between the true, the possibly true or untrue (i.e., indeterminate), and the false is one that concerns all of us.

In English-language culture information that is considered most reliable is labeled "knowledge" and described as "true." By linguistic convention, what one is said to "know" is "true." Information that is considered less reliable, of which one cannot be certain, is labeled "belief." By convention, information that falls within this category need not be true. On the other hand, neither is it false. Beliefs and believing consist of things people can neither prove nor disprove with certainty. People may one day discover that something they believed was in fact true, or false. (Information that was thought to be knowledge and labeled "true" may also turn out to be false, of course. Convention requires that people then admit that originally they made a mistake in assessing the epistemological status of that information.)

In Yoruba-language culture the two most prominent categories for classifying or rating information, akin to the English-language "knowledge" and "belief," are "*ìmọ̀*" and "*ìgbàgbọ́*."[1] At this preliminary point the word "akin" is used deliberately, signifying "comparable to" but not "the same as." When the meanings of these two terms first began to be analyzed by Western scholars, the process resulted in unflattering comparisons. For example, A. B. Ellis (perfectly correctly) identified the components of "*gbàgbọ́*" and their equivalents in English-language translation as "*gbà*" (to accept) and "*gbọ́*" (to listen) (1974, pp. 305–402). But, rather than proceeding to outline the criteria that governed their usage and thereby giving some idea of how the Yoruba *applied* these verbs to specific pieces of information, Ellis undertook etymological analyses of their supposed semantic 'roots' that brought their latent meanings more in line with the paradigm of a primitive Africa.

Both "*gbà*" and "*gbọ́*" were said to derive from the sounds "to indicate violence, exertion, whence to heat, beat to breaking, break, shatter, destroy, kill, dig, scrub, pierce. Also to make a loud sound, as to yell, cry out, crow, crash, and to produce by exertion, to make, commit, do" (Ellis 1974, p. 387). What 'loaded' semantic antecedents from which to derive cultural notions of listening and agreeing! The sad fact of the matter seems to have been that there was little interest in attempting to specify the criteria governing the application of epistemological vocabulary in African languages because of a presumption that sub-Saharan thought generally rated so low on the scale of universal rationality—was so lamentably unsystematic—that any such study would not be worth the effort.[2]

In Western epistemological theory the most problematic and controversial subcategory of information is what has come to be known as propositional knowledge.[3] Generally this is associated with information in written or oral propositional (sentential) form that is supposed to be knowledge and therefore true, but which the individual recipient is in no position to test or to verify. When one reflects upon what a member of Western society may 'learn' in the course of a lifetime, it becomes clear

---

1. The verb forms are "*mọ̀*" and "*gbàgbọ́*."

2. As evidenced by the following excerpt: "for man, however low he may be in the scale of civilisation, is always desirous of knowing the reasons for everything, and the West African negro in particular is of a very inquisitive turn of mind. Then, in order to satisfy the natural desire to know who the gods were and whence they came, the myths we have already recounted grew up, and the numerous discrepancies in them appear to show that the process was comparatively recent. It looks as if the stories had not yet had sufficient time to become generally known in a commonly accepted version" (Ellis 1974, pp. 86–87).

3. Representative is the introduction to Moser and vander Nat (1995), most of which is devoted to the issue of propositional knowledge.

that most people's "knowledge" consists of information they will never ever be in a position to confirm in a firsthand or direct manner. What they 'find out' from a history book, 'see' via the evening news on television, or 'confirm' about a natural law on the basis of one elementary experiment in a high school physics laboratory—all could be (and sometimes are!) subject to error, distortion, or outright fabrication.

Propositional knowledge is therefore generally characterized as secondhand, as information that cannot be tested or proven in a decisive manner by most people and therefore has to be accepted as true because it 'agrees' with common sense or because it 'corresponds' to or 'coheres' with the very limited amount of information that people are able to test and confirm in a firsthand or direct manner. Exactly how this coherence or correspondence is to be defined and ascertained is still a subject of endless wrangling in (Western) epistemological theory. What is relevant to this discussion is that this wrangling is evidence of the intellectual concern and discomfort (in academic parlance it becomes one of the "problems" of philosophy) on the part of (Western) philosophers about the weak evidential basis of so much of the information that people in that culture are conditioned to regard as knowledge, as true.

The distinction made in Yoruba-language culture between "ìmò̩" (putative "knowledge") and "ìgbàgbó̩" (putative "belief") reflects a similar concern about the evidential status of firsthand versus secondhand information. Persons are said to "mò̩" (to "know") or to have "ìmò̩" ("knowledge") only of experience they have witnessed in a firsthand or personal manner. The example most frequently cited by discussants, virtually as a paradigm, is visual perception of a scene or an event as it is taking place. "Ìmò̩" is said to apply to sensory perception generally, even if what may be experienced directly by touch is more limited than is the case with perception. "Ìmò̩" implies a good deal more than mere sensation, of course. Perception implies cognition as well, meaning that persons concerned must comprehend that and what they are experiencing.

The terms "òótó̩" and "òtító̩"[4] are associated with "ìmò̩" in certain

---

4. The etm (493) treats "òótó̩" as a straightforward equivalent of the English-language "truth," as it also does with "ìgbàgbó̩" and "gbàgbó̩" (233) and the English-language "belief" and "believe." Both are examples of the understandably "loose" translation equivalences that are a necessary evil for the conventional, cross-cultural translation of everyday affairs, and that cannot afford to take account of all semantic differences, even if they happen to be more than nuances. These are the kinds of approximate translations Quine has in mind when he refers to the "Procrustean variety" in his foreword to the Stanford University Press edition of KBW.

respects that parallel the manner in which "true" and "truth" are paired with "know" and "knowledge" in the English language. In English "truth" is principally a property of propositional knowledge, of statements human beings make about something, while in Yoruba "òótọ́" may be a property of both propositions and certain forms of experience. The similarities and differences in meanings these terms share, and their consequences for cognition generally, are discussed at greater length below.

The noun "ìgbàgbọ́" (and its verb form "gbàgbọ́") does in fact arise from the conflation of "gbà" with "gbọ́." The two components are themselves verbs, the former conventionally translated into English as "received" or "agreed to" (etm 229), and the latter as "heard" or "understood" (etm 248). Yoruba linguistic conventions suggest that treating this complex term as a synthesis of the English-language "understood" (in the sense of cognitive comprehension) and of "agreed to" (in the sense of affirming or accepting the new information one now comprehends as part of one's own store of secondhand information) is perhaps the best way to render its core meaning. Ìgbàgbọ́ encompasses what one is not able 'to see' for oneself or to experience in a direct, firsthand manner. For the most part this involves things we are told about or informed of—this is the most conventional sense of "information"—by others.

What makes it different from the English-language "believe" and "belief" is that ìgbàgbọ́ applies to everything that may be construed as secondhand information. This would apply to most of what in English-language culture is regarded as propositional knowledge: the things one is taught in the course of a formal education, what one learns from books, from other people, and, of particular interest in the special case of the Yoruba, from oral traditions. Whereas English-language culture decrees that propositional or secondhand information, since classified as "knowledge," should be accepted as true, Yoruba usage is equally insistent that, since classified as ìgbàgbọ́ (putative "belief"), it can only be accepted as possible (ó ṣe é ṣe).[5]

The cross-cultural ramifications of these differing viewpoints on the truth status of propositional or secondhand knowledge are worth considering. Yoruba-language speakers would likely regard members of English-language culture, who are willing to assign so much certainty to and put so much trust in information that they can never test or verify, as dangerously naive and perhaps even ignorant. Whereas members of English-language culture might criticize their Yoruba counterparts' identification of optimal knowledge with "you can only know what you can see" as in-

---

5. For "ó ṣe é ṣe" and "kò ṣe é ṣe" ("possible" and "impossible") see KBW, pp. 62, 69.

dicative of a people who have yet to discover the benefits of institutional-
ized knowledge via science and formal education.

As we continue to follow the sometimes parallel, sometimes divergent, criteria of these two cognitive systems, it will be suggested that both
of these criticisms are mistaken—mistaken because they depend upon
arguing for the truth or falsity of an entire cognitive system on the basis
of how it deals with a single issue, in this case the epistemological status
of propositional or secondhand information. The criteria that define the
respective extents of and the interrelations between ìmọ̀ and ìgbàgbọ́ stip-
ulate that any experience or information which is not firsthand, personal,
and direct must by definition fall under the heading of ìgbàgbọ́. The sense
of ìgbàgbọ́ may therefore be paraphrased as "comprehending, and decid-
ing to accept as possible (as ó ṣe é ṣe rather than as òótọ́ or 'true'), information that one receives in a secondhand manner." Ìmọ̀ (firsthand experience) and ìgbàgbọ́ (information gained on the basis of secondhand
experience) together exhaust all of the information that human beings
have at their disposal. If and when my ìmọ̀ is challenged by other persons
who have not undergone a similar firsthand experience and who therefore doubt what I say I actually saw happen, the best way to convince
them would be to arrange for some kind of test whereby they will be able
to see the thing happen for themselves.[6]

If I cannot arrange for this kind of direct testing, the next best I can do
is to ask any others who may have personally witnessed my own or a
similar experience to come forward and testify. In this case my firsthand
experience cannot become the challengers' own (ìmọ̀), but if they are
influenced by the combined testimony, they may decide to believe me or
us and accept the information on a secondhand basis, as ìgbàgbọ́. A
simple example may serve to clarify things. If I claim I have seen for myself (ìmọ̀) that a certain friend drives a specific make and model of car and
another friend challenges my claim, the best way to resolve the dispute is
to visit the friend and see (ìmọ̀) what kind of car she actually has. If the
friend lives a thousand miles away, a more practical solution would be to
ask other mutual friends who have seen (ìmọ̀) the car themselves to tell
us (ìgbàgbọ́) what kind it is, or perhaps to telephone my friend direct and
ask her to tell us (ìgbàgbọ́) what kind of car she is driving.[7]

---

6. One expression used regularly by the oníṣègùn for testing was dánwò ("try to do"; etm
142 as dọ́nwò).

7. Speaking to her directly by telephone still would not be ìmọ̀ about the car because one
is not actually seeing it. One is only hearing a voice, another form of testimony, albeit a
particularly relevant one given the circumstances.

If and when my *ìgbàgbọ́* is challenged by another person, again the best solution would be to arrange some form of empirical test. In this case since this is information I myself know only secondhand, the most reliable solution for all concerned would be to test it directly, so that the information would progress from being *ìgbàgbọ́* to being *ìmọ̀* for all concerned, myself included. Next best would again be to call upon all relevant witnesses who may have heard the same or similar secondhand information (*ìgbàgbọ́*) or, even more definitively, who may have firsthand (*ìmọ̀*) experience of what I can claim to know only on a secondhand (*ìgbàgbọ́*) basis. When agreement or a consensus among disputants is reached on the level of *ìgbàgbọ́*, the applicable term (comparable to the role of "truth" with reference to knowledge, or of "*òótọ́*" with regards to "*ìmọ̀*") is "*papọ̀*," which may be rendered colloquially as "the words have come together."[8] The antecedent process of testimony, discussion, and reflection on the basis of which the consensus is reached is described as "*nwádi*," an expression whose meaning may be compared to the English-language "let's get to the bottom of this matter."[9]

A suitably modified version of our simple example may also be helpful here. Although I myself have not seen it, I have heard (*ìgbàgbọ́*) that a friend drives a specific make and model of car. If another friend disputes my *ìgbàgbọ́*, the best way to resolve the dispute would be for both of us to go there and see for ourselves (*ìmọ̀*) what kind of a car the friend actually drives. If the friend lives a thousand miles away, a more practical solution would be for us to ask other mutual friends to tell us (*ìgbàgbọ́* + *nwádi*) what kind of car they have seen (*ìmọ̀*) or heard (*ìgbàgbọ́*) that she drives, or perhaps for us to telephone the friend ourselves and ask her to tell us (*ìgbàgbọ́*) what kind of car she is driving.

The system that emerges from these criteria appears to be three-tiered. *Ìmọ̀* is the sole category of experience or of propositions entitled to be regarded as certain[10] and as true (*òótọ́*). *Ìgbàgbọ́* that is in principle open to empirical testing, verification, and thereby transformed into *ìmọ̀* (*òótọ́*) is the next best. *Ìgbàgbọ́* that can never be verified and can be evaluated only on the basis of testimony, explanation, discussion, and reflection is

---

8. Or that the various disputants are now reconciled (etm 544).

9. According to the etm (659) "*nwádi*" is a participial conflation of the verb "looking for" or "seeking" (and perhaps finding) with the noun "*idi*" (etm 272) for "bottom," "base," "reason," or "cause." See also *KBW*, p. 70.

10. The etm translates the conflation of the verb "*dá*" (119: "fixed") with the noun "*ojú*" (eye)—*dájú*—as "certain" (123). That the *onísẹ̀gùn* see some equivalence between "*dájú*" and "*òótọ́*" is suggested by the original Yoruba-language versions of quotations (1) and (2) in the appendix. See also quotation (21) and note 6, p. 42.

the least certain. The significance of all this for cross-cultural understanding and comparisons is complex. The most obvious and perhaps important point is that the Yoruba language does employ terminology and systematic criteria for the evaluation of any type of information. This is a priority to which African systems of thought were once said not to attach special importance. Their most important knowledge was said to be preserved in the form of oral traditions, which could encompass anything from medicinal recipes to children's stories. The bias against tradition has always been epistemological—its questionable reliability as a source of and justification for knowledge.

What was said to be distinctive about African oral traditions was the relatively uncritical manner in which they were inherited from past, preserved in the present, and passed on to future generations. So regarded, traditions resembled 'rules' governing the 'game of life' that determined in a relatively absolute manner what Africans believed and how they behaved, and that they therefore had no intellectual incentive to articulate, explain, and certainly not to challenge. One problem for this (admittedly simplified) portrait of the African intellectual attitude toward tradition is that it is contradicted by the manner in which the Yoruba employ "mò" and "gbàgbó" in discourse. If my grandfather tells me that he knows the recipe for a potent headache medicine (that he in turn learned from his grandfather) and teaches it to me—this exchange of information would still be on the level of ìgbàgbó, of secondhand information. I could not be said to have ìmò of this medicine as medicine until I myself had prepared it, administered it to someone, and witnessed its curative powers. The same would hold for other traditions inherited from the past. Whether a military strategy or an agricultural technique, a tradition deserves to remain as a tradition only if it proves effective, if it does what it is supposed to do. Until this has been proven in a direct and personal manner its empirical status can be no more than hypothetical, something that may possibly be true (or false) and therefore must be classed as ìgbàgbó.[11]

There has been a great deal of technical, philosophical discussion about the epistemological underpinnings of ordinary discourse in the English language, and relatively little about Yoruba.[12] One potentially con-

---

11. As is also indicated by the various rhetorical idioms used in Yoruba discourse when reference is being made to traditions. See KBW, pp. 67–68, notes 14–16. The active rather than passive relationship that holds between the Yoruba and their traditions has been similarly documented with reference to the oral literature. See Barber (1994) and Yai (1994).

12. A representative selection of English-language philosophers and a valuable bibliography are to be found in Rorty (1967/1992). Examples of technical analytic studies based upon the Yoruba language are chapter 2 of KBW and Oke (1995).

troversial point from which to begin is the apparent emphasis placed by Yoruba on the personal element in both ìmọ̀ (putative "knowledge") and òótọ́ (putative "truth"). In English the high epistemological status assigned to both knowledge and truth arises, most importantly, from the consideration that they are more than personal. Information that is labeled "knowledge" and "true" becomes so, in principle, for anyone. Knowledge and truth thereby transcend the personal, the subjective, and assume the cloak of universality. Whereas in Yoruba, if òótọ́ for me attaches only to what I experience personally and directly, then the notions of knowledge (ìmọ̀) and "truth" that are being entertained veer markedly toward the subjective. In other words, what place is there for a truth that transcends the merely personal and becomes *inter*subjective, *inter*personal—genuinely empirical?

This point has been raised by Moses Oke in a perceptive essay (1995).[13] Oke does not dispute the substance of Yoruba discourse about perception as implying a distinctly personal and subjective basis for experience of the world. His major concern is to integrate this subjective dimension to experience with a view of mind or consciousness as also "knowing" an external world that includes other subjects, a past and a future—all with a stable order to them that can serve as a basis for inferences whose aim is objective truth.[14] I would prefer to continue following the rhetoric of Yoruba discourse about experience to see whether it suggests its own solutions to this purported problem. It certainly is the case that in other contexts, other language games, the Yoruba do talk of the world in straightforward, empirically real terms. But ordinary language—precisely because it is composed of multiple fields of discourse—cannot

---

13. "That is, if ìmọ̀ (knowledge in Yoruba language discourse) is direct perception, traditionally conceived to be fully composed of sense experience (sensation) and self-consciousness (subjective justification), then what could be known or what could constitute the possible objective of empirical knowledge would be entirely subjective sensory ideas. Consequently, the sentences in which such ideas are expressed would not be objectively (inter-subjectively) verifiable, thus failing to satisfy a minimum requirement of being empirical" (p. 209).

14. Rather than beginning from the nature of mind or consciousness in Yoruba thought, Oke begins from various beliefs the Yoruba have about the external world that imply formative inductive and deductive inferences and then introduces mind or judgment as the agency that must have given rise to them. The evidential basis for this type of mind and world is therefore indirect: "The real problem is that such a view [an apparently subjectivist (idealist) epistemology] is at variance with the observable fact that in thought and, especially, in practice the Yoruba tend to have always embraced a realist ontology which appears more plausibly ascribable to that culture than the one suggested by Hallen and Sodipo" (p. 210).

be expected to be comprehensively systematic in a philosophical sense.[15] What it imputes to the world or to experience in one context may be quite different from what it does in another. This may be the case with ordinary language in any culture in any historical epoch and should not be used as a cross-cultural index for rationality vs. irrationality, logicality vs. pre-logicality.

If the epistemic vocabulary the Yoruba employ highlights the subjectivity of human experience, this in itself is an acute observation that demonstrates a capacity for being clinically introspective.[16] One obviously relevant bit of technical philosophy is known as "methodological solipsism." A reference source summarizes this as "that knowledge about the existence and nonexistence of everything outside the self originates in the immediate experience, or "the given," which is not strictly shared [with other selves]" (Rollins 1967, p. 490). That my knowledge or belief about everything must begin from what I find myself seeing, hearing, introspecting—from what is 'given' to me by my experience—is a "fact of life" that I cannot change. Part of this 'given' is that I am not you, nor you me— our experience does not begin as shared. It begins as my experience, and from there I go on to explore whether it is somehow common to us.[17] Philosophers have tagged this solitary[18] aspect to our lives as "methodological" because it is something we have no choice but to acknowledge and with which to come to terms.

When we focus on the entire field of Yoruba epistemic discourse, on both ìmọ̀ and ìgbàgbọ́ and their interrelations, it will become clear that there is an appreciation for the importance of the intersubjective. But a preliminary concern should be with the accuracy of standardized translations (arising from the etm) from Yoruba into English of the pertinent terminology. Prior to KBW's 1986 sketch of Yoruba epistemic discourse, little attention seems to have been devoted to reviewing the interrelations between its components in translation from a systematic viewpoint.

In English-language culture the terms "true" and "truth" have been so extensively analyzed, and redefined for so many different technical

---

15. "This is not surprising because common-sense thinking is motivated by limited tasks of understanding whereas philosophy—and this applies in varying degrees and styles to all systematic disciplines—is a search for systematic coherence" (Wiredu 1980, p. 175).

16. "The study of usages of these particular words [mọ̀ and ìmọ̀; gbàgbọ́ and ìgbàgbọ́] shows the Yoruba oníṣègùn are more sophisticated epistemologically, and more critically, and indeed, empirically, minded than has been generally supposed" (Emmet 1986, p. 2).

17. "On my view truth is primarily a first-person concept" (Wiredu 1980, p. 185).

18. Another English-language derivative from the Latin roots solus (alone) and ipse (self).

contexts, that it becomes important to be precise about what meaning is being claimed as common to the two languages in a particular context. Perhaps too much is being taken for granted about the universality of meanings. If ìmọ̀ arises from a subjective base, does it make sense to couple this aspect of experience with a translation of "òótọ́"—"truth"— that in English usage implies, above all, intersubjective agreement? In KBW two passages from discussions with the oníṣègùn were introduced to justify defining "òótọ́" as "true" or "truth":

> (1) The one you see with your own eyes and which your consciousness (okàn)[19] affirms as true (òótọ́)—this is the best [kind of understanding or cognition].
>
> (2) It is clear (dá) in my eyes. This means that I have witnessed it myself. It is true (òótọ́) that he or she does this thing. . . . It was clear in your eyes (KBW, p. 60).

Using the foregoing discussion as a basis on which to reassess these two passages, a more sensible English-language translation of "òótọ́" might be "certain" or "certainty," terms which are conventionally associated in English-language discourse with subjective experience. This would mean that "òótọ́" in these contexts serves to underline the indisputability of some forms of experience (in this case veridical perception) rather than to lay claim to some paradoxical notion of subjective "truth."

This is not to say that certain or certainty is all that "òótọ́" may mean. In other contexts its sense may be more than subjective. But in those contexts where, from the standpoint of translations into English, it becomes problematic for the Yoruba to describe subjective experience with a term that really makes sense only when used for the more than subjective, this may be suggested as an alternative translation that restores translation sense, coherence, and consistency. To continue the discussion about whether "òótọ́" also incorporates a notion of genuinely epistemological (i.e., impersonal) truth, three additional passages from discussions with the oníṣègùn may be tendered:

> (3) With regards to speech (ọ̀rọ̀: etm 526): some have a gift for speaking (ọ̀rọ̀) [well], some people are known for telling lies (iró), while some will be [known for] telling the truth (òtítọ́). If you are speaking, you may be telling lies (purọ́: etm 560) or you may as well be telling the truth. When we refer to something as "possible" (ó ṣe é ṣe), what we

---

19. "Okàn" is the Yoruba word for both "heart" and "mind." In the above quotation the intended meaning is "mind" or "apprehension" (KBW, p. 61). This is that element of mental comprehension referred to previously.

mean is that you are not able to say whether it is true (òótọ́) and possible, and you are not able to say whether it is not possible (kò ṣe é ṣe).

(4) This (òótọ́) is [concerns the] thinking (èrò) of the mind (ọkàn). This is also related to "ògínrínrínginrìn" (not in etm but can be equated with "insight"). When all these small things [abilities that are instrumental to exceptional intelligence and ability] combine and other people note this (ìmọ̀) [in the person's behavior], they call that kind of person "àjẹ́"[20] because he or she always says the truth (òótọ́). His or her words never miss. They will say that if his or her dreams (àlá: etm 46) often turn out to be true (òótọ́), people will say he or she has already finished everything by [during] the night. He or she will simply say that he or she has had a dream, and it may be that this person was really dreaming.

(5) Somebody tells you something. Whether he or she tells lies or whether he or she does not tell a lie, you don't know (mọ̀). You agree (gbà) because you say that this person never tells lies. If you know (mọ̀) [from previous experience] that he or she is a truthful person (olóòtọ́ ènìyàn), you will believe (gbàgbọ́) that what he or she is saying is true (òótọ́). But if you know (mọ̀) that he or she is a liar (eléke), nobody will believe (gbàgbọ́) him or her. They will say, "He or she tells lies." They will not take him or her seriously.

(6) But if you have known (mọ̀) someone who has been behaving (ńṣe) in a truthful manner (òótọ́), if people are saying that he or she has done (ṣe) something bad, you may be reluctant to take them seriously (gbàgbọ́) because you have already accepted that he or she is a truthful person (olóòtọ́ ènìyàn). Likewise if someone is known for doing bad things and we hear (gbọ́) that he or she is doing good things. You may not want to believe [this].

Quotation (3) illustrates the Yoruba talent for articulating precise distinctions between different degrees of epistemic reliability.[21] But with reference to our continuing discussion of truth, in this quotation the referential meaning of òótọ́ is unclear. It is limited to being a property of statements, to serve as the alternative or contrary to false statements.

---

20. See *KBW,* chap. 3. The relevant point here is that "àjẹ́" is used to refer to a type of human personality.

21. With reference to spoken ìmọ̀ the oníṣẹ̀gùn introduces the alternatives of (telling the) truth (òótọ́ or òtítọ́) and (telling) lies or untruths (irọ́). With reference to ìgbàgbọ́ the alternatives are what may be possible (ó ṣe é ṣe as signifying something that has an indeterminate truth status) and what may not be possible (kò ṣe é ṣe). The two categories should not be confused: Describing something as possible means that by definition it is ìgbàgbọ́, and therefore we do not know (mọ̀) whether it is true or whether it is false or not possible.

In quotation (4) a person makes a prediction about (or 'sees') what will happen in the future. The pertinent question is at what point is the prediction true—when first expressed or when borne out by experience? If the latter, as seems to be the case, the question of truth or falsity still is determined by human experience.[22] Quotations (5) and (6) are introduced as examples of òótọ́ being used to describe a human being or a person's behavior as "true" or "truthful." This kind of usage seems as much moral as epistemic and compares with English-language vernacular when someone is described as a "true" human being, a "true" gentleman, or a "true" American—the sense being an honorable and good person whose opinions can be relied upon.

Taken together, these five quotations do not provide clear evidence of "òótọ́" as conveying a meaning comparable to Oke's desired objective truth—of truth as ultimately referring to and determined by a reality independent of human experience. Nor, in the transcripts of the discussions with the onísègùn, are there other passages in which reference is made to an "òótọ́" that may be explicitly identified with this kind of meaning. Nevertheless this does not mean the Yoruba system of cognition should be found wanting or is in some sense inferior. There are other ways of solving the 'problem'. One solution would be to argue that the workings, if not the words, of a cognitive system may evidence a notion of objective truth (or reference). For example, the sense of òótọ́ in quotations (3) and (5) where what a person is saying or telling is "òótọ́," or in quotation (4) where someone's dream becomes "òótọ́," implies that events experienced by others as well as the speaker are what determine whether these statements are òótọ́. Interpreting this term's meaning as "certain" or "certainty" in these contexts does not produce sensible translations.

That the Yoruba routinely distinguish instances in which people recount their experiences correctly from instances in which they do not indicates that on a generalized level they do have a notion of objective reference as determining what makes some statements true and others false. This kind of relatively fundamental and pure (in philosophical vernacular 'thin') notion of òótọ́ as naming the connection between language and experience, between statements and what those statements refer to, would indicate that the cognitive system in its use of "òótọ́" (in some contexts) does evidence a notion of objective reference or truth.

Critics may complain that this still does not solve the problem of how

---

22. An alternative interpretation would be to say that it may be the occurrence of the dream (as cause) that makes the event (as effect) take place.

one person's òótó may become that of another, since everyone seems to remain a 'prisoner' of their subjective experience. One alternative would be to suggest that altogether too much importance is being attached to a Yoruba representation of the English-language distinction between the "subjective" and the "objective." Perhaps the dimension to ìmò and to òótó that it is more important to highlight for intercultural translation purposes is "firsthand" experience rather than subjectivity. Another alternative would be to argue that, since for the Yoruba experience that is more than personal—that is shared and in common—is not a "given," disputed aspects to experience about which it becomes important to reach agreement must be resolved on the basis of discussion and consensus. This is the realm of ìgbàgbó (putative "belief"), and it would be a serious error to underrate its importance to the cognitive system as a whole.

Also, one must be realistic about the problems for which ordinary language makes explicit provision (via meanings):

(7) You know (mò) this is a cupboard. If another person told you it was not a cupboard, you would insist it was a cupboard and that you know (mò) it very well. Your perceiving consciousness (èrí okàn) would support you in saying that it is a cupboard. This white bottle—if they say it is black, you would know (mò) very well that it is white. It is clear in your eyes that it is white. I know (mò) that it is white.

In clear-cut situations where veridical perception is the norm, it would be unrealistic to expect discourse to provide solutions for problems that almost never arise. Five people who are sitting in that room observing the same white bottle have no need to resort to discussion (ìgbàgbó) in order to agree upon its salient points. They have no need to examine whether what is òótó about it for them individually is common to them all.

In another passage in which the onísègùn explicitly undertook to define "òótó," as relating to different individual's perceptions of the 'same' occasion rather than merely a cupboard or bottle, the situation becomes more complicated but essentially the same:

(8) This [òótó] has many meanings. If you and I discuss something, if other people should come and ask from me, I would say it is true (òótó)—that you are not telling lies (puró; i.e., that a discussion did indeed take place). That is how the matter is.

You and I have a certain discussion one morning. Later that day you tell other people that we had a discussion. Later still those people come to see me to ask whether what you said is òótó (for me). If I then respond that my òótó also is that we had a discussion, does this not express an important element of shared, common, objective truth?

Not quite, because since my òótó is mine and yours is yours, each of us will have our private version of the substance of the discussion. That it took place is something about which there may be no dispute. On the other hand, in situations where straightforward perception is not the rule, where there may be problems about precisely what is seen, what was discussed, or what is going on, people do find it helpful to discuss their differing impressions (nwádi) with a view to arriving at a more comprehensive account (papò) of what was happening. It is when recourse is had to this kind of alternative process (which surely must be relatively rare, or else endless confabs would leave no time for practical life) that there is the transition to the level of ìgbàgbó.[23]

In many other cultural contexts, the scientific included, agreeing upon what really happens also involves (ideally) a process of unbiased, interpersonal consensus. Then the emphasis is upon the process of arriving at a common (objective) truth on the basis of personal impressions,[24] and it certainly is the case that this kind of "truth" may become the laborious creation of many contributing intellects[25] rather than something obvious that is in plain view.

Critics may protest that papò is a weak and inadequate substitute for a full-blown notion of epistemological (i.e., impersonal) truth as genuinely intersubjective. To the contrary, one cannot help being impressed by Yoruba discourse's painstaking semantic depiction of perception and the basis for inferences therefrom:

> (9) The difference between what I know (mò) and what I agree with (gbà): the reason you agree (gbà) is that you may have seen (rí) that thing [yourself].

In other words, we both may have witnessed the same event, making whatever we saw ìmò and òótó for each of us individually. But when it comes to agreeing that we saw the 'same' thing, that agreement amounts to ìgbàgbó. As is the case with the sensitivity with which it records the

---

23. "The disagreements of men can in suitable conditions be resolved by rational discussion. Sadly, suitable conditions are not always available" (Wiredu 1980, p. 177).

24. This was in part responsible for the impact made by Michael Polanyi's *Personal Knowledge* (1958).

25. The role of testimony in the O. J. Simpson trial is a remarkable case in point.

"methodological solipsism" that is a 'given' for all human experience, there is a comparable appreciation here of how difficult it can become to arrive at the intersubjective, at a version of events that is representative and comprehensive (taking the experiences of all witnesses into account).

Yet another solution to the 'problem' of epistemological "truth" may be derived from the writings of Kwasi Wiredu.[26] There are two dimensions to Wiredu's discussions of truth. One is technical philosophical— to outline a cogent theory of truth that will be attractive in principle to all rational beings. The second is to explore terminology of the Akan language of Ghana, to identify how words that may compare with the English-language "true" or "truth" are used and the ramifications (if any) for cross-cultural translations. With reference to a cogent, philosophical theory of truth, Wiredu argues that whatever is called the "truth" is always someone's truth. For a piece of information to be awarded the appellation "true," it must be discovered by, known by, defended by, human beings somewhere, sometime. Furthermore what human beings defend as being "true" can prove to be false. Therefore whatever is called "truth" is more accurately described as *opinion.* Wiredu rejects the 'objectivist theory' of truth (as maintained, for example, by Oke). Rather than deriving from some transcendent reality,[27] truth as opinion in fact arises from rigorous, rational human exploration and invention: "We must recognise the *cognitive* element of point of view as intrinsic to the concept of truth" (1980, p. 115, my italics).

That "truth" as opinion needs to arise from human agency and consensus does not mean knowledge will degenerate into the merely subjective and possibly relative: "What I mean by opinion is a firm rather than an uncertain thought. I mean what is called a considered opinion" (1980, pp. 115–16). In his discussions of Akan discourse Wiredu finds a number of expressions that may serve as a basis for more generalized semantic comparisons with the English-language "true" or "truth." One such comparison would be with reference to propositions being true, which Wiredu says might pertain to an Akan rendering of truth in its purely cog-

---

26. There is a formidable selection of Wiredu publications on this subject: in Wiredu (1980), "Truth as Opinion" (pp. 111–23), "To Be Is to Be Known" (pp. 124–38), "In Defence of Opinion" (pp. 174–88), "Truth: A Dialogue" (pp. 189–232); in Bodunrin (1985), "The Concept of Truth in the Akan Language" (pp. 43–54). More recently see Wiredu (1993) and (1995d).

27. Wiredu characterizes the objectivist theory as maintaining that "once a proposition is true, it is true in itself and for ever. Truth, in other words, is timeless, eternal" (1980, p. 114).

nitive sense (1985, p. 46). This perhaps is where we may derive some inspiration for our own ruminations about a notion of "objective truth" in Yoruba discourse.[28]

When it becomes appropriate to identify the Akan terminology he has in mind as pertinent to the discussion of cognitive truth, Wiredu informs us that "here we meet with a remarkable fact, which is that there is no one word in Akan for truth":

> To say that something is true, the Akan simply say that it is so, and truth is rendered as what is so. No undue sophistication is required to understand that although the Akan do not have a single word for truth, they do have the concept of truth. (1985, p. 46)

Several points attract interest. In Yoruba discourse too it has not been possible to identify a single term that conveys a truth that is more than personal, that attaches to propositions or things independently of whoever happens to be experiencing them. For Yoruba too the possibility has been raised that, in the absence of specific terminology, it still may be possible to claim that the 'workings' of a language evidence a notion of objective truth.

However (and this is where things become a bit complex), it is also the case that Wiredu, on technical philosophical grounds, rejects the "objectivist theory" of truth. Of course, if Wiredu continues to observe the distinction here extrapolated from his analyses, the distinction between (1) a level of his own technical, philosophical argumentation and (2) the level of analyses of Akan terminology, there should be no problem. He could report that Akan discourse evidences a notion of objective truth[29] and then still disassociate himself from it, on the technical, philosophical level, as being the most satisfactory way to understand our experience. To a certain extent this is in fact what happens when Wiredu goes on to

---

28. The differences between 'cognitive truth', 'objective truth', and 'epistemological truth' are more than rhetorical. The first, as expounded by Wiredu, argues that human beings have no direct access to such a 'reality', and that truth can therefore only be determined by rigorous, careful reasoning, and experimentation—cognition. The second claims that truth must be determined by an independent, transcendent reality to which human knowledge can be shown to correspond. The last is used in this text to represent the much more modest expository notion of a truth that does involve a more than merely personal claim to "know" something of the world but does not go so far as to commit itself to a cognitivist or objectivist basis for that truth.

29. In personal correspondence Wiredu insists that he does not link Akan usage to any particular 'theory of' truth.

suggest that the notion of something's being "so" may very well be the same as something's being a fact. But if this then means that in Akan truth amounts to correspondence with fact, this would be nothing more than a restatement of elementary correspondence theory (of truth) and, as such, be less than enlightening.

Before undertaking further comparisons between Akan and Yoruba terminology relevant to "true" or "truth," we must caution against tacit presumptions that meanings are more likely to be shared in common between two African languages than between a Western and an African language. From a philosophical vantage point it is methodologically advantageous to approach each language-culture—whatever its geographical setting—initially as an intellectually independent and integral entity in its own right. If remarkable similarities between two languages emerge as a consequence of contrasts and comparisons, this may then warrant further investigation. But it is an unhelpful distraction with which to begin.

That said, one wonders whether Wiredu's suspicions about an Akan notion of "truth" in the objective sense, rendered into English as "it is so,"[30] may be of use for further explication of the Yoruba "òótọ́."[31] According to the etm "òótọ́" is an alternative (perhaps elided) form of "òtítọ́," and the latter is itself an elision of the phrase "ò tí tọ́," which may be rendered into English as "it is correct."[32] On the other hand, Wiredu's own rendering of the Akan as "it is so" could itself be experimentally reinterpreted as an Akan expression for "it is certain," as was done with "òótọ́" in quotations (1) and (2). But Wiredu has told me that he could not agree to this because interpreting "it is so" in Akan and "òótọ́" in Yoruba (when rendered as "certain") as having the same meaning would be a mistake. Entirely different expressions in Akan would have to be used to convey that sort of meaning.

The point has already been made that to choose between all of these interpretative possibilities about the philosophical prepossessions of Akan discourse about "true," more information about ordinary usage would be required. In the end the most frustrating limitation to Wiredu's termino-

---

30. The *Concise Oxford Dictionary* records this form of usage for "so" as "In that state or condition, actually the case" and cites as one example "God said 'Let there be light' and it was so" (p. 1213). The equivalence Wiredu himself favors is that "p is so" means "p is true."

31. It is relevant to bear in mind that the noun "truth" is rendered from the Akan as "what is so" rather than "that is so."

32. The various contexts in which "tọ́" may occur that are listed by the etm (650) indicate that "correct" is used in a normative or moral sense—as doing the 'right' thing or what one has the 'right' to do.

logical analyses is that he does not aim to offer a complete explanation of what is meant by saying (in Akan) that something is "so."[33] What it is the "*so*" might correspond to or cohere with is left as speculative possibilities. This is not a criticism of his analyses, by the way. It is rather another consequence of the fact that there are some questions that ordinary discourse and usage do not answer, some issues they do not resolve, because there is no need for human beings to be so technically specific about such matters at the level of ordinary, everyday discourse. However, in the other dimension to his philosophical scholarship—that devoted to purely technical philosophical problems—Wiredu has gone on to explore in detail what might be required for something to be so. This occurs in the course of a critical evaluation of the three standard theories of truth:

> Explaining "so" is the task of the theory of truth, as I understand it. It is necessary to explain what is susceptible of being "so" and what its being "so" consists in. Correspondence theory says it is a statement that corresponds, and what it corresponds to is a fact. Coherence theory says it is a statement that may be "so"; but its being "so" consists in cohering with other propositions. Classical pragmatism did not speak with one voice. But the clearest statement was in Dewey—still not very clear. What is "so" is an idea, and its being "so" is its being warrantably assertable. If warrantably assertable is understood as what is rationally warranted, I think this gives the normative definition. But "warranted" may be regarded by a given point of view in a very broad sense. Thus, a person who believes by "faith," believes, that is, without reason, would still regard their view as warranted. (personal correspondence)

His reference to the work of the American pragmatist John Dewey is noteworthy. According to Dewey[34] truth could be defined as "rationally *warranted* assertibility," and this pragmatic tone is echoed by Wiredu in his use of the phrase "truth as *considered* opinion."[35] Wiredu goes on to suggest that it is possible to make a second, generalized semantic comparison between the Akan and English terminology reference "true" or "truth" in situations where a person is said to be "truthful," as was the case with Yoruba usage on pages 23–24 above. This is a sense that Wiredu says should be construed as explicitly moral. In Akan it is ex-

---

33. In "it or that is so" and "what is so."

34. See, for example, "Propositions, Warranted Assertibility and Truth" (1946) and relevant passages in *Logic: The Theory of Inquiry* (1938).

35. Wiredu discusses the similarities and differences between himself and Dewey on this specific issue (1980, pp. 211–12).

pressed by the term "*nokware*,"[36] which is translated as "[speaking with] one voice"—"the idea being apparently that truthfulness consists in saying to others only what one would say to oneself" [i.e., in not speaking to others with 'another voice' or 'telling lies'] (1980, p. 116): "Truthfulness has to do with the relation between what a person thinks and what he says. To be truthful is to let your speech reflect your thoughts. In this, what others think or say has no particular role to play. And this was not lost upon the traditional Akan" (1985, p. 44). Wiredu's own technical, philosophical interests—perfectly understandably—influence him to concentrate more on the nature and implications of *epistemological* truth arising from Akan discourse and usage than on this notion of veracity or of being truthful.[37] Our interests will be understandably divergent since my discussion is targeting the *moral* in Yoruba thought via Yoruba discourse.

Any further contrasts between Akan and Yoruba must begin with the possibility that Yoruba usage can be interpreted as displaying a comparable distinction between "*òótó*" as an attribute of propositions ('epistemological' or, in Wiredu's terms, 'cognitive') and "*òótó*" as an attribute of persons ('moral'). In quotation (6) the sense of "*òótó*" is pronouncedly moral, but in quotation (5) both a moral and an epistemological sense seem to occur. A person is, and has a reputation for being, "truthful" (*olóòtó ènìyàn*), and because of that his or her statements can be relied upon as "true" (*òótó*). In considering this relationship between the moral and the epistemological, one assumes that its reverse may also be causally relevant—that because a person's statements are found to be generally "true," they are honored with the designation of being "truthful."

The point upon which Akan terminology and Yoruba usage appear to

---

36. J. T. Bedu-Addo's critique (1985) of Wiredu's terminological analyses is of interest, if for no other reason, as a further example of how different analyses of the same concepts can produce different meanings. He does not agree that Akan evidences separate notions of 'cognitive' and 'moral' truth ("the fact is that there is only one concept of truth; and it is an epistemological concept"; p. 73).

The most serious error he attributes to Wiredu is the failure to appreciate that *nokware*'s meaning is epistemological (in Wiredu's terms "cognitive") as well as moral—indeed, that statements which are deliberate lies constitute only a subset of the totality of false statements that represent the opposite of *nokware, nkontompo* (lies). In a language like Akan the term "lies" may stand for the class of false statements generally because, as Bedu-Addo explains, "in Akan we have no one word like the English "false" which may be used in place of *enye nokware* ("it is not true") when what is said not to be true is not necessarily a lie" (p. 71).

37. Bedu-Addo is more severe: "When Professor Wiredu argues that the Akan word *nokware* has a primarily moral connotation and that 'truth in its purely cognitive sense' is *nea ete saa*, he is in effect evolving an Akan philosophical vocabulary—albeit unconsciously—which derives from his own conception of truth as opinion" (p. 75).

part company is with reference to this interrelation between the 'moral' and the 'epistemological'. When Yoruba discourse describes a person as truthful, a good deal more is involved than merely the assessment of moral character. Describing a person in this way also means that statements made, information conveyed, by that person to others can be relied upon and used as "true" for whatever more mundane purposes to which it may prove relevant (the most cost-effective way to disinfest an agricultural crop, surviving in the 'big city').[38] In other words, the division that Wiredu makes or identifies between the moral and epistemological dimensions to "true" or "truth" in Akan appears more distinct than in the Yoruba context, even if, in the end, they agree. It is one thing for a person to have the *honorable* intention to *tell* or to *speak* the truth (moral), but in order to do so he or she must first have a correct and clear understanding of how truth is *defined* and of how to determine it *in practice* (cognitive). The earlier quotation (1985, p. 44) from Wiredu's work is a further example of this. "Speaking with one voice" may be a positive, personal, moral attribute. But the reason for its being so is that the information that comes out of that person's mouth may be shared and used by others who are trying to arrive at understanding and "truths" about the world that are more than personal.

Yoruba discourse occurs in a culture that has been typed as "oral." That the 'moral' and 'cognitive' are so intertwined is not surprising in a cultural environment where propositions only come out of mouths. In 'traditional' Yoruba culture writing discourse and/or reading discourse are not conventional pastimes. Some anthropologists and literary scholars have used orality to 'type' a particular kind of mentality,[39] which generally compares less favorably in analytically intellectual terms with its literate Western equivalents. The discussion here seeks to circumvent that increasingly controversial debate. The claim that, in 'traditional' Yoruba culture, propositions (only) come out of mouths is here an empirical observation rather than a theoretically weighted premiss. In a social context where printed books and written script may not be taken for granted, the only way in which propositions or statements may take form is for them to issue from someone's mouth. And if this is the case, it is understandable

---

38. The following quotation from Wiredu, meant to demonstrate that moral truth presupposes cognitive truth in conceptual terms, therefore does take into account the epistemologically *inter*subjective importance of the "truths" espoused by a "truthful" person: "It is important to note that *nokware* (truthfulness) involves the concept of truth. To say that somebody is speaking truthfully is to say that he genuinely believes what *he* is saying to be *true*" (1985, p. 45, my italics in part).

39. In contemporary times most seminally and famously beginning with Lord (1960).

that passing judgments upon a proposition's reliability or upon its likeli-
hood of being "true," purely on an instrumental (pragmatic) ground, may
involve assessing the moral character of the person who is its source,
whose mouth it issues out of.[40]

With this 'linking' of the epistemological and the moral in Yoruba
discourse, we move a step closer to value theory. If what a statement
means and is taken to mean by others also depends upon whose mouth
it is coming out of, then any speaker's reputation, their moral character,
as defined by others becomes one prominent consideration to the epistemological rating of their statements. Reciprocally the statements made by
an individual, in principle on any subject, may be treated as firsthand
evidence of the individual's moral character. In addition to a statement's
'objective' terms of reference, that, how, and why it is made by a particular person in a particular situation may also be interpreted as reflecting
the moral values of the person concerned. As Wiredu has pointed out,
however, this should always be with the qualification that good (or, for
that matter, bad) intentions are never enough if the person involved does
not also have a correct (cognitive) understanding of what truth means and
how to go about determining it.

Before fully undergoing the transition to value theory, something
needs to be said about the negative influence of Western paradigms when
it comes to unraveling the epistemological and moral nuances of Yoruba
discourse. When the outline of Yoruba cognitive criteria that constitutes
the heart of *KBW* was completed and it became obvious that system was
different in significant respects from what the Western paradigm stipulates
a cognitive system should be, it would have been possible to carry the
argument one step further and demand that the Yoruba system be granted
prima facie equal consideration as a non-Western, epistemological alternative for imposing order on human experience.

Another philosopher who happened to read and review *KBW* at the
time (Stich 1987) did appreciate this dimension to the text, and it is to his
reading of it (Stich 1990; Haack 1993) that I owe the inspiration for this
final, introductory harangue. From the outset African philosophy has been
haunted and handicapped by the possibility that the indigenous African
mentality does not measure up in intellectual terms: Whether it is presented as essentially poetic and symbolic in nature, and thereby denied
the analytic skills that are fundamental to any Western definition of the
intellect; or whether it is presented as the product of tradition(s), a source

---

40. In a literate context, an analogous assessment process takes place when comparing the
reliability of news reported in *The New York Times* and *The National Enquirer.*

that has been judged epistemologically suspect when it comes to the justi-fication of knowledge. Once one appreciates the point of these less than subtle intimations of intellectual inferiority, it becomes clear that it will be on the battlefield of epistemology that the legitimacy of African philos-ophy must most importantly be established. Considerations of how and what people claim to believe and to know are always fundamental. They underlie every aspect of human endeavor: aesthetic, commonsensical, moral, political, technological, scientific.

But the orthodox Western paradigm of what a cognitive system should be in order to be considered "rational" so dominates that battlefield of today that it is difficult to secure even a modest space for any non-Western alternative.[41] Every contemporary philosophical text having to do with epistemology defines "knowledge," "belief," "true," or "truth" exclusively in terms of the Western paradigm. The 'trick' to much of this, of course, is that the word "Western" is not made explicit when the para-digm is presented. Consequently it is discussed as if universal, as the high-est expression of rationality for any culture, as what every human being and society should emulate and imitate.

If African philosophers do not challenge the universality of this para-digm when they pursue an interest in things epistemological with refer-ence to African systems of thought, they will find themselves in a compro-mising situation. If they identify processes of reasoning that the paradigm rejects as 'deviant' or 'substandard', they are forced to admit that this kind of reasoning needs to be changed, that these are areas where Africans have not succeeded in arriving at as clear standards of rationality (super-stitions), or to argue that the apparent differences are superficial, and that on closer examination it will turn out that African modes of thought are not so different after all.[42] With his concern that Yoruba cognition be at-tributed a notion of "objective" truth that complies with the stipulations of this orthodox (Western) paradigm, Oke falls into this trap.

There is an alternative strategy that will hopefully be illustrated by this study. This involves reassessing academic philosophy's supposedly universal paradigms as Western paradigms. It involves arguing that any non-Western system of cognition deserves an equal hearing, prima facie

41. Richard Rorty has extensive discussions of what he regards as Western philosophy's obsession(s) with notions of culturally and historically transcendent knowledge (1991a, b).

42. "In the matter of the philosophical problem of truth the deepest problem, it seems to me, is whether the world contains cognitive beings and their thought and perceptions and the objects of their thoughts, plus something over and above all these which confers truth on their thoughts" (Wiredu 1980, p. 175).

credibility in its own right as an alternative pathway to the "true" or "truth." In this way, at the very least, they can become the subjects of detailed study and analysis by philosophers that they deserve to be. There will be complaints that this kind of attitude opens the door to relativism and the loss of objective knowledge altogether. That complaint is perhaps a lesser evil than the virtually uniform denigration of the African intellect that has become conventional. Why else is it that academic philosophy to date has exhibited such minimal interest in African systems of thought? If not because they had been assigned so lowly a ranking on the cross-cultural scale of rationality that they did not merit serious interest? But surely it is within academic philosophy that the sanctum sanctorum of rationality still reposes? If so, then it should also be the responsibility of the academic philosopher to assess and to define the rational in any culture.

To that end analytic philosophers concerned with Africa must engage in systematic presentations of African cognitive systems, moral systems, aesthetic systems. "Systematic" is the key term here. It has not proved an effective intercultural, philosophical strategy to extrapolate single beliefs from African systems of thought, single words from African languages, for comparisons with purported Western equivalents. Treated in isolation it is not possible to demonstrate the evidential basis from which a belief arises, the semantic contexts from which a word derives its meanings. An African system of cognition, or system of values, must be described and analyzed as something that is intellectually credible ab initio in its own right. It must be treated as a 'statement', if you will, made by human beings in a particular culture about how best to understand or to deal with experience.

The same must be done to the orthodox paradigms (or systems) that predominate in academic philosophy today. As a cultural statement in its own right, academic philosophy is overwhelmingly Western in orientation. A first step toward liberating non-Western systems of thought is to accept this as a 'given'. Reigning paradigms of rationality and morality, once labeled explicitly "Western," can then be reassessed as just other alternatives human beings have devised to explain and to order their experience. More importantly for philosophers in and of Africa, the door is then open for them to claim 'equal time' for the representation and analysis of African alternatives. This could lead to relativism, and, to go one step further, it might also involve pluralism. Even so, it would still be possible for an African system of cognition, or an African system of morality, when sited in its own geographical, historical, and social contexts to be awarded just as high marks as Western alternatives when assessed as an instrument of explanation, prediction, and control.

ME,
MY SELF,
AND MY DESTINY

THE GODS ARE NOT TO BLAME

Narratives of African worldviews often claim that the distinction between the spiritual and the natural, the mystical and the mundane, is not as sharp as in the West. The African consciousness is said to be steeped in, suffused with, a suprasensory sensitivity. This sensitivity is more crudely portrayed by some scholars as a diverse population of deities, spirits, and personified natural forces that sustain their vitality because of their participation in and influence upon the world of human experience. Wole Soyinka is one of the most sophisticated and eloquent exponents of this view of the metaphysically more expansive African consciousness. It becomes relevant here insofar as any account of the moral in an African context is obliged to take the metaphysical into account. For Soyinka is well aware of the tendency on the part of the analytic approach to create artificial divisions in human experience, to "compartmentalise"[1] as he likes to put it:

> one important, even vital, element in the composition of the elaborate interiority of such a world [the African] is, of course, its moral order. This

---

1. "What Western European man later reduced to specialist terminologies through his chronic habit of compartmentalisation" (1976, p. 6).

must not be understood in any narrow sense of the ethical code which society develops to regulate the conduct of its members. A breakdown in moral order implies, in the African world-view, a rupture in the body of Nature just like the physical malfunctioning of one man.

Where society lives in a close inter-relation with Nature . . . the highest moral order is seen as that which guarantees a parallel continuity of the species. We must try to understand this as operating within a framework which can conveniently be termed the metaphysics of the irreducible: knowledge of birth and death as the human cycle; the wind as a moving, felling, cleansing, destroying, winnowing force; the duality of the knife as blood-letter and creative implement; earth and sun as life-sustaining verities, and so on. These serve as matrices within which mores, personal relationships, even communal economics are formulated and reviewed. Other "irreducible" acceptances may evolve from this; for instance, the laws of hospitality or the taboo on incest, but they do not possess the same strength and compulsion as the fundamental matrix. They belong to a secondary category and may be contradicted by accident or human failing. (1976, pp. 52–53)

Any disciplinary study, as Soyinka certainly appreciates, will be "guilty," to some degree, of treating its subject matter in relative abstraction from broader cultural or scholastic contexts. The analytic approach has achieved unfair notoriety in this respect, a victim of its explicit use of the term "analysis," which connotes 'breaking up' a subject matter into component pieces or elements. Perhaps the most constructive way to reconcile this study with Soyinka's criticism is to agree with it—analysis does, by definition, compartmentalize. And, from there, go on to be candid about the positive, if limited, results that may result from this kind of methodological approach. In doing so, let me target critically two other species of African worldview narratives whose reductive abstractions have become so commonplace as to be stereotypical. As a result they distort certain elements, said to be "key," totally out of proportion to their real significance.

One such narrative is the progeny of the poetic-symbolist school. It gives the impression that the African consciousness, at the proto-rational level to which it has evolved, is a maelstrom of ancestors, cults, demons, divinities, incantations, magic, masquerades, sorcerers, witches, and agencies of predestination over which the individual can never exert sufficient control. In such interpretations the spiritual dimension and the dramas it carelessly inflicts upon the merely human become of such exaggerated importance that the role human intelligence plays in imposing order upon human experience becomes of secondary, virtually minor, importance. That humanity is the victim of forces it cannot fully understand and certainly cannot overcome becomes in fact the defining characteristic of the African worldview.[2]

A second type of narrative treats the beliefs inherent in African cultural traditions as a set of rules that are embalmed in the social fabric. Behavior becomes semiconscious, rote, governed by a memory that is unintelligent. How traditions first arose and retain their force is attributed, by scholars on a 'scientific' basis, to instinctive concerns with the survival and welfare of the species or community. To say the African intellect is portrayed as minimally cerebral would be a slight exaggeration. To say Africans are regarded as incapable of reasoning about their beliefs in conscious, articulate, analytical fashion would not.[3]

One of the defining points of this study is that philosophy should concern itself with defining whatever it is that is regarded as the rational in a particular cultural context. That ordinary language or African discourse is a major instrument to this end, in that it imposes order upon ordinary experience, is another. From this it follows that the study of moral discourse, as illustrated and explained by Africans, outlines the kind of order to be desired in and of human behavior. The value of such a study, restricted and restrictive when compared with the two previous types of narratives, is that it is a healthy corrective to tendencies to underrate the role of articulated, conscious, systematic thinking in the African cultural context.

2. Christian missionary accounts of African 'traditional' cultures are representative. Part of the message of Christian salvation that was thought to be particularly relevant to the African context was that individual human concerns, expressed via prayer and devotion, could become of transcendent importance, could prevail. Generous generalizations about the influence of the religious, benign and malicious, upon Yoruba life are commonplace: (1) "The keynote of their life is their religion. In all things, they are religious. Religion forms the foundation and the all-governing principle of life for them" (Idowu 1962, p. 5); (2) "Religion permeates all facets of their lives, and constitutes the foundation and the all-governing principle of life for them. They firmly believe that the full responsibility for all the affairs of this life and the one beyond belongs to the Supreme Being (God); their own part in the matter is to do as they are ordered through the priests and diviners whom they believe to be the interpreters of the will of the Supreme Being" (Kayode and Adelowo 1985, p. 233).

3. "A great number of beliefs and practices are to be found in any African society. These are not, however, formulated into a systematic set of dogmas which a person is expected to accept. People simply assimilate whatever religious ideas and practices are held or observed by their families and communities. . . . In traditional religions there are no creeds to be recited; instead, the creeds are written in the heart of the individual, and each one is himself a living creed of his own religion. Where the individual is, there is his religion, for he is a religious being. It is this that makes Africans so religious; religion is their whole system of being" (Mbiti 1970, p. 4).

One point in Soyinka's presentation from which this study will dissociate itself is that it is possible to generalize about a "metaphysics of the irreducible" that is cross-culturally African—that may be attributed to all African cultures. It may be another sign of the "compartmentalist" mentality, but one hesitates to embrace yet another generalized, semiconscious network of concerns for all Africans until there is better evidence that it too is not a product of hasty generalization. Anthony Appiah voices a similar reservation:

> I think we should ask what leads Soyinka astray when it comes to his accounting for his cultural situation. And part of the answer must be that he is answering the wrong question. For what he needs to do is not to take an *African* world for granted but to take for granted his own culture—to speak freely not as an African but as a Yoruba and a Nigerian. The right question, then, is not "Why Africa shouldn't take its traditions for granted?" but "Why I shouldn't take mine?" The reason that Africa cannot take an African cultural or political or intellectual life for granted is that there is no such thing: there are only so many traditions with their complex relationships—and, as often, their lack of any relationship—to each other. (1992, pp. 79–80)

That Soyinka's arguments then become directly relevant only to accounts of Yoruba culture may seem to make their impact upon this study even greater than before. But that need not be the case. Ordinary language pertains to everyday life, and the stuff of everyday life is so often relegated to the pedestrian, the banal, that people are not excited by the prospect of making a special study of it. It is when the everyday is disrupted, when the usual becomes unusual, that ordinary discourse must have recourse to extraordinary discourse, to those further dimensions to experience that transcend yet infuse the ordinary. This study does not deny that those dimensions inform the Yoruba consciousness in an important manner, and that their influence pervades Yoruba culture. But it also insists, stubbornly if need be, that paying excessive attention to them can divert attention from the rational texture of the everyday discourse that governs normal life. And when the role of the ordinary goes under-reported, the importance of extraordinary elements such as the spiritual or metaphysical, which in cross-cultural terms are comparatively exotic, becomes enhanced and inflated.

MORAL CHARACTER

In discussions with the *onísẹ̀gùn* the moral dimension of persons (*ènìyàn*) was most frequently ascribed to their character (*ìwà; etm* 328). It was described in a variety of ways:

(10) If you are doing (*ṣe; * etm 606) what is good (*dáà; * etm 127), they will say your character (*ìwà*) is good (*dára*). If you are doing what is bad (*burú; * etm 118), they will say your character (*ìwà*) is bad. They know (*mọ̀*) your character (*ìwà*) from the way you behave (*ṣíṣe; * etm 609: "act of doing").

(11) Ìṣeṣí (etm 607: behavior)!

(12) We use our eyes to see many things. We observe (*wò*) the behavior (*ìwà*) of many people.

(13) We know these things by means of a person's behavior (*hùwà; * etm 328).

"Behavior" could become a problematic term in English-language translation if its terms of reference are not clear. But the *onísègùn* were prepared to be more specific:

(14) This is related to our actions (*ṣe*) and to what we say (*ọ̀rọ̀ ẹnu; * etm 526 and 191: literally "words of the mouth"). . . . There is no other thing we know (*mọ̀*) . . . apart from behavior (*ìwà*)[4] and the way we talk (*ọ̀rọ̀ ẹnu*).

(15) Before you can identify a bad person (*èníyàn burúkú*) you must see their acts (*iṣẹ́; * etm 609). You cannot know them until you see (*rí*) 'the work of their hands'.

(16) A good person (*èníyàn rere*) says (*sọ̀rọ̀*) good words (*ọ̀rọ̀ rere*), and a bad person speaks bad words (*ọ̀rọ̀ burúkú*).

(17) They will say that he doesn't take time [hesitate] to kill a person [as an example of 'doing']. They will say good words never come out of his mouth [as an example of 'saying'].

(18) The thing the person is doing (*ṣe*) is not good.

To be frank, the parallel between Yoruba usage and the philosophical position known as behaviorism that emerges from these definitions is almost too good to believe. 'What a person says' and 'what a person does' rather neatly convert into the standard behaviorist categories of verbal and nonverbal behavior. At this still preliminary stage there is no need to go so far as to say this amounts to some form of ethical behaviorism. Exegesis is still in that liminal transition region between epistemology and ethics. What is cropping up here again is the Yoruba penchant for hard evidence, for firsthand certainty, for only being able to "know" what you witness in a firsthand manner:

---

4. There is sometimes circularity in passages where *ìwà* is used to convey "behavior"; and "behavior" (*ìṣeṣí*) is used to convey *ìwà*, but that is to be expected with definitions obtained from numerous discussions that took place over an extended period of time.

(19) [You cannot really know 'it':] Unless you use your own eyes to see (*rí*) it [*ìwà*].

(20) If you don't want to be a liar (*eléke*), the thing which has not been done in [before] your eyes [firsthand], you should not say "I believe" ("*Mò gbàgbó*"). Before you say "I believe," you ought to have seen the person who has done it in your eyes. It is the thing you see that you can say, ["I know" ("*Mò mò*")].

(21) I believe you (*gbà ó gbò*) when I know (*mò*) your character (*ìwà*). But it is what you see (*rí*) that is "bigger" [more convincing]. I see it with absolute certainty (*dájú dájú*). I [may] believe you (*gbà ó gbò*) when I did not see the thing.[5] But what I see clearly (*kedere*) I know with certainty (*dájú*).[6]

With reference to being certain (*òótó*) about what someone says or does, the same firsthand-secondhand criteria arising from the distinction between "knowledge" (*ìmò*) and "belief" (*ìgbàgbó*) will be found to apply. This is something to be considered in detail below. For the moment the relevance of this passage is the connection it makes between knowing a person's character (*ìwà*) and firsthand observation.

Quine relates behaviorism and empiricism in a manner that is compatible with this line of thought:

> When I dismiss a definition of behaviorism that limits it to conditioned response, am I simply extending the term to cover everyone? Well, I do think of it as covering all reasonable men. What matters, as I see it, is just the insistence upon couching all criteria in observation terms. By observation terms I mean terms that are or can be taught by ostension, and whose application in each particular case can therefore be checked intersubjectively. Not to cavil over the word "behaviorism," perhaps current usage would be best suited by referring to this orientation to observation simply as *empiricism*. (1976, p. 58, my italics)

Since this form of behavioristic empiricism explicitly connotes a thing being publicly (i.e., *inter*subjectively) observable, and we have yet to resolve finally the matter of the "true" (*òótó*) as arising explicitly from *personal* observation, some readers may think the relevance of this passage is

---

5. With this sentence the *oníṣègùn* is introducing the distinction between "knowledge" (*ìmò*) and "belief" (*ìgbàgbó*): If the information you receive from another person was not witnessed by you in a firsthand manner, it can only qualify as secondhand (*ìgbàgbó*).

6. This passage also is of interest because it introduces another term for "certainty" which the etm (123) reduces to the component "*dá*" + "*ojú*," literally "fix" + "eye." This again promotes that paradigm of firsthand observation.

questionable. For those who remain unpersuaded by any of the proposed alternative solutions to the "truth" or "certainty" problem (òótó; see chapter 2), here is another: that the Yoruba allow for a wide variety of *uncontested* (personal) observations of numerous objects or events witnessed simultaneously by numerous observers implies at least a 'thin' notion of intersubjective truth (see also chapter 2 for a discussion of this usage of 'thin').

MY SELF AND MY CHARACTER AS "OBJECTS" OF FIRSTHAND (INTROSPECTIVE) KNOWLEDGE

The importance Yoruba discourse attaches to the personal element of experience means that the knowledge I have of my own character (ìwà), as arising from *my* conscious self, is privileged. When it comes to others I may have to rely upon verbal and nonverbal behavior. But for the self that I am, consciousness privileges me with introspective awareness. My behavior follows upon thought, and my thought originates in my conscious self, my 'inside' or inú:

(22) It is where we think (okàn) of [going] that we usually go (ńlo). That is why we say [the proverb] that "wherever the head directs us, the legs should follow the person (ènìyàn) to that place" ("*ibi tí orí bá ti gbé ní lo kí esé máa sin ènìyàn lo*"). Before we do (se) anything the thinking (ńro) comes from inside (inú). We think from inside.

(23) This (èrò okàn)[7] is what you think (rò) about doing before you do (se) it.

(24) It is very difficult to identify (mò) . . . [bad people] because we don't know (mò) what their [innermost] thoughts (èrò) are.

(25) The church (sóòsì; etm 623) we attend is established as a society (egbé) or a place of meeting, but as members we don't know (mò) the innermost thoughts (inú) [of the members]. You don't know (mò) my 'inside' (inú). I don't know (mò) your 'inside' (inú).

(26) We human beings are just existing (wà; etm 660: used here in the sense of getting along as best we can, without still really understanding many things). I don't know (mò) your 'inside' (inú), and you don't know mine.

(27) It is only the person himself or herself who can know (mò) whether he or she is the enemy (òtá) of another person.

---

7. Etm 571 and 512; literally "thinking" of the "mind."

With reference to my personal knowledge of my personal character (*ìwà*), it is best to be cautious of excessive reification. That character (*ìwà*) is a term that may be used to represent the moral dimension to others' words and actions, does not mean that when I 'look' inside myself I find a distinctive psychological 'object' clearly labeled "character" ("*ìwà*"). Instead character (*ìwà*) may be a looser term of reference for whatever moral consciousness is involved (or immorally not involved) in my thinking. Here again it may be unrealistic to expect ordinary usage to be so precise, even if the terms of reference for the conscious self (*èrí okàn*) to be discussed shortly do involve the making of moral judgments.

Yoruba vocabulary pertaining to consciousness and its various faculties is rich. So as to provide a more clear understanding of moral character (*ìwà*), and the conscious self which has firsthand experience of its own moral character, that vocabulary will now be discussed in some detail. In doing so I will make reference to a study entitled "The House of the '*Inú*': Keys to the Structure of a Yoruba Theory of the 'Self'" (Hallen and Sodipo 1994), although the exposition of that paper will be revised and expanded upon here.

"*Inú*" (etm 309) is a general or comprehensive term the Yoruba can use to refer to the psychological self, psychological in the sense of that "inner, private, 'mental', enduring conscious element or dimension to the person" (Hallen and Sodipo 1994, p. 5). Some of the mental faculties or capacities that constitute the *inú* are the "mind" (*okàn*), "wisdom" (*ogbón*), the "intellect" (*opolo*), "judgment" (*èrí okàn*), the "eye" of the *inú* (*ojú inú*), in part akin to "insight," "self-consciousness" (*iyè inú*), "character" (*ìwà*), and "patience" (*sùúrù*). Patience (*sùúrù*) will become of importance considerably later when considering more specific types of moral characters that are preferred:

> (28) In the most common use (*nípàtàkì*) of the word ["*inú*"], when we say that someone has 'got'[8] *inú* we mean that he or she is a good person (*omolúàbí;* etm 414): anybody who is wise (*gbón*) and who can know (*mò*) via eyes (*ojú*) and body (*ara*) at the same time [again the conjunction of seeing, saying, and doing the right thing at the right time].
>
> (29) If the innermost self (*inú*) of someone is good, bad things will not have a place there. If we [try to] teach (*kò*) him or her to do bad things, he or she will not accept (*gbà*). Whenever a person is taught

---

8. Technically every human being has 'got' an *inú*. The approbation implied here inclines this expression toward the idiomatic.

(*kò*) to do bad (*ìkà*) things, if he or she agrees, this means that he or she wants to do bad things (*fé ṣe ìkà;* perhaps here expressing something akin to "will").

That more general reference is made to the "self" (*inú*) rather than a person's character (*ìwà*) when it comes to doing bad or good things is not unusual in some contexts, for the involvement of character (*ìwà*) is implied in such references to the self (*inú*):

(30) People will say that the innermost self (*inú*) of such a person is good. . . . That is character (*ìwà*).

(31) All of a person's character (*ìwà*) and actions (*iṣẹ́*) are gathered [located or originate] inside the innermost self (*inú*).

"Èmí" (etm 187) is another term that is frequently used to refer to the "self." Sometimes the *onísègùn* appear to use "*inú*" and "*èmí*" almost interchangeably. Sometimes the contexts in which "*inú*" tends to occur suggest that it may have more in common with English-language notions of the mental or conscious self, while "*èmí*" is used more frequently to refer to that spiritual element of the person the Yoruba believe survives death to be reincarnated for an indefinite number of further lifetimes.[9]

This discussion will concentrate on the life of the person when incarnate, when living in the world. To that end the remarks made by the *onísègùn* in which "*èmí*" appears to be virtually interchangeable with "*inú*" will be of primary interest:

(32) This is the self (*èmí*). A person with a bad *èmí* will behave badly. So also a person with a good *èmí* will behave well. Bad actions have their origin inside (*inú*).

(33) It is the self (*èmí*) which makes man behave (*hu ìwà*) as he is. It is the self (*èmí*) which makes a man behave in a good manner or in a bad manner. As you come to see me now, it was your self (*èmí*) which made you think of coming to see me. It is the self (*èmí*) which causes (*mún;* etm 429) people [to do good or bad].

(34) They [character (*ìwà*) and the self (*èmí*)] are one, because both good thoughts (*èrò*) and bad thoughts come out of the self (*èmí*).

(35) It is the people who possess bad (*burúkú*) selves (*èmí*) who do cruel (*ṣe ìkà*) [things].

(36) When a person has a self (*èmí*) and it is a good self (*èmí*), he or

---

9. In Hallen and Sodipo (1994, p. 5) the sense of *inú* is said to be more often psychological, and that of *èmí* to be more often metaphysical. In religious literature "*èmí*" is regularly translated as "vital spirit" or "soul."

she will behave (*hùwà*) well. If he or she has a bad (*burúkú*) self (*èmí*), he or she will behave (*hùwà*) in a bad manner.

(37) If the life of someone is bad, it comes from [is the product of] her own hand (*owó*) [doing]. If it is good, it comes from his or her hand. If the life of a person is good or bad, it comes from their 'insides' (*inú*). This is the self (*èmí*).

"*Okàn*" (etm 512), here rendered into English as "mind," is another element constitutive of the self (*inú* or *èmí*). In the same way that character (*ìwà*) may serve as a more specific reference for moral character, *okàn* is used when "mind" or "cognition" in particular is specifically being made reference to:

(38) You know that hearing is in the mind (*okàn*). When you use the ear to hear what they teach you, it goes into the mind (*okàn*). If your mind goes there [listens or pays attention], you must know (*mò*) that thing. If your mind (*okàn*) does not go there [fails to listen or to pay attention], you cannot know it. It means that you are just 'looking' (*wò*) [i.e., not concentrating] (Hallen 1979, p. 312, note 15).

(39) Our self changes in the way that the clock changes. You know that it is impossible for a person to stand [in any place] without thinking of anything. When he or she stands quietly, and they ask of him or her "Where is your self?" for him or her to say he or she is not thinking of anything—the self cannot rest without thinking of something. As we are speaking together at this moment, our self is 'working' for us in another place [also thinking about something else].

(40) I think that the self (*èmí*) should know (*mò*) this because, apart from the discussion we are having now, our minds (*okàn*) are also somewhere else, even far-off [thinking of what we would rather be doing, daydreaming]. But as we are [physically present] here, it appears as if the self (*èmí*) also is [here] with us. If it is possible for one not to talk at all, his or her self (*èmí*) cannot be where he or she is. The mind (*okàn*) will be wandering (*lo sí ibi gbogbo*) here and there. As you are here now, your mind (*okàn*) could be in [thinking of] Lagos. This is because you once lived there. Your self (*èmí*) may be looking for [thinking about] all the things you knew before.

In terms of a faculty psychology, mind (*okàn*) serves as the locus or repository of thought (*èrò*):

(41) He could not have done it under any influence if the idea (*èrò*) had not been in his mind (*okàn*).

Within the self (èmí or inú), within the mind or consciousness (okàn), as indicated, reference may also be made to a number of more specialized and refined capacities:

a. "Ogbón" (etm 249: "intelligence," "sense") is frequently rendered into English as "wisdom." This appears to refer to being unusually informed about the traditions pertaining to Yoruba culture and, for that matter, for being reliably informed generally. In an oral culture it could obviously be important to stress the positive attributes of such individuals:

> (42) When you have a child you begin to teach it wisdom (ogbón). When the father becomes old, then he will begin to say [to the child] 'this and this' are the things which they told us [things inherited from the past]. Whatever he has seen or heard, he will be saying the same things [in turn] to his son. But the son has not seen all of this [firsthand for himself]. Whatever we have not seen but which we are told of, are what we call "this and this are the things they told us."

It is relevant to recall the earlier discussion (see chapter 1) about the truth status of traditions. When they have the status of information that has not been tested or verified, their epistemological status can be no more than hypothetical, than possibly true. But knowledge about traditions, and being an accurate source of information generally, need not imply that such persons are regarded as relatively passive repositories, sort of living libraries. It also implies being able to discriminate among traditions and information to choose whatever is particularly relevant to a situation, and being able to reason on the basis of that information, being able to apply that information, so as to determine what would be the best thing to do. It is this final dimension to "ogbón" that causes it to overlap or to intersect the usage associated with the intellect (opolo).

b. "Opolo" (etm 524: "brain") is sometimes used by the Yoruba to refer to the brain as the physical organ it is. But it would be a gross oversimplification to infer from this that the physical locus of human intelligence is as cerebrally oriented as in the West. For the physical location of the self (inú) and the origin of its various faculties is said to be the stomach or belly.[10]

---

10. Or as expressed by the oníṣègùn: "the intellect (opolo) is living inside the self (inú) before it moves to the head" (Hallen and Sodipo 1994, p. 7).

The sense of "opolo" that is more relevant to our interests is its use as something comparable to the English-language "intellect." As well as the ability to recall information in an accurate manner,[11] saying someone is intelligent (opolo) implies that he or she also is able to use that information to think in an original and creative manner:

> (43) For example, if a person is saying that this town should have water [pipe-borne] or a bank, or that our hospital should be changed to a general [one], the way in which this could happen is that both men and women would contribute money. People may [at some point] ask, who made the [original] suggestion? They would say that he or she has 'got' intelligence (opolo). This is the way that we use that word.

c. In *KBW* "èrí okàn" (etm 192 and 512: "conscience") was rendered literally as "the witnessing or evidence of the mind (okàn)"—"witnessing" or "evidence" in the sense that, if the paradigm for knowledge (ìmò) is veridical perception + mental comprehension, this expression represents the latter element of (mental) comprehension and judgment about what one is seeing without which knowledge (ìmò) would not be possible. At the time, in a separate note (p. 61, note 9) we commented on Christian missionaries' use of this expression as an equivalent for their notion of "conscience," lamenting the fact that reducing the Yoruba meaning to this deprived it of significant content.

Several colleagues have since complained that our lament and comparatively amoral rendering of èrí okàn as "judgment" pure and simple has the unfortunate consequence of depriving the Yoruba of any critical moral sense (Bello 1988; Oke 1995). That was not our intention. In some contexts the onísègùn clearly do assign judgment a moral role:

> (44) Whatever you do (se) in the absence of any person and which nobody knows (mò), your mind (okàn) will be telling (jélérí) you that you have done (se) this thing. This may be a bad thing or a good thing.
> (45) If he or she is a real person (ènìyàn gidigidi), he or she will know

---

11. As expressed by the onísègùn: "If they say about ten sentences in your presence today, and you are able to repeat exactly the same words tomorrow, and in three days you can repeat the same without taking away any one [word] out of it, and you can say it again even when it is five months' time when you have not written it down, this is what is called someone who has 'got' intellect (opolo)" (Hallen and Sodipo 1994, p. 7). Here "got" is used with the same sense of approbation as in note 8 above.

(*mò*) that what he or she has done that time [when he or she did not do as he or she should have] was not good.

But in others where *èrí okàn*'s influence also is determinate, the situation appears to be one in which there is no apparent *moral* choice. Here it makes sense to render its function as akin to the morally neutral but still crucially important role of a critical sense, good sense, or judgment. For example, in the following passage "good" and "bad" seem to be used in pragmatic or instrumental senses, as what it may have been advisable or inadvisable to do on other than moral grounds:

(46) This [*èrí okàn*] can be divided into many parts. . . . For example, if you are doing something which is always right without anyone telling you [what to do], your judgment (*èrí okàn*) is helping you to do it. You can be invited to go and visit a person. You could say, "If you are going to so-and-so's house, I'm not going." Your good sense (*èrí okàn*) tells you not to go. And if you are dragged there, and it happens that there is a quarrel, you will say that you did not want to come, that your good sense (*èrí okàn*) told you not to come there. It is your own judgment (*èrí okàn*) which tells you whether something is good (*dára*) or bad (*burú*), and this is more important than accepting advice from someone. If your own judgment (*èrí okàn*) speaks with you, it will be difficult for another person to persuade you from doing what you want to do. The *èrí okàn* is the [part of] the self (*èmí*) which sustains the person (*ènìyàn*). Those who have no faculty of judgment (*èrí okàn*) are those who are always doing the wrong thing at the wrong time.

The result is not to deny the Yoruba a sense of moral judgment. It is to suggest that the view of judgment underlying this expression is broader than the English-language "conscience," so that moral deliberation becomes only one type to be subsumed under this more general heading.

d. It is the "*ojú inú*" (etm 460 and 309; literally "inside eye" or "eye of the self") that the *oníṣègùn* was describing in quotation (4). As this quotation indicates, this capacity is frequently linked to the ability to 'picture' something internal to one's consciousness. As such it shares some meaning in common with the English-language "imagination."

The 'picturing' powers of this faculty are sometimes linked to the paranormal, so that it takes on vestiges of 'second sight', or of foreseeing the future in a supernatural manner (Bodunrin 1978; Oluwole 1978). But the remarks of the *oníṣègùn* give equal weight to rendering the *ojú inú* into English as "insight," when defined by the *Concise Oxford Dictionary* as "penetration [via the intellect] into character, circumstances, etc. with the understanding" (p. 630). One of the most valued consequences of such insight would be more acute predictive powers.

Nevertheless this ability to 'see' more in an event than what is superficially obvious to the casual observer indicates that we are here entering the domain of true intellect, of being able to assess and interpret one's experience in an acute and independent manner:

> (47) We can look at a person. You can even look at a crop [on a farm]. If it is not good, you will say [perhaps only to yourself] that the soil of the place is bad. If you see a child working sluggishly, you will say that she is a sick person. If the child is restless [not serious about what she is doing], you might say this is a bad child. We are looking at these things with insight (*ojú inú*).

e. "*Iyè inú*" (etm 334; literally "inside thought or understanding" of the self) is used to name the consciousness *of* self in self-consciousness. This is the "me" that witnesses and chooses to deliberate about a particular experience, that suffers the pain of a headache, that chooses to exercise insight (*ojú inú*), judgment (*èrí okàn*), or the intellect (*opolo*) upon a given occasion. In part this understanding is said to be "inside" because I may decide not to share it with anyone else. My self-consciousness is private, and as such I may keep such thoughts to myself:

> (48) They [the various psychological faculties already enumerated] have separate 'keys' [controls] which open [activate] them when you need them. If you want to make use of [exercise] wisdom (*ogbón*), you take it out of [find it in] this innermost self (*inú*). If you want to have [exercise] patience (*sùúrù*), you take it from [find it in] the self (*inú*). Everyone of them has got its own place. . . . All the 'keys' [the initiatives and conscious decisions to make use of any human faculty] that work in the [human] body are inside the self (*inú*).
>
> This [*iyè inú*] is where the 'keys' live. The conscious self (*iyè inú*) is the thing which directs or advises (*júwe*) a person about what to do. If you want to do something, the understanding (*iyè*) of your self (*inú*) will show you how to do it. This [*iyè inú*] is different from *inú* and *èmí*, but they all live inside the *inú*.

It is a commonplace in much of the literature dealing with sub-Saharan Africa's cultural and intellectual patrimony that the terms "pre-reflective" and "pre-critical" feature prominently. One fundamental presumption underlying the use of these terms is that African theoretical thought as evidenced by African discourse has little to offer when it comes to *introspective* analyses of the individual, conscious self and the intellectual faculties at its disposal—faculties associated, most importantly, with cognition or understanding. Consequently Africans generally have been characterized as peoples who care much more about what human beings *do* than about what (and how) they *think*.

Perhaps this presumed emphasis upon the importance of *doing* (the 'right' thing) in an implicitly social context has contributed to the impression that it is the community which is responsible for how the individual behaves, and therefore in effect for morality, in African societies. This general line of thought—that in 'traditional' Africa the community is by definition much more important than the individual—will be discussed in greater detail later. What is relevant here is to point out that the above passages from discussions with the *oníṣègùn* provide ample evidence that Yoruba discourse makes explicit reference to conscious states and experiences that could only be named on the basis of explicit introspective reference, and that also are regarded as important prerequisites to moral or immoral behavior.

In these passages there are references to the "mind," to "reflection," to the importance of self-conscious decision-making *preceding* action, that make mention of the individual's responsibility to think through and thereby also be responsible for those actions. This emphasis placed upon thought processes that precede action should serve to redress any imbalance created by a relatively one-sided emphasis on the importance of communitarian values and sanctions for governing individual behavior (especially where the part played by thought is, sometimes, not even taken into account).

MY DESTINY AND MY CONSCIOUSNESS

During each lifetime the self (*èmí*) is embodied in the world as human being, it has an "'inner' head" or personal destiny (*orí*):

(49) For a long time we've been saying in our land that men end up doing (*àkúnlèyàn*) what they have chosen in 'heaven' (*òrun*). This shows that everybody has made his destiny (*ìpín*), even before they come to the world. And this kind of destiny cannot be rejected (*nkò*) during the person's lifetime.

(50) It is destiny (*ìpín*) that is called the "'inner' head" (*orí*)—what we choose (*pín*) from 'heaven' (*òrun*). It is said that (*nwán ma ńṣo wípé*) it is the "'inner' head" (*orí*) which makes the choice (*ṣe pín*) [of the type of life a person will live] before the person (*ènìyàn*) comes to the world. When people say that a person (*ènìyàn*) has a bad destiny (*orí burúkú*), they are making reference to the destiny (*ìpín*) which they chose in 'heaven'.

(51) It is the destiny (*ìpín*) that we choose that we call the "'inner' head" (*orí*). People may say someone has made a 'bad choice' (*ìpín burúkú*). They mean the same thing as when they say a person has a bad destiny [i.e., *ìpín burúkú* equals *orí burúkú*]. They may also say that a person has made a 'good choice' (*ìpín rere*). This means the same thing as saying someone has a good destiny (*orí rere*). "'Inner' head" (*orí*) and "destiny" (*ìpín*) refer to the same thing.

(52) What you are referring to as "destiny" (*ìpín:* etm 355) is *kádàrá* (etm 357: "destiny," "fate").

(53) All the things we do on earth are according to our destiny (*ìpín*). If a person behaves (*se*) badly, this is what their destiny (*ìpín*) wishes. This [destiny] is what has been created (*se*) along with them.

More studies have been made of this component of the Yoruba psychology than any other, no doubt in part because of its comparative novelty in cross-cultural terms.[12]

The self (*èmí*) is said to choose its destiny, evidently still as some form of conscious self, each time before returning to the world for its next incarnation.[13] Its choice is said to be free because the supreme deity (*Olórun*) puts at its disposal innumerable possible future lifetimes, with attendant moral characters (*ìwà*) ranging from as bad as bad can be to the opposite extreme of good. Whatever choice the self (*èmí*) finally makes will be approved without comment.[14]

(54) It is the person who has chosen for himself or herself what he or she has come to do (*se*) on earth. . . . The supreme deity (*Olórun*) merely says that it should be so [the *àse*].[15]

---

12. The efforts of translators to come to terms with this novelty are responsible for the remarkable variety of suggested equivalents for it in English: "guardian spirit" (Ellis 1974, p. 127); "god of fate" (Johnson 1921, p. 27); "guardian deity" (Talbot 1969, p. 283); "deification of good luck" (Lucas 1948, p. 283); "ancestral guardian soul" (Bascom 1956, p. 401); "personality-soul" (Idowu 1962, p. 170); "locus of intelligence "(Verger 1971, p. 63); "human destiny" (Abimbola 1971, p. 80); "bearer of human destiny" (Makinde 1988b, p. 90); "spiritual entity . . . to account for the phenomenon of destiny . . . [that] determines the personality of the individual" (Gbadegesin 1991, p. 40).

13. There is a philosophically astute and culturally informative discussion of the various factors involved in choosing a destiny and the relationship between an (otherworldly) afterlife and (earthly) reincarnation in Gbadegesin (1991). See especially pp. 46–56.

14. To quote the *onísègùn:* "It [*èmí*] . . . chooses what it will come to do. . . . So also it is the act (*isé*) of the self (*èmí*) when it is with the supreme deity (*Olórun*). There are very many different kinds of selves (*èmí*), and they ask for different kinds of things."

15. *Àse* here has the significance of the power employed by the supreme deity to join a particular destiny to a particular self (*èmí*).

Does the disembodied self (èmí) that makes this choice itself have a moral character (ìwà) when choosing its new destiny? This is one of those 'logical consequences' questions philosophers can ask that it may be unfair to put to ordinary usage.[16] Nevertheless if the self (èmí) has to select the future lifetime it prefers, the process of favoring one over others would seem to involve some kind of character to influence the decision.

The degree of predetermination to which the Yoruba lifetime is subjected by this notion of destiny (orí) has been summarized as follows: "the orí is, in a sense, my meaning—is what I shall become while I am in the world this time. It limits my possibilities and provides me with a course to follow" (Hallen 1976, p. 60). This way of expressing it has been endorsed by a subsequent study (Gbadegesin 1984, p. 181):

> (55) Destiny (ìpín) is everything that the person (ènìyàn) will do on earth. The self (èmí) chooses all the things that the person (ènìyàn) will do, without leaving nothing aside.

The complications that may ensue from such a notion of predetermination for a moral system can be serious. According to quotation (53) "everything" a person does is determined by their destiny (orí), and as quotation (53) also indicates, some kind of linkage is made between morally correct and incorrect behavior and an individual's destiny (as orí or ìpín). If all of a person's words and actions may be construed as predetermined from the moment they are born, how morally responsible may they be held for them? Destiny (orí) introduces the possibility of a determinism that would absolve everyone in Yoruba society of direct moral responsibility for whatever good or ill they do or say. How the belief system may be seen to resolve this question becomes of crucial importance to whatever system of values it enunciates:

---

16. For instance, does the tree that falls in the forest make a sound when there's no one there to hear it? Nevertheless the oníṣègùn did remark that "the self (èmí) brings its character (ìwà) to the world"; "people are born with character (ìwà)"; "You were born (bí) with your character (ìwà). You do not come to the world to choose it"; "The character (ìwà) goes with him [when a person dies]. It doesn't leave you behind." But one oníṣègùn dissented: "We don't know whether they [èmí] can distinguish good from bad, because we are not there [i.e., we cannot 'see' the afterlife or, as one Nigerian aphorism famously put it: 'No telephone for heaven!'] when they choose [a destiny]." Also, "Yoruba philosophy regarding ìwà, character, is that one's character, either good or bad, is not interned with the deceased; even after death character continues to exist here below and in the hereafter" (Delano 1969, vol. 2, p. 366).

(56) It [orí] is the most important (pàtàkì jù) [thing to a person]. It is the creator (elédà) [in the sense of a force that will 'carve out' a lifetime for us] with whom we come to the world.

When it comes to integrating this notion of predestination with every-day life, a variety of otherworldly beliefs play supporting roles. It is said that, when finally settling upon a particular destiny, it is very difficult for the self (èmí) to foresee the multifarious consequences of any lifetime it chooses. The self (èmí) that honestly desires a lifetime of doing real good can make a poor choice and even end up as morally corrupt. Furthermore from the time it is reborn into the world, the self (èmí) is said to lose the memory of whatever destiny it *thought* it chose. In other words, once I become sufficiently self-conscious to be held responsible for my actions, I can no longer remember what I've supposedly come into the world pre-destined to do:

(57) Nobody can really know (mò) what his or her destiny is. If it were so, one might be able to go directly [to what they've chosen to do]. . . . But no person can say with accuracy what someone has chosen.

(58) No person can know the kind of choice he or she made (ńkan tí o yàn). He or she cannot remember when he or she is in the world. If he or she could, he or she would be able to go straight into the course [life] which he or she chose.

(59) We usually say the person (ènìyàn) will not do other things apart from those he or she has chosen (pín). But when one is in the world he or she does not know what he or she chose.

My destiny is still somehow with me, guiding me, but not as something of which I may be conscious:[17]

(60) It is when the person (ènìyàn) is created that the destiny (ìpín) is also created with them. But it is the self (èmí) which has to do all the things we do.

How any latent inconsistencies—between this notion of a 'fixed' destiny and the efforts of individuals' striving to become something more or even other than they find themselves to be—are regarded and possibly re-solved by the onísègùn is an issue that will be discussed below.

---

17. Robin Horton (1983) draws interesting parallels between the Yoruba destiny (orí) and the unconscious of Freudian psychiatry.

WHEN INDIVIDUAL DETERMINATION
MEETS SOCIAL MATRIX

When all of these beliefs about the self are combined and interrelated with all of the various faculties and abilities that constitute the self, what becomes the 'human condition' from a Yoruba point of view? How, for example, is a passage like the following now to be interpreted:

> (61) This is the self (èmí). A person with a bad self (èmí) will behave badly. So also a person with a good self (èmí) will behave well. Bad actions have their source inside (inú) [the person].

Can the self be held *morally* responsible independently of its destiny (orí)? Or is it more fundamentally *morally* responsible because it chose the *orí*? Or is it less *morally* responsible when it finds itself the unwilling victim of a lifetime it finds morally repugnant? Indeed in certain contexts a person's destiny (orí) is referred to as the behavioral and moral surrogate of the self (èmí):

> (62) There is something we call "destiny" ("orí inú"). This is related to our behavior (ṣe) and speech (òrò enu). Whenever things happen [e.g., a problem arises] and one begins to behave unusually and say things that we do not expect of him or her . . . they would say that my destiny (orí inú) was worrying [influencing] me because I picked a quarrel . . . without any reason. There is no other thing we know of destiny (orí) apart from behavior (ìwà) and the way we talk (òrò enu).[18]

When it concerns the individual coming to terms with the vicissitudes of life, carving out an identity and struggling to succeed, how is the moral to be interrelated with all of these various faculties and forces? How important can moral imperatives be—even that basic query, Why be

---

18. The explicit linkage of behavior and destiny is noteworthy. From a conceptual point of view it would appear that the provenance of a good moral character (ìwà) must overlap or intersect that of a good orí (destiny), as in the conventional Venn diagram. But a healthy portion of each would also not overlap, as in the cases of the morally good who endure unhappy and unsuccessful circumstances, or the corrupt businessman whose success becomes the envy of his peers. Also, "bad" in some contexts need not mean *morally* bad. A decision might also be bad for purely strategic, tactical, or instrumental reasons: "The one [orí as destiny] we are talking about is 'inside'. If the 'inner head' (orí) is good, it starts from 'inside'. . . . If your 'inside' [head] is good, you will get out of any problem (ònà rè di tìtì tì) you come across, and people will be saying that your 'inner' head (orí inú) is good. . . . Whenever anybody does bad things, it means his or her 'inside' is bad."

moral?—in a context where, potentially, every action of significance is said to be determined by a power (one's destiny) whose essential nature is unknown? On the other hand, one might wonder whether the *discon-nection* of predestination from conscious life does not effectively undermine any *practical* consequences the *belief* could have for moral discourse? If I no longer know what I am predetermined to do, does my practical situation vis-à-vis making the decisions of everyday life not become the same as that of a person who has no such belief? To answer this last question in the affirmative would be a serious error. Given the frequency with which the Yoruba make reference to their destiny (*orí*), propitiate their destiny (*orí*), petition their destiny (*orí*), and consult diviners about the nature of their destiny (*orí*), collecting information and evidence about the type of lifetime one is meant to follow remains a major preoccupation of Yoruba discourse.[19]

From the epistemological perspective, once an individual is born into the world, although he or she is presumed or believed to have a destiny, the nature or character of that destiny may only be adduced or inferred (*ìgbàgbó*) from a variety of sources:

a. From the successes and failures we experience in life:

(63) This means that the destiny (*orí*) of the person (*ènìyàn*) takes him or her to where he or she goes (*ńlo*). Destiny (*ìpín*) is what we've chosen (*yàn*) from heaven. We cannot change (*yí*) it when we come to the world. This is what will happen (*se lè*) to us in this world. If the person should achieve a very high office, it is his or her destiny (*orí*) which will push him or her to that place.

(64) When we come to the world and we find things easy, we may take pride in the fact that we chose a very good thing in 'heaven' (*òrun*).

(65) For example, someone going to school may not know what he will study when he leaves home. But he will take to the one [subject] in which he performs the best (*mú ò kè jù*).

(66) Some persons, when they get to the world, may realize that they're doing very bad things (*ìkà*) and they want to be good (*rere*), but despite their efforts they will not be able to change the *àse*[20] of the supreme deity (*Olódùmarè*). Because this is what he or she himself

---

19. One could persist in asking, Why does it remain as a preoccupation? Why don't the Yoruba en masse just sit back and take things as they come, saying "What will be, will be"? This is another of those 'logical' lines of thought to which ordinary language is unable to provide an answer.

20. See note 15 above.

or herself [the self as èmí] has chosen (yàn), upon which he or she has agreed with the supreme deity (Olódùmarè) [as that self's preferred choice of destiny].

b. From the prescriptions of diviners if and when individuals feel the need to consult them about how they can 'change' their lives: The onísègùn or babaláwo[21] play a number of roles in Yoruba society. What is of interest here is the one they play in the lives of individuals who consult them about their destiny. There can be many reasons for this, but the most relevant are cases in which persons feel that they are failing to succeed and become unhappy, dissatisfied, frustrated by anything ranging from their present situation to their general lot in life.

It is not necessary to detail the machinations of the divination process. The point of consulting a diviner, of course, is to identify the source, the cause, of failure and to obtain a prescription that will correct it, remove it. One can still ask what is the point of even consulting diviners if everyone's life course is predetermined? What is the point of trying to 'do' something about a past, present, or future which cannot be changed? In the remarks of the onísègùn there are two lines of thought that may be relevant here. One concerns the relative mixture of happiness and unhappiness, success and failure, that everyone has a right realistically to expect from life:

(67) But both good and bad things follow each other [are intertwined during the course of a person's life] ("Ire àti ibi ní o ntele ara nwon."). There are no persons who can accomplish good things all the time without having any difficulties (ibi).

(68) Bad and good things work together [are intertwined]. It is impossible to choose one good thing for a person that might not have any bad concomitants ("Búburú àti rere ní ó nrín pò.").

(69) It seems to us that someone has good (rere) fortune (sáà), but there are some aspects (ibi tí oti je; literally "places where") of his or her life which are good and some which are bad. The person who is

---

21. In Yoruba culture generally the two professions most prominently associated with divination are that of the babaláwo (literally "father" or "guardian of secrets") and that of the onísègùn. In the literature the term "babaláwo" is conventionally rendered into English by the word "diviner," and onísègùn by "herbalist." The literature devoted to the study of the babaláwo and the exegesis of the literary corpus of which they are said to be the "guardians"—Ifá—is substantial and well worthy of study in its own right. Study of the methods used by the onísègùn has, by comparison, been considerably less intensive. In Ijan there was no resident babaláwo, and so divination too was a prerogative of the onísègùn.

experiencing the bad (*búburú*) sees (*rí*) it [is the one who really knows it]. When we say life is bad for one person, there are places where it is [also] good for him or her. A person cannot be unfortunate (*búburú*) in all respects.

The second line of thought arises from an expression that has bedeviled any number of studies intent on reconciling the belief in predestination with the practice of consulting diviners, if the latter implies that an individual may exercise some independent control over, effect upon, his or her life once in the world. That expression has been popularly rendered into English as "to miss [the] road" or "missing road," frequently taken to mean that one has lost one's way in the world—strayed from the path for which predestined:

(70) He has just 'missed road' (*sínà*). . . . As I told you before, when the fellow realizes his folly, he will go to the diviner (*babaláwo*) to ask which path (*ònà*) to follow on earth. And the diviner (*babaláwo*), who has insight (*rírán*), will explain to him that he has left the path. It is then he will come back to the right path. To 'miss road' (*sínà*) is like when a stranger comes to a town with many roads and does not know exactly where he is going. If such a stranger has no one to direct (*tó si ònà*) him, he could 'miss road'. Suppose someone is coming from a distant place. His intention is to come to Ijan. But he takes the road leading to Enugu. When he gets to Enugu and asks for the road to Ijan he must be directed here. This is the job of the diviner (*babaláwo*).

(71) It is the destiny (*orí*) which makes the choice (*pín*) of all these things. When a person 'misses his or her road' (*sì lónà*) and has someone to redirect him or her, he or she says that it is his or her destiny (*orí*) which has directed him or her to the person who shows him or her the road. If the supreme deity (*Olórun*) wants someone not to 'miss road', he or she will meet people who will tell him or her the way wherever he or she goes. He or she will always say that his or her destiny (*orí*) has helped him or her so that he or she is able to meet good persons (*èníyàn rere*) who are always helping him or her.

(72) There is not any important thing that the diviner (*babaláwo*) can do (*se*) here. What happens is that one (*ení*) is bound to suffer during the early part of his life [if that is as he has chosen]. And when, after he has seen the diviner (*babaláwo*), life becomes more abundant for him, that also is what he has planned (*yàn*) for himself. It is not the effort of the diviner (*babaláwo*) that has made him be prosperous. In fact, we could regard the work of the diviner (*babaláwo*) as the person who redirects (*júwe ònà fún*) a man who has 'missed his road' (*sínà*) in the street. You would acknowledge that

there are children of rich men who are poor, regardless of whatever efforts their rich father may have made to help them. Yet such children might not reach a high place in life. Usually people say such a child chose to be a poor man when he was choosing his destiny.

(73) If someone misses his destiny (ńsìnà ìpín), another man will come to redirect (kò sìnà) him. The supreme deity (Olórun) made this provision for such and such a man to do this. And it's possible for a person (ènìyàn) to have a destiny (ìpín) with which he or she will 'miss road' (sínà) for a certain part of his or her life, but in which he or she will come to the path in a later part of his or her life.

The semantic sense of "missing road" generates problems because it is difficult to reconcile the idea of having a fixed destiny with the notion of losing touch with that destiny for a portion of one's life. To further complicate matters, quotations (70) and (71) might seem to imply that the diviner can carry the destiny-tampering one step further by putting the person back onto the path on which they are meant to be.

The more fundamental sense of these passages is that the 'missing road' is actually a constituent part of the destiny as originally chosen, as is the decision to 'go' and consult a diviner, as is the greater degree of success that may follow thereafter. The sense of 'missing road' that underlies all of this is that it may be used to describe a period of apparent or genuine misfortune. It is persons who fail, who are dissatisfied, and who are unhappy who think that they (or by others are said to) have 'missed road'. To 'miss road' does not mean that one has strayed from one's "true" destiny, so much as that one is experiencing a period of comparative hardship in the overall destiny one has chosen. That periods of unhappiness may be equated metaphorically with missing one's way makes good sense in a semantic context where the underlying strategy is that the point of choosing a 'good' destiny is that one will then be happy, content, and successful for as much of a lifetime as possible.

When the oníṣègùn reflected on the range of clients or patients who came to consult them about undesired misfortune, and then generalized about the kinds of causal explanations with which they provided them, the cases fell under two headings:

a. Dissatisfaction or failure attributed directly to one's destiny: Attributing failure directly to one's destiny is the more unpalatable and far less frequent of the two. To borrow, with rhetorical misgivings, an expression from computer terminology: This implies that there is a problem with the hard drive rather than just the software:

(74) There are certain persons who, even if other people wish them good fortune, will continue to follow bad ways. People are likely

to say to them that such persons have chosen a bad destiny from heaven, and they will call them that—"bad destiny choosers" (olórí burúkú).

(75) There are ways in which we can know whether our medicines are effective (ṣe ènìyàn dáda). When we prepare a certain kind of medicine for a person, the medicine will heal him if he himself is a good person. But there are some people who do it to themselves (ṣe ara rè; i.e., are the cause of their own bad fortune). No medicine can cure such people.

(76) Of such persons [suicides] we say their destiny (orí) 'turned back' [seemed as if lost] from them. . . . He or she thinks about what is happening today but forgets that it might change tomorrow. His or her thought is too narrowly focused.

(77) Any person with a bad destiny, and who realizes that it cannot be changed, will simply conclude that the next time [incarnation] when he or she comes to the world he or she will have a good destiny, because now he or she cannot change the one he or she has.

Evaluating someone's destiny as a whole in terms of whether it is good or bad is a momentous undertaking. When the verdict is negative, that effectively condemns the individual concerned to a lifetime, rather than merely an episode, of failure.

b. Dissatisfaction or failure attributed to other persons ("òtá"; etm 529: enemies) who do not have your best interests at heart: For this reason failure that is attributed to the relatively temporary conflicting interests of other persons—competitors or malevolent types—is the much more common type of explanation provided by diviners:

(78) When a person is not able to reach the level [of achievement] he or she desired, if he or she says it is the work of an enemy (òtá) it is because of some signs (àmì) [of this] which he or she has experienced (rí). If he or she engages in a certain occupation without success [one kind of 'sign'], he or she will say this is the influence (iṣé) of an enemy (òtá). If he should marry 'outside' [a wife who is not from the locality] and others should take his wife away [another kind of 'sign'], he will say this is the influence (iṣé) of an enemy (òtá). A person whose child is killed [as if] by àjé[22] [yet another kind of 'sign'] will know that this is the influence (iṣé) of an enemy (òtá).

(79) Other people can cause (dàrú) one to miss [one's destiny]. For in-

---

22. For àjé see pages 90–97.

stance, a man may acquire property and, when he is not around, it could be stolen. In this sense, such a thief has spoiled the 'plan' of the man who acquired this property. From the origin of the world there have been some people who do bad things (*aba nijé*), whose business is just to disrupt another man's plans. Such people could spoil another man's destiny.

(80) Let's say there were two trees, side by side. The larger could fall on the smaller. It could remain [resting] on the smaller tree for several years, which would retard the growth of the smaller tree. This is the same situation as that of people whom an enemy (*òtá*) has over-shadowed.

Attributing problems to the intervention of other persons leaves the individual with some hope that their influence may eventually be countered, that some of the destiny remaining may be good:

(81) There are very few people who would say they had made a bad choice in "heaven" (*òrun*), even when living an unhappy life on earth. What such people usually say is that this [their undesirable circumstance] is the work of the 'people of the world' [*òtá*].

From the moral point of view what is of special interest about the category of the enemy (*òtá*) and about their intervention as a conventional explanation for misfortune is that it brings the role of other persons, rather than just the self, into prominence. Although I may well blame myself for some of my shortcomings, the "other" as a potential source of my more serious problems provides an opportune narrative transition to the interpersonal or social dimension of Yoruba moral discourse. The types of behavior taken as symptomatic of the antipersonal become the antisocial. But care must be taken not to present the use of the "other" as a cause for more-than-ordinary misfortune in an unflattering light. Personalized causal elements need rate no higher nor lower on the intellectual scale than impersonalized ones. To quote from Jeanne Favret-Saada's study (1980)[23] of the witchcraft belief in contemporary France:

Whenever folklorists or reporters talk of witchcraft in the country, they always do so as if one were facing two incompatible physical theories: the pre-logical or medieval attitude of peasants, who wrongly attri-

---

23. Valentin Mudimbe chided (1987) the authors of *KBW* for failing to make an explicit comparison (Favret-Saada's book was listed in the bibliography) between Favret-Saada's study and our own. That sin of omission is, I hope, hereby corrected.

bute their misfortunes to imaginary witches; and ours, the attitude of educated people who know how to handle causal relations correctly. It is said or implied that peasants are incapable of this either because of ignorance or of backwardness. In this respect, the description given of the peasant and the "*pays,*" the canton, that determines him is governed by a peculiar set of terms which necessarily imply that he is incapable of grasping causal relations. Witchcraft is put forward as a nonsense theory which peasants can afford to adopt because it is the local theory. The folklorist's job is then to underline the difference between his own theory (which also happens to be a "true" one) and the peasant's, which is only a belief.

But who can ignore the difficulties involved in postulating the coexistence of two incompatible physical theories which correspond to two ages of humankind? Do you really have to do thirty months of fieldwork to be in a position to say that country people are just as well able to cope with causal relations as anyone else, and to make the suggestion that witchcraft cannot be reduced to a physical theory, although it does indeed imply a certain kind of causality? (p. 5)[24]

One must tread carefully when topics like witchcraft or the "enemy" (òtá) are introduced. Too often their existence in a society is used primarily to imply that the culture concerned is somehow intellectually backward. Indeed, Favret-Saada's findings provoked angry denunciations and denials from a French cultural establishment that refused to accept the popular survival of a belief that had been relegated to its archaic, medieval past.

My position on the reality of witchcraft as a cross-cultural phenomenon is articulated at length in *KBW.* It is argued there that the personality type in Yoruba society known as the àjé, conventionally rendered into English as "witch" by Christian missionaries and a disappointing number of social anthropologists, may more specifically be interpreted as referring to persons of extraordinary intellect rather than this folkloric bugaboo immediately associated with the devil and pacts with incubi and succubi, magic, and the black mass.

It is also relevant to note that Favret-Saada eventually concluded that,

---

24. The significance of Favret-Saada's title, *Deadly Words,* is that in France's Bocage region malevolent words directed by one person against another become the weapons that inflict the damage. Words become more than performative utterances. They become performative missiles. The power of words in Yoruba culture, particularly with reference to incantations, is the subject of O. L. Osatuyi's M. A. thesis (Obafemi Awolowo University, Nigeria, 1985) titled "'Ofò': An African Issue in Philosophy." An astute ethnophilosophical work, it merits publication in its own right.

even for the prelogical "peasants" who were the subjects of her study, there were no clearly identifiable human beings in these communities who could in fact be considered witches. What did exist, more importantly, for these contemporary citizens of France were (1) undesired and undeserved misfortunes which (2) were attributed to the malevolent thoughts of indeterminate "others," and (3) which could be reliably disarmed via the ministrations (rather than "witch hunts") of local healers. At some point it might be interesting to test the limits of this model against Yoruba culture—that it is not necessary to have witches in order to have a belief in something resembling the witchcraft phenomenon.

Once the pejorative slurs associated with the witchcraft belief have been bracketed it is possible to concentrate, from an explicitly methodological point of view, on the type of causal model involved. The relevance of Favret-Saada's study is her discovery that serious misfortune is causally attributed to the influence of other, sometimes malevolent, persons. What is most interesting about this as an explanatory model is that it is apparently a product of reasoning from effect to cause. Undesired misfortune, as a phenomenon, could not be denied. That the persons concerned then conjoined it with a semantic and causal network that attributed it to other human beings is a point that may invite further comparisons as this study proceeds.

c. Of particular relevance to the moral, from our behavior as observed, interpreted, and morally defined by others: Morality is more than a matter of personal conscience (èrí ọkàn). The moral is determined in a context that is by convention social. My efforts to fulfil my destiny, including those involving the most agonizing, personal, introspective turmoil, take place in a society. That society itself rewards certain forms of behavior and punishes others. This means that my moral self is defined as much by others as by myself.

Whatever inclinations I may have that are inborn, whatever predispositions are peculiar to my self (èmí or inú), in whatever directions I may conclude that my destiny (orí) is leading me—the moral dimension to my behavior, in particular, must also come to terms with the social matrix:

> (82) The reason is that we come to meet [know] ourselves in the world. We don't know if any [prior] change takes place. We don't know the kind of destiny other persons chose in heaven. It may have been good or bad. We just find the child in the world. We may say a child should behave one way and then it behaves in another. If we were to kill a child because we think it might be a bad person (èni-yàn burúkú), the Creator (ẹlẹ́dà; etm 172; here used as another

expression for *Olórun,* the supreme deity) will punish us for such an action. This is the reason why we try to educate them [children]. If when we teach them they [still] refuse to listen to us, we cannot do anything.

(83) Some people will appear to be behaving (*hu ìwà*) very well [from all external signs], especially when they are in public (*àárín agbo*). But when they get back [home alone] they will begin to do bad things. Those who know his or her secrets will be saying that he or she says (*sòrò*) good things, but he or she is a bad person.

The experience I have of the moral self I know myself to be is privileged. No other person is privileged to know me in the immediate manner definitive of introspective awareness. Therefore how others come to define me as a moral person, and I them, involves a further set of epistemic criteria. The standards that apply to the gathering of evidence about the *ìwà* of the "other," and the relevant behavioral (verbal and nonverbal) values enunciated and enshrined in Yoruba discourse are the subjects of the next chapter.

THE GOOD
AND THE BAD

KNOWLEDGE AND BELIEF ABOUT THE MORAL
CHARACTER OF THE 'OTHER'

I have suggested that it is helpful to use epistemological concerns, as articulated in discourse, as a wedge or key or vantage point with which to
approach the analysis of Yoruba moral meanings in a systematic manner.
As such the epistemological could amount to nothing more than an expository tool, a narrative device. It may provide a point of view from
which to tell the story, but that needn't mean it represents the breadth and
depth of real Yoruba concerns. As our analysis now proceeds, eventually
to consider some of the specific values articulated in an emphatic manner
by the *onísègùn,* I believe it passes beyond using the epistemic merely as
a narrative device. I believe that the epistemic becomes a kind of master
key, a *passe partout,* to the value system.

From an empirical rather than an introspective point of view, the distinction between "knowledge" (*ìmọ̀*) and "belief" (*ìgbàgbọ́;* i.e., between
firsthand and secondhand experience) means that a person's verbal and
nonverbal behavior are construed as firsthand evidence of their moral
character (*ìwà*). To recapitulate the criteria that must be satisfied in order
for any experience to be firsthand: I must witness it directly, and I must
think that I understand or comprehend what is going on. Information
about anything that comes to me in a comparatively indirect manner, that
I do not personally witness when it happens, is therefore secondhand and
cannot be certain (*òótọ́*). Although comparatively less attention has been
paid to this category of information in my exposition, that will no longer
be the case. For the caution and care with which secondhand discourse

(which, after all, includes even gossip) about persons is evaluated is a testament to Yoruba prudence about human fallibility.[1]

This prudence is amply reflected by innumerable passages in which the *onísègùn* explain what can and cannot be known (firsthand) and what can and cannot be believed (secondhand) about a person from the moral point of view. What I find remarkable about these passages, despite their semantic convolutions, is the absolute rigor and consistency with which the distinction between "knowledge" (*ìmò*) and "belief" (*ìgbàgbó*) is sustained:

(84) If they say someone did (*se*) something, and if the second person says it is clear in his own eyes [*ìmò*] that the first person could not do such a thing, he or she will say, "I believe (*gbàgbó*) he or she could not do such a thing." Or he or she will say, "I believe (*gbàgbó*) in that person, that he or she would not do such a thing." Or he or she may say that "I believe (*gbàgbó*) he or she could do it." This is [means] that he or she knows (*mò*) his or her behavior (*àdìn*).

(85) If you have been noticing the behavior (*ìwà*) of a person, we can say, "He or she can do (*se; is capable of*) a certain kind of thing." But if he or she has not done (*se*) such a thing in [before] your eyes [*ìmò*], you will say, "I believe (*gbàgbó*) [he or she could do it]." But if he or she has done such a thing in your eyes [*ìmò*], you will say, "I know" ("*Mo mò*"). This means that it is clear in your eyes [*ìmò*]. If he or she says that he or she believes (*gbàgbó*) something, and if they [people] ask him or her why he or she believes (*gbàgbó*) such a thing, he or she may say that the behavior (*ìwà*) of such a person makes him or her know (*mò*) [it could be possible].

(86) Somebody tells you something. Whether he or she tells lies or whether he or she does not tell a lie, you don't know (*mò*). You agree (*gbà*) because you say that this person never tells lies. If you know (*mò*) that he or she is a person of truth (*o l'óòtó ènìyàn*), you will believe (*gbàgbó*) that what he or she is saying is true.[2] But if you know (*mò*) that he or she is a liar, nobody will believe (*gbàgbó*) him or her. They will say, "He or she tells lies." They will not answer him or her.[3]

(87) But if you have known (*mò*) someone who has been acting as a truthful person (*ńse òótó*), if people are saying that he or she has done (*se*) something bad, you may not want to take them seriously

---

1. And, some may say, perfidy!
2. True for him, not for you.
3. This is a repetition of quotation (5).

[gbàgbọ́], because you have already accepted that he or she is a truthful person (olóòtọ́ ènìyàn). And the same if someone has been doing bad things and we hear (gbọ́) that he or she is doing good things. You may not want to believe (gbàgbọ́).[4]

(88) Because I have been spending time with someone, I know (mọ̀) his or her character (ìwà). I know (mọ̀) what he or she can do and what he or she cannot do. If another person should come and tell me that he or she does certain things, since I know (mọ̀) his or her character (ìwà) I know (mọ̀) whether he or she could do them or not. I will believe (gbàgbọ́) that he or she does them. But if I do not know (mọ̀) his or her character (ìwà), then I will say I do not believe (gbàgbọ́).

(89) I believe you (gbà ọ́ gbọ̀) when I know (mọ̀) your character (ìwà). But it is the one you see (rí) that is bigger [most convincing]. I see it with absolute certainty (dájú dájú). I believe you (gbà ọ́ gbọ̀), but I did not see the thing. But what I see clearly (kedere) I know (mọ̀) with certainty (dájú).[5]

(90) We don't take them [strangers] as bad or good, because we have not been living with them and don't know (mọ̀) what kind of person they are.

A person's moral character (ìwà) is not as readily or easily observable as everyday material objects, such as a tree or a table. Obviously a process of inference is involved in order to move from observing a multiplicity of individual actions to making a generalization about a person's character (ìwà). The interplay between knowledge (ìmọ̀) and belief (ìgbàgbọ́) in such contexts appears to be as follows. On the basis of a number of specific previous occasions when you have had the opportunity, firsthand (ìmọ̀), to verify the truth (òótọ́) of a person's statements, you are justified in using these firsthand experiences as the basis for a generalization about their moral character. This generalization may then serve as a kind of character reference for evaluating the reliability of future statements made by this same person, but strictly speaking, such evaluations must remain hypothetical or tentative (ìgbàgbọ́) until also confirmed in a firsthand manner.

When the criteria stipulated by these passages are stitched together, a kind of sliding scale for epistemic certainty about the moral character of other persons may be postulated:

---

4. This is a repetition of quotation (6).

5. This is a repetition of quotation (21).

Best: You *know* (*mò*) the other person well entirely on the basis of your own *firsthand experience* (*ìmò*), and this enables you to make a comprehensive assessment of that person's moral character—how he or she is *likely to behave* (*ìgbàgbọ́* because predictive)[6] in any situation.

Next best: You *don't know* (*mò*) the other person well, but you have *observed firsthand* (*ìmò*) how he or she behaves in certain situations, and so you can make a partial assessment of that person's moral character—how he or she is *likely to behave* (*ìgbàgbọ́* because predictive) in certain types of situations.

Next best: You *don't really know* (*mò*) the person, but people you *know* (*mò*) well and can *believe* (*ìgbàgbọ́*) say they *know* (*mò*) the person well, and this enables them to make a comprehensive assessment of that person's moral character—how he or she is *likely to behave* (*ìgbàgbọ́* because predictive) in any situation.

Next best: You *don't really know* (*mò*) the person, but people you *know* (*mò*) well and can *believe* (*ìgbàgbọ́*) say they have *observed firsthand* (*ìmò*) how the person behaves in certain situations, and this enables them to make a partial assessment of his or her moral character—how he or she is *likely to behave* (*ìgbàgbọ́* because predictive) in certain types of situations.

Worst: You *don't know* (*mò*) the person, and you *don't know* (*mò*) anyone else who *knows* (*mò*) the person, so you can say nothing about that person's moral character—what he or she is likely to do or to say in any situation.

A person who makes an informative statement may be obliged to recount the precise circumstances in which he or she came by it. A person is expected to say whether there is any cause for uncertainty or imprecision about the information. Determining whether the information is derived from the speaker's firsthand (*ìmò*) or secondhand (*ìgbàgbọ́*) experience is part of this process. A person's diligence in doing all of this is considered important evidence of their moral character (*ìwà*) as well as of their intelligence (*ogbọ́n, ọpọlọ*).

It now becomes appropriate to introduce into our narrative three

---

6. Predictive as in the following: "Before you believe (*gbàgbọ́*) it, you will have tested (*dán wò*) it. A person can say he can drink this [pointing to a cup on the table]—ten of these [filled with] palm wine. They may say it is not true (*òótọ́*). But anybody who saw (*rí*) [in the past] the man drinking this quantity would say, 'I believe' ('*Mò gbàgbọ́*') [it is possible]."

specific values to which reference was made by the *oníṣẹ̀gùn:* listening (*gbọ́fọ̀*) well, speaking (*sọ̀rọ̀*) well, and patience (*sùúrù*). Listening and speaking well are frequently paired in symmetrical fashion:

> (91) Someone who does not listen (*gbọ́fọ̀*) to others has a bad character (*ìwà*). Someone who listens to others has a good character (*ìwà*). A good person (*ènìyàn rere*)[7] speaks (*sọ̀rọ̀*) good words (*ọ̀rọ̀ rere*), and a bad person speaks bad words (*sọ̀rọ̀ burúkú*).
>
> (92) If we say that a person has 'got' *inú,*[8] it means that person will not tell (*wí*) to others what you have told (*sọ̀rọ̀*) him or her [not break a confidence]. This means that he or she has 'got' *inú* into which to put words (*ọ̀rọ̀*).[9] This can also refer to a person to whom you ask a question [and] who is able to give you a satisfactory answer. And since he or she can give you a satisfactory answer, you will say that person has 'got' *inú,* because he or she has answered your questions.

One reason for emphasizing these as values is that one should not 'tell lies', deliberate or careless, about what one knows. I shall consider the negative extreme of the liar shortly, but, in the present context, the point of listening and speaking *well* are that one should neither misrepresent nor misreport. In an oral culture one might expect that special importance would be attached to what people hear and what people say. Certainly elocution and phrasing one's remarks in an intelligent manner are matters of concern to the Yoruba. But that is not sufficient to explain the emphasis placed upon speaking *well* and hearing *well* as values.

People in Western societies have become concerned about exercising control over the media. In the Yoruba society with which the *oníṣẹ̀gùn* were conversant, the media were mouths. Doing these things well involves setting 'broadcasting standards' for those mouths. "Speaking well" and "hearing well" may be euphemistically popularized as not to 'tell lies'. But not to 'tell lies' means providing accurate information or useful advice and telling the truth about what you really do have firsthand expe-

---

7. The differences between the expressions for a "true person" (*ol'óòtọ́ ènìyàn;* as in quotation 86) and a "good person" (*ènìyàn rere*) are a matter for further inquiry, although it would seem that the latter is more explicitly moral in character. One could at least imagine the possibility of a socially unpleasant personality that still earned a reputation for speaking the truth.

8. See note 8, p. 44 for *inú* and for this idiomatic usage of 'got'.

9. In other words, saying someone has 'got' *inú* is an idiom used to describe a person as both intelligent and responsible.

rience of, what you have only heard about secondhand, and what you have only heard about secondhand, and what you have no information about at all. "Speaking well" and "hearing well" are not, then, *moral* values in any conventional sense. They are rather *epistemological virtues* because of their *instrumental value* for ensuring the accuracy of information.

It is as a secondary consequence that they may also be used to provide evidence that other people may use to assess your moral character, or that you may use to assess theirs. This moral dimension to the epistemological brings us back to the point, first articulated in chapter 2—that when propositions issue out of mouths, inevitably the moral character of a speaker becomes a condition (necessary or sufficient?) and now, it appears, also a function of their accuracy. Nowhere is this clearer than in the case of the liar (*eléke*). The definitions of "lie" (*iró*) and "liar" (*eléke*) are quite straightforward in epistemic terms:

(93) This [lying] is what a person does not do (*ṣe*) while people continue to say that he or she did it. You can say that they tell lies (*iró ní wón pa*) against such a person.

(94) Apart from some people who will tell lies (*puró*)—what they don't know (*mò*) they will say they know (*mò*). These are liars (*eléke*).

The epistemic conditions for not 'telling lies' also are made clear:

(95) If you don't want to be a liar (*eléke*) [in a discussion about predicting behavior], the thing which has not been done in your eyes, you should not say, "I believe it" ("*Mò gbàgbó*"). Before you say, "I believe it" ("*Mò gbàgbó*") you ought to have seen that person do it in your presence. It is the thing you see that you can say, "I know" ("*Mo mò*").

It is also clear how damning it can become to be labeled a "liar," for its practical and moral consequences:

(96) Somebody tells you something. Whether he or she tells lies (*puró*) or whether he or she does not tell lies, you don't know (*mò*). You agree (*gbà*) because you say that this person never tells lies. If you know that he or she is a truthful person (*o l'óòtó èniyàn*), you will believe (*gbàgbó*) that what he or she is saying is true (*òótó*). But if you know that he or she is a liar (*eléke*), nobody will believe (*gbàgbó*) him or her. They will say, "He or she tells lies." They will not take him or her seriously.

The sanctions that can be invoked against a reputed liar are formidable. Imagine what the life of a person might become if no information he or she vouchsafed would be received as reliable. A person's credibility as both talker and actor, as witness and reporter, of his or her own or other's experience, becomes suspect.[10] Whether his or her 'lies' are careless or malicious,[11] his or her covert motives become matters for speculation, especially if they indicate an unfounded antagonism or animosity toward other people.

The emphasis placed by the Yoruba upon patience (sùùrù; etm 602) as a value was, I believe, first commented upon in Western scholarship by Robert Farris Thompson. The oníṣègùn also underscored this by assigning patience (sùúrù) a place of distinction in the self (inú):

(97) A moral character marked by patience (ìwà sùúrù)—this is the best of all forms of good character (ìwà).

Thompson linked the importance of sùúrù to a person's being "cool" in his account of a Yoruba aesthetic. The reason for the cool being an important value in Yoruba culture was said to be its connection with dignity and kingliness: "Yoruba, in brief, assume that someone who embodies command, coolness, and character is someone extremely beautiful and like unto a god" (Thompson 1971, P/5). But rather than being a value arising from demeanor or appearance, the oníṣègùn link patience (sùúrù) to the èmí or inú, to the innermost self:

(98) There are some people who will stay among others and will not talk [but they do listen!]. And there are some people who will continue to stand and talk for three to four times [who talk too much and fail to listen!]. Some people have the self (èmí) of patience (sùúrù) and some have not.

This suggests that its importance as a behavioral criterion is more epistemic than it is aesthetic. A 'cool' temperament, the patient person, is far more likely to listen to and observe carefully what is happening, and to speak with apperception and perspicacity. If patience (sùúrù) becomes an aesthetic value associated with certain norms of appearance in Yoruba culture, the more profound reason for its becoming so is the instrumental

---

10. "If you hear (gbó) well (dájú dájú), you will know it. But if you are a liar (eléke), you can say you don't hear."

11. One common example of the malicious liar is "someone who talks (rojú; etm 572) of [against] another person when the person is not there."

benefits that derive from it *as an epistemic virtue*. A character (*ìwà*) that assigns a high priority to patience (*sùúrù*), especially in difficult or problematic situations, informs a consciousness that maintains self-control and optimal communication with its environment.

A further, derivative, paired variation upon "listening" and "speaking" as epistemic virtues and moral values is "listening to advice" and "giving (good) advice." The difference between "listening well" and "listening to advice" is more than one of emphasis. The latter highlights the importance of reflecting upon and assessing efforts by others to influence ones behavior:

> (99) Destiny (*ìpín*) is everything that a person (*ènìyàn*) will do on earth. The self (*èmí*) chooses all the things that the person (*ènìyàn*) will do without leaving anything aside.[12] For example, if a man tries to make trouble, if everyone begins to appeal (*ńbẹ;* etm 100: "beg") to him, if the thing working inside (*inú*) him refuses absolutely (*dandan;* etm 142 as "*dọn-dọn*") to listen, he will let these people beseeching (*bẹ̀*) him go their own way and do (*ṣe*) [whatever he wishes]. But if he is able to think (*rò*) with this something inside him (*inú*) and decide not to behave (*ṣe*) in a bad way, this would mean that his destiny (*orí inú*) yields to their appeal. If someone is really upset, and people put their hands on his [physical] head to 'pet' [placate] him, he will not yield if his destiny (inner head)[13] refuses to listen. If he accepts the plea, this means that his destiny (*orí inú*) has accepted it. It is then that people will say his destiny (*orí*) is good because he listens to advice.

This passage also is of interest for the behavioral connection it makes with a person's destiny. The person who responds to well-meant advice, who decides not to do what others are convinced would not be in his or her best interests, may be said to have a good destiny (and the opposite is certainly implied as well). Giving good advice also involves more than merely "speaking well." Here the emphasis is upon the importance of reflecting upon the welfare of the 'other', upon considering what may and may not be in the best interests of the person concerned:

---

12. To this point this is the same as quotation (55).

13. The expression for "destiny," "*orí inú,*" does literally mean "inner (*inú*) head (*orí*)" or "inside head" and is frequently rhetorically contrasted with the word "*orí*" when used to refer to the physical head.

(100) Yes, if he or she has some good people to move with. When they advise him or her, he or she could change. This would mean that he or she has *ronúpìwàdà* (literally "thinks deeply and changes behavior [*ìwà*]"). People are born with a moral character (*ìwà*). But it can change—because there are some people, when they want to do bad, if there is anyone to speak to them, they may change[14] and not do such a thing. This means that they think deeply upon the matter and decide to change their behavior (*ronúpìwàdà*).

BAD ADVICE, BAD MOTIVES, BAD PEOPLE

The true-to-life moral world of the Yoruba, the one in which both "bad and good things follow [upon] each other,"[15] does contain its share of bad—in the sense of *morally* bad—behavior. The analysis of the forms of discourse the *oníṣẹ̀gùn* associate with the "bad" (*búburú, burúkú*) will be facilitated by presenting them in a systematic format. To be compatible, any form of systematization must be based upon some theme common to the majority of these forms of discourse. The one selected here is that morally bad behavior may be ranked or graded from lower to higher, from less to more, from peccadillo to iniquity. And the common element that determines where a particular action should fall on the scale is the intention, the motivation, of the perpetrator, ultimately as defined by others on the basis of the offender's verbal and nonverbal behavior.

This moral scale, as represented here, may also be described in terms of three steps or stages of immorality. The first or lowest stage is that of the morally bad *act* by a person whose overall character (*ìwà*) is rated as good (*ènìyàn rere*). Such actions are often said to be the product of poor judgment (error) or the bad influence of other persons. The second and third stages are assigned to the person whose overall *character* (*ìwà*) is rated as bad (*ènìyàn burúkú*). These divisions are not meant to be absolute; they are meant to provide a basis to work from and with. Some behavior may involve motivations arising from more than one of the stages. Some motivations may be inexplicable by any of them, as seems to be the case with behavior attributed to the 'spirit' (*ẹ̀mí*) of *Èṣù*:

---

14. Again one can ask whether such "change" is in accordance with one's destiny or represents an actual change in that destiny. The interpretation favored here, for consistency if nothing else, is that change too is a part of everyone's destiny.

15. See quotations (67)–(69). See also the following: "There need to be both bad things and good things. . . . A person (*ènìyàn*) cannot exist without enemies (*ọ̀tá*)."

(101) It is the Èṣù[16] which makes a person get annoyed (bínú; etm 104) [without good reason]. You know a person can just get annoyed without anyone offending (ṣe; etm 614) him or her. When the 'spirit' (èmí) of Èṣù goes away (kúrò; etm 398) from his or her mind (okàn), he or she will say that he or she doesn't know (mọ̀) what happened to him or her.

(102) This is the 'spirit' (èmí) of Èṣù. If it is not the 'spirit' (èmí) of Èṣù, he or she will begin to explain what happened to him or her. He or she will say that "such-and-such" a person did (ṣe) something to her that he or she didn't like.[17]

Conventional examples of immoral behavior, as spelled out by the oníṣègùn, contain few surprises: telling lies (purọ́; etm 316), quarreling (jà; etm 337: "fighting"), stealing (jalè; etm 339: "commit theft"), and parsimony[18] (ahun; etm 32: "miser"):

(103) You know, there are some people who are hot (gbónó) [tempered]. If you play with [tease] them, they will become quarrelsome (ìjà). There are some you can joke with who will not become annoyed. People will say that the innermost self (inú) of such a person is good. Some people are miserly (rorò). That is character (ìwà). Character (ìwà) is divided into many other parts [has many facets].

Murder (ìpànìọ̀n; etm 311, 357: "murderer") is described as the worst single act of which an individual is capable.

On the first or lowest level of moral culpability, immoral behavior on the part of a person is the exception rather than the rule. The character (ìwà) of such persons has previously been witnessed on numerous occasions and rated as good. Some of the more common explanations, ex-

---

16. The Èṣù is a Yoruba deity associated with indeterminacy and the inexplicable—situations that, whatever the circumstances happen to be, don't make sense. The "spirit (èmí) of Èṣù" may therefore be an idiomatic expression for the inexplicable rather than a reference to the direct intervention of the deity into everyday affairs.

17. "Character (ìwà) and behavior (iṣẹ́) are based in the innermost self (inú). Sometimes they say that the innermost self (inú) of someone has broken (fọ́). This means that the person no longer knows what they're doing. . . . Sometimes also some people are referred to as having an innermost self (inú) of ashes (eérú). This means that their innermost self (inú) cannot turn to the right direction [behave in a correct or sensible manner]."

18. That this may be regarded as an immoral 'act' may come as a surprise to some. The English word popularly used as the equivalent to "ahun" is "miserly," being a miser: "The Yoruba despise a miser" (Eades 1980, p. 145). But I would suggest that the disapproval expressed about parsimony is also because it is interpreted as a possible symptom of avarice, of irresponsible greed, of the person who also covets the property of others.

cuses actually, for such untoward behavior are therefore either errors in judgment:

> (104) He or she didn't think things through. He or she thought that he or she had no other way to go[19]

or the temporary influence of bad company, immoral others:

> (105) There are some people who have not stolen (*jalè*) before, but come to steal because they keep bad company (*ẹgbẹ́*).
>
> (106) If he or she has been a good person before, people will say certain forces, such as *àjẹ́* or bad *àlùjànún*,[20] are influencing (*tì*) him or her.

Such patterns of explanation should not be taken to imply that immoral behavior by otherwise good persons is always somehow rationalized and excused. Assessments of *intentionality* and *responsibility* also play a prominent part in ordinary moral discourse. First, intentionality:

> (107) All people who do (*ṣe*) bad things know (*mọ̀*) what they're doing. For instance, if a person kills (*pa;* etm 536) another, he or she will definitely know (*mọ̀*) he or she has done a bad thing (*ṣe búburú*). If a person tells lies (*purọ́*) about others, he or she will know (*mọ̀*) he or she has done a bad thing. Thieves (*olè*) know (*mọ̀*) that what they do is bad (*kò dára*).
>
> (108) Many people would say that he or she does it on his or her own recognizance, because they believe (*gbàgbọ́*) that he or she could not have done it under any [other] influence if the thought (*èrò*) had not been in his or her mind (*ọkàn*).[21]
>
> (109) If his or her words lead to lies (*irọ́*), they will punish (*jẹ ní ìyà;* etm 332) him or her—that he or she did it intentionally (*ó mọ̀ọ́mọ̀*[22] *ṣe;* etm 425: "deliberately," "intentionally").[23]

---

19. As a further explanation or excuse for erroneous judgment: "If he's a drunkard (*ọ̀mùtí*), they might say he was under the influence of wine."

20. *Àjẹ́* and *àlùjànún* are the names of specific personality types to be discussed later on in this chapter. The relevant point here is that they refer to other human beings.

21. Part of this quotation was used in a different context as quotation (41).

22. A word that is interesting etymologically to the epistemologist for its apparent doubly reflexive use of the verb "to know" (*mọ̀*).

23. Non-philosophers may find it takes an effort to remember that "behavior" in this text is being used to refer to "speech" (verbal behavior) as well as to "actions" (nonverbal behavior). This passage is included because it makes explicit reference to immoral words—lies.

Then responsibility:

>   (110) If other people see (*rí*) him or her doing it, they would not believe (*gbà*) him or her [if he or she denies responsibility for his or her behavior].
>   (111) [Quotation (109).]
>   (112) People (*wọn*) would not believe (*gbàgbọ́*)[a person's denial of responsibility]. They will ask him or her to go and think (*ronú*) about it, because perhaps he or she was drunk (*ọmọ ẹmu*) then. Or maybe he or she is about to go mad (*orí rẹ ní ó dàrú*). If he or she was not drunk or crazy, they would say he or she is telling lies.

The standards and forms of punishment also may vary, depending upon the person's moral 'reputation' or *ìwà* as defined by prior behavior:

>   (113) [Quotation (109).]
>   (114) They would warn (*kini ní lọ̀*) the good person (*ènìyàn rere*) and punish (*ìyá*) the bad person (*ènìyàn burúkú*).
>   (115) The bad person (*ènìyàn burúkú*) would receive more punishment (*ìyá*), while they may warn (*ìlọ̀; etm 304*) the good person or make his or her punishment less.
>   (116) The punishment of (*ìjìyà; etm 332: "suffering"*) the bad person (*ènìyàn burúkú*) would be double that of the good person, because people are aware that he or she is a bad person. They will say that there are external forces pushing the good person (*ènìyàn rere*), and they will not make him or her suffer (*ìyá*).

This first or lowest stage of immoral behavior, blame and punishment, constitutes the domain of those whose overall character (*ìwà*) continues to be rated "good" (*ènìyàn rere*). If a person comes to be *characteristically* regarded as a liar, quarrelsome, a thief, or miserly, their character (*ìwà*) will eventually be 'elevated' to the second stage of the immoral, and they will be labeled an "immoral person" (*ènìyàn burúkú*). But if such behavior constitutes only the occasional lapse in an otherwise unblemished moral character, a good moral reputation may be sustained.

   With the introduction of the immoral or bad person (*ènìyàn burúkú*), we make the transition to the second stage of immoral behavior. This second stage is the domain of those who deliberately and consistently choose to prey upon others in an immoral manner in order to satisfy their own desires. When they have a specific need they target a specific person or situation to victimize in order to satisfy it. Their own self-interest is defined at the expense of others. One such illustrative type is motivated by a mixture of envy and greed. Such people tend to dislike anyone who seems more successful than themselves, and they seek to victimize them by stealing, for example, the fruits of their labor. In other contexts they might seek to 'steal' their good moral character (ìwà) by 'telling lies' against them. But all of this is meant to be done with an honest face, which makes these immoral persons (ènìyàn burúkú) a hypocritical lot. Obviously they cannot announce their immoral intentions in a forthright and public manner, or they will be shunned by all who are moral:

> (117) Some people will appear to be behaving (hu ìwà) very well [from all external signs], especially when they are in public (àárín agbo). But when they get back [home alone] they will begin to do bad things. Those who know his or her secrets will be saying that he or she says (sọ̀rọ̀) good things, but he or she is a bad person (ènìyàn burúkú).[24]

They therefore try to behave as if moral persons (ènìyàn rere), as if morally good. They pretend to have as much concern for the general welfare as anyone else. How the Yoruba go about identifying these hypocritical individuals, behaviorally and otherwise, constitutes a key dimension to their moral discourse. For, from the standpoint of *moral* persons (ènìyàn rere), such people become the "enemy" (ọ̀tá).

Providing an adequate introduction to this notion of the enemy (ọ̀tá) requires a brief digression from our principal narrative about immoral persons (ènìyàn burúkú). For the category of "enemy" (ọ̀tá) covers a very wide spectrum of antagonisms that may vary considerably in intensity. A healthy rivalry between two friends that deteriorates into petty animosity because of increasingly bitter competition may result in their regarding one another as enemies (ọ̀tá):

> (118) Those whom we call "enemy" (ọ̀tá) may be friends (ènìyàn rere) to other people.
> (119) And someone may be bad in the hands of [in the opinion of] one person and be good in the hands of another.

For this degree of discord it is questionable whether referring to someone as an enemy (ọ̀tá) involves a *moral* judgment. Yet it is a part of discourse. In the 'give and take' of everyday life, of rivalry and competition between associates and siblings, everyone tends to view their own interests as privileged. Anyone who stands in the way of those interests could receive the

---

24. This is a repetition of quotation (83).

appellation "*ọ̀tá*," but in such circumstances it is applied in a relatively shallow and harmless manner.

Yoruba psychological discourse is of interest for the fact that it does not replicate the conventional Western distinction between the rational and the emotional (Hallen 1979, p. 305). The rational may be equated with the mind (*ọkàn*). But emotion is not attributed to any single source in the 'deeper' self. As we have seen, the 'deeper' self, if indeed there is a 'deeper' self, has been equated with a person's destiny.[25] A person's emotional nature is generally regarded as a function of their character (*ìwà*). Allowances are made for the hot-tempered (*gbónó*) person (quotation 103), seen as the 'victim' of a temperament that becomes something with which their friends have to put up. But the high value placed upon patience (*sùúrù*) implies that the more reliable type of persons keep their tempers and emotions under control.

When envy, greed, and animosity exceed the ordinary and are thought to become deep, abiding dominant motivations (still meant to be covert,[26] bear in mind), the *oníṣègùn* are remarkably candid about the fact that human beings don't require any extra-human assistance (from the Devil,[27] for example) to become so unpleasant:

> (120) The supreme deity (*Ọlọ́run*) is not the enemy (*ọ̀tá*) of human beings (*ènìyàn*). People (*ènìyàn*) are their own enemies (*ọ̀tá*). . . . There is not any enemy (*ọ̀tá*) [deriving] from the supreme deity (*Ọlọ́run*). *People* [italicized because emphasized] hate one another and become enemies.
>
> (121) Anyone can be an enemy (*ọ̀tá*). . . . Even ordinary people can be an enemy (*ọ̀tá*) to other people.

To acknowledge one other divergent possibility: The *oníṣègùn* do appreciate that some people are their own worst enemies. As one has already remarked (quotation [75]): "There are some people who do it to

---

25. See note 17, p. 54.

26. "But if a person wakes up very early in the morning and goes to do (*ṣe*) something with another, and returns home before others wake up, and it seems as if he did not even go out that day."

27. Despite the determined attempts of Christian missionaries to co-opt the *Èṣù* (see note 16 above) for the role of the Devil, the spiritual indeterminacy of this deity has enabled it to evade such cross-cultural typing. In fact, the *Èṣù* is enjoying something of a renaissance in African American literary theory as the symbol of systems of African and African American meanings and beliefs and their distinctive means of (rhetorical, literary) expression and transmission (Gates 1988).

themselves." These are individuals who evidently chose a bad destiny at the very beginning because they don't require the assistance of enemies (òtá) to do themselves in:

(122) An enemy (òtá) can trouble a person (yọ ènìyàn lẹ́nu) for a while, but he is not able to change their destiny (ìpín) if that person has not made a bad destiny himself or herself.

A related point to stress is that being regarded as having a bad destiny is not a sufficient condition for being regarded as an immoral person. Someone can struggle and fail at a variety of conventional enterprises for an entire lifetime and still preserve their reputation as a moral being. "Bad destiny chooser" (olórí burúkú) need not be equivalent to "bad" in the sense of an "immoral" person (ènìyàn burúkú).

To resume our narrative, in their descriptions of the enemy (òtá) as immoral person (ènìyàn burúkú) the onísẹ̀gùn go beyond the level of petty animosities when they speak of individuals who are 'by nature' or 'by disposition' generally dissatisfied and envious of others who seem better off:

(123) People (ènìyàn) are the enemies (òtá) of themselves. There is no special [type of] person who is referred to as the "enemy" (òtá). These are people who are not satisfied with [the behavior of] others. . . . It is people who do not like (féràn) others who are referred to as enemies (òtá).

(124) "Enemy" (òtá) is not a special kind of person. These are the kinds of people who are not happy when they see people behaving well. It might be that the work of others is better than their own.

(125) "Enemy" (òtá) is a general name given to anyone who behaves badly [most dangerously in a covert[28] manner] to other people. They may not be an enemy (òtá) just to certain specific people, but to many people. They might be an enemy (òtá) to more than sixty people. Bad people (ènìyàn burúkú) are not usually kind, both to animals and to human beings (ènìyàn). Any bad person can be referred to as an enemy (òtá).

(126) They [òtá and ọmọ aráyé] are generally bad people (ènìyàn bur-

---

28. "You know during the time of the war there were some people who were the enemies (òtá) of [then Governor of the Western State] Akintola and who killed him, despite the fact that they had been eating together [i.e., were close associates and friends]. Then they turn back [against him] and conspire to kill [assassinate] him. And they say it is death which can bring peace!"

úkú), and bad people (èníyàn burúkú) have chosen[29] to be such in 'heaven' (ọ̀run).

It is when it comes to the third stage of the immoral that one encounters the truly immoral person. This class of immoral persons (èníyàn burúkú) was sometimes referred to by the onísẹ̀gùn as the "children of the world" (ọmọ aráyé; etm 61: "wicked people") or "people of the world" (àwọn aráyé). Such people are frequently identified with the English-language "sorcerers and witches" (Eades 1980, p. 121). Rendering their meaning into English with these terms immediately suggests that one is being transported into that 'realm' of superstition and spirit(s) that is still supposed to dominate 'traditional' African cultures. But this is also because terms like "witch" and "sorcerer" have attracted a pejorative penumbra in 'modern' Western cultures that makes their imputation to any African system of belief(s) equally pejorative. Yet, unless one is a very firm believer in the universality of meanings, there is little reason to presume that the Yoruba have devised precisely the same set of beliefs as medieval Europeans. And because these kinds of imputations affect the entire subject matter, for purely methodological considerations they make the analysis of a subclass like "children of the world" from the moral point of view much more difficult. So for the time being, I will treat the class of "children of the world" as if a new phenomenon that cannot be so rudely reduced to Western cultural anachronisms.

It is in fact the human-ness, the *this*-worldliness, of immorality[30] that recalls my discussion of Soyinka's portrayal[31] of the Yoruba consciousness as more metaphysically oriented than its Western counterpart(s). Scholars who exaggerate the 'metaphysicality' of the Yoruba consciousness (Parrinder 1970)—for example, interpreting a phenomenon like the "children of the world" (ọmọ aráyé) as yet another manifestation of a cross-cultural phenomenon called "witchcraft"—present a grotesque caricature of their own creation if they portray Africans as living in a world where the innocent are regularly and remorselessly spiritually 'zapped' by demonic forces, as if on the orders of the Evil Emperor Ming in the old Flash Gordon movies. This is an example of that kind of antisystematic, anti-

---

29. These are people who have chosen a destiny that results in their being bad or immoral and for which they may be criticized, as distinct from those whose destiny entails failing to succeed in life but remain moral.

30. People as *their own* worst enemies, and so forth.

31. See pages 37–40.

empirical stereotyping of the African consciousness that has heretofore inhibited the serious pursuit of studies such as this.

This third and highest (or worst) stage is reserved for the morbid few (one hopes) who derive their principal satisfaction from victimizing others in a more or less indiscriminate manner. These are individuals whose motivating desire is to make other people suffer rather than to benefit materially from their deprivations. Hence, they may target anyone and everyone. The *oníṣẹ̀gùn* had the following to say about these "people of the world" (*àwọn aráyé*):

> (127) There are some people who are cruel (*ìkà*), and they will do things without regard for anyone. These people have chosen (*nyàn*) this from 'heaven' (*ọ̀run*).[32]

> (128) These also are human beings (*ènìyàn*) who are very cruel (*ìkà*). Who make bad plans against others. They are those who do not want other people to progress (*ànfàní*: etm 78: as "*àùnfàní*").

> (129) From the origin of the world there have been some people who are bad-doers (*abanijé*; etm 4, 94), whose business is just to disrupt another person's plans.

The dominant motives attributed to this more lethal variety of enemy (*ọ̀tá*) intermix vengeful envy with indiscriminate malice. At the same time it is important to bear in mind that part of the power of such individuals derives from the fact that they try to appear as perfectly normal, ordinary, working, walking-talking members of the human race. Indeed they may even be members of one's own household:

> (130) People sometimes say the enemy (*ọ̀tá*) is outside the house, but "the person who will do bad things is inside your house" ("*èhìn-kùlé ní ọ̀tá wà, ilé ní aseni ńgbé*," which etm: 182 renders as "one is sometimes betrayed by one's nearest and dearest"). They also say that "a person is the enemy of himself; the people of your house are your enemy" (*ènìyàn ní ọ̀tá ara rẹ̀; ará ilé ẹni ní ọ̀tá ẹni*). . . . Dangers are much more common at home. If they say that something is happening to the person, it [frequently] has its source in his or her own household.[33]

---

32. Perhaps it is worth noting again that one's destiny or the idea of having chosen from 'heaven' is not enough to excuse or protect a person's moral or immoral reputation.

33. It is relevant to bear in mind that the notion of the 'extended' family in Yoruba society is significantly different from what Western society typically defines as the "nuclear" family.

How does one recognize one's enemies as enemies? Introspectively each of us has immediate access to our own motives, to our feelings of enmity toward and malicious designs upon other persons:

> (131) It is only the person himself or herself who can know (mọ̀) [intro-spectively] whether he or she is an enemy (ọ̀tá) to any other per-son. Because if a person could know who their enemies (ọ̀tá) are, they would do as much as possible to avoid them, but the mind of an enemy (ọ̀tá) may be very dark [difficult to identify, much less access].[34]

But that is not the case when it comes to knowledge of the mind of the 'other'. Behavior then becomes an important alternative:

> (132) Before you can identify a bad person (ènìyàn burúkú) they must behave badly to you. You cannot know them until you see 'the work of their hands'.

What kind of behavior on the part of a person can lead to their being labeled this variety of enemy (ọ̀tá)? The following example is illustrative rather than definitive:

> (133) If you don't offend a person, yet they are always annoyed with you and turn against you and tell lies against you and are cruel to people, we can regard this as an enemy (ọ̀tá).

Another alternative is to infer the malicious influence of bad persons (ènì-yàn burúkú) from the fact that one is suffering undesired and unwarranted misfortune. This possibility was treated in a different context in chapter 3:

> (134) When a person is not able to reach the 'level' [of achievement] he or she desired, if he or she says it is the work of an enemy (ọ̀tá) it is because of a sign (àmì) [of this] which he or she has experienced (rí). If he or she engages in a certain occupation without success [one kind of 'sign'], he or she will say this is the influence (iṣẹ́) of an enemy (ọ̀tá). If he should marry 'outside' [a wife who is not from the locality] and others should take his wife away [another kind of 'sign'], he will say this is the influence (iṣẹ́)

---

34. This is a more expansive version of quotation (27).

of an enemy (òtá). A person whose child is killed [as if] by àjé[35] [yet another kind of 'sign'] will know that this is the act (iṣé) of an enemy (òtá).[36]

As has already been mentioned,[37] and may be reiterated here as a further intriguing complication, the causal influence of bad or immoral persons (èniyàn burúkú) may be invoked to explain and to excuse *one's own* malicious or morally wrong behavior, especially when caught out by others:

> (135) We say [when a person's responsibility for a malicious act is being debated] that an enemy (òtá) pushes (tì; etm 641) him or her to do it, and sometimes we say that it was his or her own thoughts (èrò). These are the two possible ways of describing (ṣọ) it.

In other words, people may seek to avoid responsibility for malicious behavior, now recast as undesired misfortune, by blaming *it* on the outside influence of immoral persons (èniyàn burúkú):

> (136) There are very few people who would say they had made a bad choice in heaven, even when living a bad life on earth. What such people usually say is that this [misfortune] is the work of the "people of the world" (àwọn aráyé).
> (137) There is nothing bad done by a person that could not be regarded as the work of the "people of the world" (àwọn aráyé).

What perhaps needs to be reiterated at this point is that the importance of the underlying *personalized* model[38] for the explanation of undesired and unwarranted misfortune should not be exaggerated out of proportion to its real influence. That model is said to be personalized because such misfortune is attributed to the causal influence of other human beings, to immoral persons (èniyàn burúkú). But that *exceptional* misfortune is explained by the influence of other persons does not mean that normal or everyday misfortune is as well. This is an important point—the

---

35. This is the term frequently translated into English as "witch." The shortcomings of using European witchcraft terminology for Yoruba translations will be discussed in further detail later in this chapter. The possibility that such 'effects' might also involve extra-physical—supernatural—'causes' will also be discussed.

36. This is a repetition of quotation (78).

37. See pages 40–41.

38. See the discussion of Favret-Saada's *Deadly Words* in chapter 3, note 24 (p. 62).

personalized model is invoked in exceptional rather than normal circumstances. Falling down the stairs, being assaulted by armed robbers, breaking an arm, an automobile accident, are not automatically elevated to the status of the exceptional. There is still a sizeable chunk of reality that is left to the ordinary. The *context* in which misfortune occurs is as important as the misfortune itself.

In any case, that my misfortune may be the product of another person's influence does not necessitate that I will go that one step further and try to identify who the person may be. The causal model may 'be' there, but latent, dormant, in the background. For identifying the immoral person (*èníyàn burúkú*) is not a simple process. If the system is marked by a tendency to attribute serious, unwarranted misfortune to others, it is marked equally by the talents of those others to conceal themselves. Furthermore, by the very fact that the more harmful immoral persons (*èníyàn burúkú*) are motivated by pure malice, by a desire not to see *any* of their fellow human beings progress, that malice becomes unfocused, impersonal, or, better, omnipersonal. When a person is believed to be (secretly) against the progress of mankind generally, it becomes a formidable task to establish that, in this particular instance, on this specific occasion, the indiscriminate malice of that particular bad person was directed against me. Perhaps this is the point at which the Yoruba personalized causal model most closely approximates Favret-Saada's suggestion that it is not really necessary to have witches in order to have something like the witchcraft phenomenon occur in a society.

With regards to comparisons between African and Western models of causal explanation, the importance and role of so-called 'personalized' models of causal explanation in Africa is sometimes unfairly exaggerated. At the same time a similar exaggeration occurs regarding the West's attachment to a causal model derived from *mechanism* (science as technology). For example, a building collapses, killing several members of a family of good reputation. On what may serve as a level of commonsense explanation common to both cultures, the same kinds of observations would be made—inadequate maintenance and dangerous overloading of the upper story. But it is then said that the West and Africa part company when it comes to explanations about how the structure came to collapse at that precise moment so as to kill those specific individuals. The former supposedly would speak only of things like load factors and force vectors reaching intolerable limits. The latter would speculate about the reasons why that family could have attracted the attention of bad persons (*èníyàn burúkú*), or about why bad persons (*èníyàn burúkú*) would attack the family by targeting those particular individuals, and so forth.

However, this is not so clearly the case. There is evidence of the personalized in Western discourse too when remarks are made about the recurrent misfortunes of the family involved, or about how those who behave badly toward their fellow men and women eventually receive their just deserts. Such Western interpretations of misfortune are not really so different from comparable, personalized, causal explanations in African cultures. A point to emphasize again is that the function of a personalized causal model, such as that articulated by the *oníṣẹ̀gùn,* is to provide a *theoretical* framework for the intellect as much as it is to serve the *practical* purpose of cautioning the envious and aggressive against sawing through someone's rafters or playing arsonist with their property (i.e., people will also think about who might have done these things deliberately). This does not mean that the Yoruba are revealed to be an anxiety-ridden, neurosis-plagued 'folk' who are obsessed with scrutinizing every detail of one another's behavior for any possible sign that can be interpreted as evidence of animosity. For it is at this point that the stabilizing role of the diviner (*babaláwo*) or *oníṣẹ̀gùn* becomes of critical importance. But before proceeding to that important topic, we must attempt a comparably general outline of the morally good person (*ènìyàn rere*), and then of several special personality types identified by the *oníṣẹ̀gùn,* whose members also may be either morally good or bad on an individual basis.

JUST LIKE A WHITE CLOTH

(138) But among all these different types of people we've mentioned, there is no one which is better than the good person (*ènìyàn rere*). The good person is just like a white cloth which you keep [aside] so that people will not touch it with hands covered with oil.

If I attempt to collate the positive virtues and traits that have received special attention in the course of this narrative, it is possible to arrive at a fairly comprehensive moral paradigm of the "good person" (*ènìyàn rere*). Such a person would be

- scrupulous about the epistemological basis for whatever they claim to know, to believe, or to have no information about
- a good listener (with the emphasis more upon cognitive understanding rather than polite and respectful demeanor)
- a good speaker (with the emphasis upon speaking in a positive, thoughtful, and perceptive manner rather than mere elocution)
- patient (calm and self-controlled in judgment and intellect rather than merely in manner or demeanor)

- able to demonstrate all of these qualities via one's verbal and nonverbal behavior, this taken as indicative of a high level of intelligence and ability, which means that one's self (*inú* or *èmí*), mind (*ọkàn*), judgment (*èrí ọkan*), insight (*ojú inú*), destiny (*orí inú*), and moral character (*ìwà*) all are judged to be of superior quality
- an astute judge of the motives and morals of others on the basis of what they do (*iṣesí*) and say (*ọ̀rọ̀ ẹnu*)
- someone that does not become a party to quarreling, fighting, lying, stealing, or parsimony, unless it is to countermand them in a productive manner.

The moral commitment that is expected from this kind of person toward his or her fellow human beings also is made explicit:

(139) Good persons (*ènìyàn rere*): These are the people who help (*ràn;* etm 576) others, who do not want bad things to happen to their fellow human beings

as is the recognition and appreciation they receive from their fellow men and women:

(140) There are some persons, whenever they say something, it is true. And whenever they behave, they behave in a very correct way. There are some people like this who themselves are not aware of it. Other people recognize [them].

DEMONS OR INTELLIGENTSIA?
SPECIAL PERSONALITY TYPES

At several points during the course of this narrative reference has been made to the *àjẹ́* as a name for a class of human beings that is somehow distinctive in its own right. This kind of specialized typing also occurred in conjunction with our discussion of the "children of the world" (*ọmọ aráyé*). There it was implied that exceptionally nasty dispositions may be linked with exceptional personal 'powers'. I complained that the hasty reduction of such special Yoruba personality types to "witches" and "sorcerers" fails to take adequate account of their uniqueness and moral significance as products of a non-Western culture. It introduces a pejorative, demeaning element that impairs intercultural communication and respect.

The *oníṣẹ̀gùn* described a variety of such types, two of which will be discussed here: (1) àjẹ́ and (2) àlùjànún. Their English-language equivalents, as suggested by the etm, underscore my concern to liberate them from the semantic domains of Western magic and superstition: àjẹ́ is translated as "witch" (38), and àlùjànún as "evil spirits" (52). I am going to suggest that, rather than beginning from a presupposition that each of these types represents a different kind of *super*-natural, we experiment with approaching them as various types of *natural* human beings who are distinguished by superior intelligence and ability. I suggest this comparatively empirical alternative because I believe it will serve to correct the cognitive imbalance that results from their being treated as forms of superstition, and because I believe this gives better representation to some of the discussions with the onísẹ̀gùn about how these terms are used in Yoruba discourse.

To clear the narrative field of spirits and shades, perhaps the first point with which to begin is that all of the special personality types identified by the onísẹ̀gùn are persons (ènìyàn), are human beings:

> (141) These [àjẹ́, àlùjànún] are different types of persons (ènìyàn), some black, some yellow (*pupa*), and some light in complexion [drawing an analogy between different personality types and different skin tones].

That there can be special types of persons should also imply that there is a nonspecial or ordinary type of person (ènìyàn). This too is something about which the onísẹ̀gùn were explicit:

> (142) The person with one self (òní inú).[39]

Within the general class of all human beings, that there can be extraordinary personality types should also imply that there is some common measure or basis on which they may be distinguished from one another and from the ordinary person. It is the ẹ̀mí, inú, or self of the person that provides this basis:

> (143) It is the self (ẹ̀mí) which makes man behave (*hu ìwà*) as he does. It is the self (ẹ̀mí) which makes a man behave in a good manner or in a bad manner.[40]

---

39. See quotations (171), (180), and (228) for further references to the "ordinary" person as having only one inú.

40. This passage was used in a different context as part of quotation (33).

It is the number of èmí or inú, the number of selves, attributed to a single person that becomes a definitive characteristic of every personality type:

(144) There are some [ènìyàn] with two selves (èmí); àjé has two selves (èmí). The oṣó[41] has three [èmí]. Those we regard as wise people have four [èmí]. The strongest àlùjànún has seven selves [èmí], and every one [of the èmí] has its own duty to perform. Someone with seven selves [èmí] will be more powerful than someone with [only] one. It's like someone who has many servants, because they can do much more work than someone with no servants.

(145) There are many kinds of selves (èmí). People like Awolowo[42] and others, there is a certain self (èmí) which uses them. We hear some people have got about seven [èmí], or more.

(146) A person can have two selves (inú),[43] or three.

Extraordinary types of persons are said to be distinguished from the ordinary because they possess multiple selves (èmí or inú). The form of diagrammatic representation suggested is that of an inverted pyramid, with ordinary persons, described as having one self (òní inú or èmí), at the bottom and the most extraordinary, described as having seven selves, at the top.

Another distinguishing characteristic of the various personality types is said to be their "powers" (agbára; etm 26):

(147) This is power (agbára). A person can have two selves (inú) or three. . . . That is the way in which he or she can make use of his or her own power (agbára).[44]

(148) This is the point where the supreme deity (elédà) has limited some person's powers (agbára), while it does not limit the powers of others. We both have selves (èmí), but he makes theirs more powerful. He made their selves (èmí) double. You know there is some

---

41. A personality type that will not be discussed, but that is characterized by avarice.

42. The late Chief Obafemi Awolowo was the most important political and intellectual leader of the Yoruba in post-independence Nigeria. Former premier of the Western Region of Nigeria, leader of the Action Group political party, and author of any number of books and articles detailing what he believed to be the most satisfactory social and political philosophy for his country and for Africa generally. A detailed synopsis of Awolowo's thought can be found in Makinde (1988b, pp. 59–86).

43. I include this brief passage as evidence that the oníṣègùn in this context too can use the terms "èmí" and "inú" interchangeably.

44. This is a slightly longer version of quotation (146).

cloth which will cost one Naira[45] a yard, while there is another kind which will cost double that. There are many things we use, such as the bicycle, which are superior to others. We can compare this to those who have more power (*agbára*) than the rest [i.e., they have a special kind of self (*èmí*) that is superior to others].

But such power is also said to be a *consequence* of intelligence and ability:

(149) This is their thought (*èrò okòn*), which they use to do everything.[46]

(150) I don't know (*mò*), but those who are intelligent (*gbón;* etm 249: "intelligence") [would]; that is, those who know 'here' and 'there' [have more than one *èmí* or *inú*].

(151) There are very few people who can do this. Because it can be done [only] by people who are very intelligent (*gbón dáadáa*).

(152) The Europeans (*òyìnbó*) support themselves with selves (*inú*) which they 'turn' [control; apply] to certain kinds of power (*agbára*) to make certain things [technology like the airplane and the automobile] which surprise us. . . . There are some people who have that kind of power, but they use it to make rain.[47] And there are some people who also know the medicine to prevent the rain from falling. There are medicines which are used to do all these things, and this kind of wisdom (*ogbón*) has been in the world for a long time.[48]

What might be the reasoning underlying discourse which attributes superior intelligence, ability, and invention to the presence of multiple selves? Are we faced with *The Seven Faces of Eve* and the Yoruba semantics for multiple personality disorders? Choosing that as our course would introduce unnecessary and erroneous complications. Although it certainly is true, as is the case with the Western psychological "self," that the *èmí* or *inú* is not regarded as materialistic or physical in conventional terms:

---

45. The Nigerian currency.

46. This is the statement immediately following upon quotation (145).

47. It is what such power(s) and intelligence may be used to do, or how they may be evidenced in empirical terms, that tests the limits of Western credulity. Such disputed limits to the empirical will be the subject of a further study devoted to the cultural relativities of the distinction between the natural and the supernatural.

48. These are successive statements to quotation (147).

(153) If it were possible to see the self (èmí) physically, the [Western] doctors would have tried to remove the self (èmí) of a good person (ènìyàn rere) who was about to die and use it to replace the self (èmí) of a bad person (ènìyàn burúkú), so that the bad person (ènìyàn burúkú) would turn into a good one (ènìyàn rere). I think this would change the behavior of someone who did not behave well. Then I think he or she would behave as a good person (ènìyàn rere).

To continue, why choose this form of discourse to express extraordinary intelligence and ability? Reasoning again in terms of a personalized causal model, it would make good sense and certainly be consistent to express the remarkable attributes of unusually gifted individuals as the consequences of additives to the base rate of the intelligence and ability attributed to the ordinary person. How do people express analogous meanings in Western vernacular? Someone has *more* brain cells? A *higher* I.Q.? An *egghead*? A *high* forehead? *High*brow? *Cervellone*?[49]

To return to the subject of values, the standards governing moral and immoral behavior that have been detailed thus far must obviously apply to the ordinary person in Yoruba society, the person with one self (èmí). What becomes of importance is that individuals who fall within each of the extraordinary personality types also are judged by the same standards. What also become of greater consequence are the uses or ends, for good or ill, to which they are able to apply their remarkable intelligence and abilities.

a. Àjẹ́

KBW argues at length against the summary reduction of the àjẹ́ phenomenon to being essentially the same as that of English-language culture's "witch," and against Western scholars using African cultures as testing grounds for their theories about Western witchcraft. I cannot help but refer interested readers to that discussion as a useful background to what follows. What this narrative can try to do in greater detail is to be more precise about the behavioral dispositions the onísẹ̀gùn associate with the àjẹ́ as a personality type, and to demonstrate that such people's behavior is judged by the same moral standards that have already been outlined.

KBW also suggested that there is a popularized stereotype of the àjẹ́ phenomenon in Yoruba society itself. In the literature it is this stereotype, a polyglot mixture of African and Western (mainly via missionaries) su-

---

49. Italian for having a 'big' brain.

perstitions, that became the subject of Parrinder's[50] *Witchcraft: European and African.* Some of the false distortions worked upon the àjé personality type by this misguided stereotype are as follows: àjé generally are portrayed as "evil," as always immoral; àjé always are women; àjé tend to be identified with Halloweenish trappings of Western witchcraft (pacts with the Devil, flying off at night to meet with their coven, and so forth):

(154) They are persons (ènìyàn), just like you and me.[51]

There is therefore a need to demolish these false generalizations, one by one. First, the onísègùn made it clear that there are male àjé as well as female:

(155) (Interviewer:) Is it true that àjé is more common among the women?
(Onísègùn:) This is not true. We call àjé the "mother of children" (ìyá àwon omodé), but this is just because of fear [it is a euphemism that provides a discreet way to refer to a potentially dangerous person]. We do not say the "father of children" because that is not how we refer [not the phrasing of the conventional idiom] to the àjé.

(156) And they [women] have àjé more than men.

(157) The same [proportion of men are àjé as are women]. But there may be many among men.

(158) Only the supreme deity (Olórun) knows that [whether more àjé are women or men].

They also stated that the àjé personality can be eminently moral:

(159) Àjé are [can be] good persons (ènìyàn rere). Not all the àjé are bad persons (ènìyàn burúkú). There are some good ones. Since they do not talk (sòrò) [about it], that is why we cannot differentiate (mò sòtó) whether this àjé is good or whether this àjé is bad. If you and I are going out in [wearing] the same clothing, people will think that I am someone who 'knows book' [can read] because they see us in the eye [together]. They will not know (mò) that I do not know book. That is the case of àjé.

(160) Not all of them [àjé] are bad persons (ènìyàn burúkú). There are some of them . . . who do not say any cruel (ìkà) thing. If he or

---

50. Who, I have repeatedly been reminded by anthropological colleagues, is not a social anthropologist.

51. Included to reinforce the point that they are *human* beings.

she sees a person who wants to be cruel, he or she will warn them not to do so [i.e., warn off another àjẹ́ who is a bad or immoral person (ènìyàn burúkú)]. And he or she may tell other persons that the people of that place are bad—do not go there. There are some good àjẹ́ who may want to warn people, but the listeners will say, "Do not mind him or her," that "He or she [only] wants a favor from you." They may say that he or she is saying that [giving the warning] because he or she wants palm wine. And some may say he or she is drunk, whereas he or she wants to say the truth (òótọ́). But it may be that this person does not have many things in hand [i.e., that he or she is not important and so others don't take his or her warnings seriously]. There are some people who have something in hand [i.e., who are well-off] who have àjẹ́. There is nothing which can spoil their things; they can predict how a matter will be in a day and it will happen.

(161) There are some [àjẹ́] who do good things. . . . Àjẹ́ is not meant to be used in bad ways. Àjẹ́ is created so that the world may progress.

(162) The àjẹ́ behaves according to how its self (ẹ̀mí) is. Not all of them do bad things. There are some of them who use their own [intelligence and ability] to develop life.

(163) A good àjẹ́ (àjẹ́ rere) who does not do bad things—he or she doesn't kill children. He or she doesn't create fear in the minds of children. . . . They can say he or she is a good àjẹ́. Good àjẹ́ (àjẹ́ rere) cannot do anything bad. He or she will be looking for good things.

(164) There are some [àjẹ́] who behave well, if they have chosen to be so from 'heaven' (òrun). This type of àjẹ́ will not associate themselves with others [àjẹ́] who are known to be bad.

(165) There are some àjẹ́ whose moral character (ìwà) is good.

(166) Sometimes they do good things.

The point of introducing so many quotations to refute this notion is that, if there can be both bad and good àjẹ́, this means that there can be both immoral *and* moral persons who have whatever this extraordinary ability is. In terms of our inverted pyramid, àjẹ́ generally rate on the level just above ordinary human beings in that they are said to have two selves (ẹ̀mí):

(167) These are the people who we can refer to as having two selves (ẹ̀mí)—àjẹ́.

(168) Àjẹ́ have two selves (ẹ̀mí).

This implies that their 'powers' for good or ill are rated as roughly twice those of the ordinary person. But again such 'powers' are clearly linked to superior intelligence and ability:

(169) There are some persons [who], whenever they say something, it is true. And whenever they behave, they behave in a very correct way. There are some people like this who themselves are not aware of it. Other people recognize [them]. People may call them . . . àjẹ́, and it is possible that they are . . . [not]. There are some àjẹ́ who recognize themselves as such and [other] people know that they are àjẹ́. There are some people who receive great profit from whatever they do. These [people] may not be àjẹ́ or any of these [other special types of] people.

(170) This [ojú inú][52] is [pertains to] the thought (èrò) of the mind (ọkàn). This is what we call "ọ̀gínrínrínginrìn" [not in etm but can be equated with "insight" and "predictive ability"]. When all these small things combine to increase the knowledge of someone, they call that kind of person "àjẹ́" because he always says the truth. His words never miss.

(171) There are some people who are not àjẹ́, but they behave (húwá; etm 328) like àjẹ́. The supreme deity (Ọlọ́run) has given some people intelligence, even more than the àjẹ́. Some people are not àjẹ́, but they have supporters who are àjẹ́. These are the kinds of things which make it difficult to recognize àjẹ́. Some àjẹ́ reveal secrets and things that will happen [in future] to other persons (ènìyàn). They give warnings to other persons (ènìyàn) that they will deal with them if they do not behave in the way they like. It is very easy for àjẹ́ to deal with other persons who are not àjẹ́. . . . This shows how powerful they are. It is very difficult to know [distinguish] an àjẹ́ from an ordinary person (òní inú).

(172) As some people are more powerful (lágbára jù) than others, so also their intuitive insight (ojú inú) is more powerful. There will be two [eyes] outside and two inside. We call them "àjẹ́." You see (rí) that he or she will be more powerful than someone with [only] two [two eyes, not two ẹ̀mí!]. Some people can sit down here and may know what is happening down there [on the other side of the town]. Some people may open their eyes now [speaking of àjẹ́ and referring to their physical, normal eyes]—they have gone. Their intuitive insight (ojú inú) may be seeing other places. We call them "àjẹ́."[53]

At this point I would like to elaborate a thesis intimated in *KBW* (pp. 115–16). All of the *onísẹ̀gùn* concurred that the superior intelligence and

---

52. See pages 49–50.

53. Whether this is interpreted as evidence of natural (exceptional insight and an acute predictive ability) or supernatural (clairvoyance, prescience) talents need not be a point of concern for this discussion. See note 47 above.

ability associated with the àjẹ́ cannot be taught. It is inborn, pertaining to what in English-language culture is sometimes referred to as "native" intelligence. It is a fact of life that human beings do differ, sometimes markedly, from one another in terms of their native intelligence or I.Q. It is perhaps in part to account for these differences that the Yoruba attribute such disparities to a person's destiny (orí inú):

> (173) These [àjẹ́] also are persons (ènìyàn). But the àjẹ́ [ability] has been created with them when they were coming from 'heaven' (òrun). They chose this [as a destiny] because they liked it.

This makes perfect sense as a way to explain how two different persons (ẹ̀mí), who in principle should somehow be equal simply by virtue of each one's being a person (ẹ̀mí), can turn out in the course of a single lifetime to display very different levels of inborn or native intelligence, with all the consequences that may entail. That such differences may be attributed to their respective destinies is certainly a way of representing intelligence as inborn. In a belief system where every individual is said to undergo an indefinite number of reincarnations, who would want to be faced with the prospect of being a less intelligent person throughout them all? Hence, each choice of a new destiny also gives the self a chance[54] to improve upon its "native" intelligence and abilities.

If the foregoing serves to rehabilitate the àjẹ́ as a general, if exceptional, personality type, we may now proceed to detail the more specific types of immoral *and* moral behavior associated with it. What should distinguish such behavior is its scale or degree, in that the àjẹ́ is capable of doing greater good or greater bad than the ordinary person. I have already suggested that the àjẹ́'s talents may be applied to advance positive moral interests. Here are some examples of immoral behavior that the onísẹ̀gùn associated with the àjẹ́. Although it may seem redundant, the first point to establish is that the àjẹ́ personality can be associated with a morally bad person (ènìyàn burúkú):

> (174) The "enemy" (òtá) and the àjẹ́ are types of persons who are not happy when one is progressing.
> (175) The àjẹ́ may also be an immoral person (ènìyàn burúkú).
> (176) The àjẹ́ do bad things because they don't like people (ènìyàn).
> (177) The difference between them is that the àjẹ́ behaves badly to other

---

54. In certain respects trying to choose a good destiny becomes as daunting as trying to choose the winning number in a lottery.

persons without any cause at all, while the ordinary person will have a reason for their behavior.

This then explains a great deal about their having to conceal themselves from *moral* persons:

    (178) Àjẹ́ are just like thieves, because no one who is a thief would tell others that he was. So also *àjẹ́* will not reveal their identity to any person.

    (179) Yes, but there are some people [who are *àjẹ́*] who appear dull (*gọ̀;* etm. 256: "stupid," "dull," "foolish").[55]

    (180) It is very difficult to know [distinguish] an *àjẹ́* for [from] an ordinary person (*òní inú*).[56]

Consequently the bad or immoral *àjẹ́* become very difficult to identify:

    (181) They spoil the work of other people, but people cannot see them because they follow the path of darkness.

    (182) It is very difficult to recognize *àjẹ́* . . . because we don't know what their thought is [what they're thinking 'inside'].

Another relevant topic that was raised in *KBW* is why it must be the case that *moral* persons who are 'blessed' with these superior abilities also apparently must conceal themselves from the general public. For it certainly is the case that people do not go about in conventional Yoruba society introducing themselves as *àjẹ́*! The explanation suggested for this then was as follows:

> Extraordinary ability also demands extraordinary responsibility. The good *àjẹ́* recognizes that ordinary people cannot be expected to understand or to accomplish as much as he can. For this reason he cannot expect that, if he were to reveal his knowledge to them, they would use it responsibly and at the same time honor him as the intellectual and spiritual leader he would deserve to be. More likely, because the basis for his special abilities is something that cannot be shared or taught [i.e., is the product of inborn or native intelligence], ordinary people would come to fear him and take whatever steps they could to contain or to destroy him. So, even the good *àjẹ́* must conceal himself. He may still exercise his powers for the benefit of the community, but only in a deliberately discreet and indirect manner. (*KBW,* p. 116)

---

55. As a ruse to disguise themselves.

56. This is a repetition of the final sentence of quotation (171).

Supplementary remarks made by the *oníṣẹ̀gùn* seem to support this interpretation:

> (183) But it is the *àjẹ́* who knows the ones that are not good (*kò dára*) [who can recognize other immoral *àjẹ́*], but they cannot say it openly. If he says it openly, people will say that he or she is 'prophesying' (*kà;* etm 356 A.2(c)–(d)).

However, as I shall indicate shortly, there are certain firsthand manifestations of good moral character (*ìwà rere*) that may be attributed to the *àjẹ́*.

Certain forms of immoral behavior can be associated with the *àjẹ́* as a personality type:

> (184) They will behave like *àjẹ́*. For instance, if people complain that *àjẹ́* are troubling them, rather than sympathizing with them the *àjẹ́* will say they are not concerned, that no *àjẹ́* could come to them, that they are free from all *àjẹ́*.[57]

Certain forms of moral behavior can as well:

> (185) If he or she sees a person who wants to be cruel, he or she will warn them not to do so [i.e., warn off another *àjẹ́* who is a bad or immoral person (*ènìyàn burúkú*)]. And he or she may tell other persons that the people of that place are bad—do not go there. There are some good *àjẹ́* who may want to warn people.[58]
>
> (186) Some *àjẹ́* reveal secrets and things that will happen [in future] to other persons (*ènìyàn*). They [also] give warnings to other persons [*ènìyàn*] that they will deal with them if they do not behave in the way they like.[59]

---

57. As quotation (160) indicates, being *àjẹ́* in a particular lifetime is not sufficient to ensure a good destiny with everything that might entail (moral character, prosperity, happiness). It is possible to choose a destiny that involves being (or in more empirical terms to be identified by others as) *àjẹ́* and still have an unfortunate and unhappy life.

It appears that *àjẹ́* may also be used, perhaps idiomatically, to characterize some unfortunates whose 'powers' to inflict misfortune upon themselves are perceived as exceeding the ordinary: "There are some kinds (*ènìyàn míràn*) of persons (*ènìyàn*) who are unfortunate (*ènìyàn burúkú*), who don't cut their hair. Some people may say that they are bad *àjẹ́*. Then they will call them 'wretched *àjẹ́*' (*àjẹ́ òsì*). There is nothing which can 'have eye' (*ojú*) when it gets to his or her hand [i.e., they will fail in everything]. . . . People will say that his or her *ẹgbẹ́* (fellow *àjẹ́* in the world) do not allow him or her to be prosperous (*kò ní láárí;* etm 403: 'it is valueless'). If he or she puts something in his pocket, he or she may lose it without even knowing when. If he or she plants yam, it will not yield well."

58. This is a restatement of a portion of quotation (160).

59. This is a restatement of a portion of quotation (171).

I anticipate that this attempt to rehabilitate the intellectual and social standing of the àjẹ́ will be received with grave reservations by some scholars who are persuaded by the more orthodox portrayals of the àjẹ́ as the "witch." I would remind them that the onísẹ̀gùn with whom I was privileged to hold these discussions were themselves once stigmatized with the title "witch doctors," with all of the intellectual scorn that term implied. If use of that term has been suspended because of a better appreciation of their genuine abilities, why should not the same be the case with the use of "witches" as a name for the persons (reflecting the personalized causal model) associated with important or momentous events during an individual's lifetime? It was Jack Goody (1977) who posed the topical question: "Intellectuals in Primitive Societies?" His response on the basis of, as always, literacy was not very positive. And perhaps because the title "intellectual" is so directly associated with the "book" in Western culture, this particular term does not provide a comfortable cross-cultural frame of reference. Yet if "intellect" as a term is also used to refer to cognition, to the power(s) of human understanding, certainly the àjẹ́ exercise these in a superior manner—with all that implies about "knowing" and "believing"—in comparison to ordinary persons. In this case perhaps it is the connotations that have come to be attached to use of the term "intellectual" in Western culture that must be chastened, so that its meaning can extend to oral cultures and to persons like the àjẹ́. I have searched my thesaurus for semantic alternatives and intermediaries that fall anywhere between "smart" and "genius," but I have not found any other that expresses optimal cognition in a more suitable manner.

b. Àlùjànún

The àlùjànún personality type becomes my candidate in Yoruba discourse for the equivalent to "genius" in English-language usage. This is the term the etm recommends be translated as "evil spirit." The etm goes on to suggest that the word in Yoruba derives from the Hausa-language "al-jannu," which in turn is said to derive from Arabic. The Arabic word apparently involved would be "janna," which in turn is derived from "yajinnu," which a footnote to my copy of the Koran defines as "to be covered or hidden" (p. 319, note 929). And yajinnu also happens to be the root of the Arabic jinn[60] or jinni, from which the English-language "genie" and eventually "genius" evolved!

---

60. "Some people say that jinn therefore means the hidden qualities or capacities in man" (Koran, p. 319, note 929).

In setting out the evidence from the discussions with the *oníṣègùn* to support this interpretation, I will follow the same general schema as was used with the *àjẹ́*. The first point to establish is that the *àlùjànún* are persons (*ènìyàn*), human beings:

> (187) How they appear (*awo*) is just like the ordinary person appears. They don't have four eyes. We are not different from them.

Second, that they can be both morally good and morally bad:

> (188) Persons who are *àlùjànún* . . . some are worse (*burú jù*) than others. There are bad ones. There are good ones.
>
> (189) Yes, they can be bad persons (*ènìyàn burúkú*). If the *àlùjànún* is a bad person in himself or herself.
>
> (190) There are good ones and there are also bad ones. There are some of them who will be using (*lo*) their own [special abilities] for good work, and there are some who will be doing bad (*búburú*) things.
>
> (191) Some of them are bad, because there are no persons with extra powers who [on some occasions in their lives] are not cruel. . . . They can do good things, and bad things as well. The same as with the ordinary person.
>
> (192) There is no one among them [the different 'types' of persons (*ènìyàn*)] where we could not find bad or immoral persons (*ènìyàn burúkú*). The ones who are good are more numerous (*pọ̀jù*) than those who are bad.[61]

Introductory remarks about their 'powers' were certainly intriguing:

> (193) The persons we call "*àlùjànún*" are those who can do extraordinary things (*iṣẹ́ ìyanun*; etm 677: "surprise," "something wonderful"). Whenever we would see something mysterious or marvelous in the olden days, we would refer to it as the work of *àlùjànún*.
>
> (194) *Àlùjànún* is a type of person who does extraordinary things (*iṣẹ́ ìyanun*). You know that I am one of them.[62]
>
> (195) They [*àlùjànún*] are the people who developed the world [the very wise ones].

---

61. This remark is also interesting as a generalization about the relative proportions of the morally good and bad.

62. An admission made in confidence, of course.

On the inverted pyramid used to rank the relative 'powers' of the special personality types, the *àlùjànún* get the highest rating with "seven selves"[63] and therefore occupy the topmost stratum. That having 'seven' selves is equivalent to superior intellect and ability becomes clear from the behavioral characteristics[64] recounted by the *onísègùn:*

> (196) Those that can know (*mò*) things best are those we call *àlùjànún.* These are the people whom others will come to and ask whether the path they want to trace [the plans they have made] is good.
>
> (197) There are some people who will say something, and it will be [happen] like that. When he or she says so, it will happen like that. And you can call this kind of person any kind of name. They will say he or she is *àlùjànún.* . . . That he or she has 'seen' everything before he or she pronounces upon it. Later on nobody will try to disprove whatever he or she says. They will not want to conclude a discussion until he or she is there. They will say he or she is in the best position to say which one is good [e.g., which plan or program].
>
> (198) But those who have *àlùjànún* usually possess the most effective medicine (*òògùn*), and the people [general public] will be making comments that those people are not ordinary herbalists or diviners (*babaláwo*), that they do not use the 'naked' [ordinary] eye to do what they are doing.

That they can be identified by their superior intellectual powers as displayed via (verbal and nonverbal) behavior means that there are certain forms of behavior associated with 'being' *àlùjànún:*

> (199) This is only possible by listening to their words and knowing (*mò*) what they're doing. [Recognizing] that they behave differently and can do extraordinary things. It is through their works that we know they are a different kind of person (*ènìyàn*).
>
> (200) These are the people we call "*àlùjànún.*" They will say, "That man is *àlùjànún*"—those who see (*rí*) how he behaves (*húwá*) and how he talks (*sòrò*). People will say he is a good *àlùjànún.*

That such superior intelligence and ability is inborn or "native" also is made clear ("You cannot just become *àlùjànún* [via lessons, teaching, etc.]").

---

63. See quotations (144) and (145).

64. I was reliably informed that no one under the age of thirty is likely to be referred to as *àlùjànún.*

What is remarkable about these passages is how clearly they reiterate the evidential criteria involving what people 'do' (ṣe) and what people 'say' (sòrọ̀) that served as the basis for defining moral character (ìwà). Only now they extend to personality types as well. The consistency in this regard evidenced by the remarks of the onísẹ̀gùn is undeniable. Although valued for their good counsel generally, one aspect to their superior intelligence that was especially appreciated by the onísẹ̀gùn was their predictive powers, for the dissemination of which they may be morally praised or blamed:[65]

> (201) Some of them are bad, because there are no persons with extra powers who [on some occasions during their lifetimes] are not cruel. For example, if an àlùjànún becomes aware of something that's going to happen in the future, it might refuse to inform the people who are going to be injured. If it refuses to do this, we think it is a bad person. They can do good things, and bad things as well. The same as with the ordinary man.

In other words, àlùjànún too can err. But the occasional mistake will not result in the general attribution of a bad moral character (ìwà burúkú).

What more precisely is it about their 'seven selves' that was thought to enable such genius to demonstrate its superior ability (without having recourse to 'spirits' and the supernatural)? When one of the onísẹ̀gùn was trying to express, admittedly with obscure phrasing, what goes on in the self (èmí or inú; and by implication the mind [ọkàn]) of the àlùjànún he said the following:

> (202) They merely 'listen' and 'hear' the 'voice', but they don't see (rí) and they don't know (mọ̀) [in the conventional, everyday manner].

The phrasing again is remarkable. One cannot help but be struck by the epistemic framework he invokes for his terms of reference. The ideas the àlùjànún comes by are not knowledge (ìmọ̀) in the conventional sense— what one perceives and comprehends. It is much more intimate, personal, cerebral, intellectual:

---

65. As was also the case with the àjẹ́. See quotations (185) and (186).

(203) He should have 'seen' the root of the problem (*ìdí:*[66] the reason
behind or the "bottom" of the matter) that he wants to use the
medicine (*òògùn*) for. If you come to ask something from me now,
I can tell you to go and come back. I will put that thing in mind
(*okàn*). And when I foresee (*ríró̩n;* etm 317: "sight," "vision") it, if
it is something that will not be possible, I will say so [i.e., in the
interim he will use the *àlùjànún* to look into it (*ríró̩n* here having
the sense of assessing something's future feasibility and efficacy)]
and be able to tell the person the answer—whether it is possible
or not—when they return. If it is good, I will tell you to go
ahead—that there is nothing [no problem]. It means that I've used
my [cognitive powers of] understanding and insight (*ojú inú*) to
see (*wò*) it. As *àjé̩* and *àlùjànún,* any medicine which I put my
hands on must be good.

Why might this not amount to the description of an intellectual process
similar to what the genius undergoes when reflecting deeply on a problem, eventually to arrive at a solution on the basis of his or her own superior intellectual prowess? The rhetorical trappings of Yoruba discourse,
the metaphors and images, used to describe a person's intellect and reflective powers (*ojú inú,* and so forth) may differ, but their sense when
viewed in a systematic context such as this argue for understanding and
intellect providing the basis for knowledge.

THE MASTERS OF MEDICINE

During the thirteen years that I tried the patience of the *onís̩è̩gùn,* quib-
bling over the correct usage of the same term time after time, I don't think
I ever appreciated how important a role they actually played in the epistemic and moral system(s) they were helping me to understand. In part this
was because they seemed (to me) so unpretentious in appearance and
manner. If these were men whose knowledge was 'power', whom other
members of the community consulted about serious matters, whom an
informal communal consensus had advised me to consult for the most
profound knowledge of their culture, in physical terms they were also
men of 'low profile'. Their bodies were not adorned with exceptional
robes, and their homes were not festooned with medicines. When I finally
did inquire about this I was told that they did not need to "advertise" their

---

66. See the discussion of "*nwádì,*" which is a contraction of *nwá* (finding) and *ìdí,* on
page 18.

distinction in so vulgar a manner. Their reputations 'spoke for themselves' via the relief and success had by individuals who came to consult them.

On the other hand, their demeanor—their manner, their behavior—was impressive. But here, once again, I mean to refer more to their words, the contents of their speech, than to the way they sat in a chair or gestured with their hands. They were reserved, serious, calm, patient—and whatever else is required by the paradigm of the person with good moral character as previously outlined in this chapter. But what was impressive about their speech was the intelligence it reflected. This was what informed their behavior and, indeed, my role in the circumstances. For I became the student and they the teachers.

I have previously indicated that the oníṣẹ̀gùn, among themselves, preferred the title "adáhunṣe." The meaning of this complicated contraction may be rendered as "the ones who can really do[67] something," a title whose significance was not overlooked by those who had to turn to someone else for help:

(204) They [the oníṣẹ̀gùn] take care of people (ènìyàn). They prepare medicine (òògùn) for people (ènìyàn). Second, they help persons and deliver them from the hands of their enemies (òtá) so that they cannot harm them.

(205) He [the oníṣẹ̀gùn] can make medicine (òògùn) which will prevent them [ènìyàn burúkú] from doing harm to a person.

(206) You see, those oníṣẹ̀gùn, they chose it [as their destiny] from 'heaven' (òrun). They are powerful wherever they go. Whatever happens, they can be powerful [able to solve people's problems] wherever they go. Either in the afternoon, in the morning, or in the night. The supreme deity (Olórun) has created them as "the persons to 'repair' [protect] the town" (a túnlúse; to make good things for it).

(207) They [immoral persons (ènìyàn burúkú)] have an enemy (òtá). The oníṣẹ̀gùn are their enemy (òtá).

Destiny (orí inú), of course, may also be involved with the decision to 'consult' an oníṣẹ̀gùn. The person who is experiencing 'hard times', undesired and unwarranted misfortune, may feel that he or she is in that precarious state that has been described as 'missing road' (chapter 3). Yet, as was the case with 'missing road', the oníṣẹ̀gùn had no problem with integrating the decision to consult them as part of a person's overall

---

67. "Do" (dá) here has the sense of innovation.

destiny. That the apparent inconsistency between a 'fixed' destiny and 'changing' one's destiny may be resolved in this manner would indicate that the overall concern of the individuals who are involved is more with the 'pattern' of their lives than it is with rather specific incidents in them. While that overall pattern appears to remain positive, a lifetime is considered generally good. When it does not, a valued part of the pattern itself is that it will become so:

> (208) But if it is the test of the "people of the world" (àwon aráyé) [i.e., if your problems are caused by immoral others], his or her good *inú* [here having the sense of *orí inú* or "destiny"] will cause him or her to meet someone [*oníṣègùn*] who will help him or her solve the problem.
>
> (209) And when, after he or she has seen the *oníṣègùn* and life becomes more abundant for him or her, it is also what he or she has planned for himself or herself.

What does the *oníṣègùn* do during the course of a consultation? In the case of a person who is caught out in an immoral act and denies responsibility for it, for whatever reasons, the *oníṣègùn* may be involved:

> (210) Before they could believe [the disclaimer] they would take him or her to the *oníṣègùn,* who will say whether he or she is responsible for his or her actions or not.

The principal task of the *oníṣègùn* in this kind of situation is to rule on the possibility of mitigating circumstances. If there are none, then the person remains principally and morally responsible for the action.

What do the *oníṣègùn* 'do' for either of these two categories of clients or patients: (1) one who has committed immoral acts for which he or she denies responsibility, and (2) "bad destiny people"? As the title "master of medicine" indicates, they prescribe medicine (*òògùn*) that will serve to correct or to mitigate the underlying problem:

> (211) The *oníṣègùn* can do this through medicine (*òògùn*).
>
> (212) Yes, he [the *oníṣègùn*] can help them by preparing medicine (*òògùn*) which the person will put in his body. This will make the immoral person (*ènìyàn burúkú*) keep away.

This preparing of medicine is a central element to the intelligent application of the *oníṣègùn*'s art and therapy:

(213) If one has a powerful self (èmí), he can use this to support a deity (òrìṣà),[68] and people will think that it is the deity (òrìṣà) that is doing something special for the man. Some people [oníṣègùn] also support their deity (òrìṣà) with medicine, and in this case they can perform extraordinary feats (iyùn). Deities (òrìṣà) on their own are nothing until they are supported by the owner [worshipper].

So much more is involved than with the white-smocked pharmacist who fills a doctor's prescription in the typical Western pharmacy. For in Ijan the oníṣègùn was the doctor as well as the pharmacist and thereby dominated the entire consultation process from beginning to end:

(214) This is the main reason why people go to oníṣègùn. The oníṣègùn will tell the person to go and make sacrifice, that he may become a 'good-headed' man [as if a person with a good destiny]. For instance [an analogy], if you offend me and I've written your name down, but later on you come to apologize to me, this kind of apology is what we refer to as "sacrifice" (ètùtù; etm 168: "atonement"). If I take your apology, I will forgive you, and I will cross out your name in my book. This is [means], I've agreed to forgive you. This means that the sacrifice (ètùtù) has been accepted, and the fellow will come to the right path and his life will be prosperous.

(215) These also are immoral persons (ènìyàn burúkú). . . . People are always afraid of them. . . . All these kinds of bad things [the immoral human beings that fall within the various special personality types] are persons (ènìyàn). This is the reason why people should 'sacrifice' (ètùtù), so that these kinds of people will not have influence over them.

(216) The diviners (babaláwo)[69] are the oníṣègùn who heal people through leaves and roots.

(217) Only the babaláwo can do this. They will give medicine to the victim which will decrease the power of these bad forces [ènìyàn burúkú].

---

68. Òrìṣà generally are the lesser divinities of the Yoruba pantheon. His point is that, in such circumstances, many people would not credit the oníṣègùn for the skill of his medicine. They would attribute the efficacy (or 'power') of the medicine to the 'divine intervention' of a deity.

69. In Ijan there were no Ifá babaláwo, but the oníṣègùn would sometimes refer to themselves as "babaláwo." That is also the case in ensuing quotations when use is made of the term "babaláwo."

The significance of these passages is important. The point of the entire consultation process—whether with reference to an immoral act or for advice about a 'bad destiny'—is to effect what will be better for the client or patient. The point is not to initiate a 'witch-hunt', to provide patients, via the consultation process, which may also involve a form of divination, with the names and addresses of persons who have been causing their misfortune so they can be tracked down for 'termination'. One reason for consulting the onísègùn, and for the kinds of prescriptions[70] they make (whether for a medicine to take or for a sacrifice to make), is to prevent that kind of thing from happening. Professional reputations depend upon whether the "medicines" they prescribe provide effective protection (itself a form of relief) against further influence from immoral others or misfortune.

This seems an appropriate point at which finally to discuss in some detail the relationship between the natural and the supernatural (or extra-physical) implied in some of the above quotations (204, 205). For when there is reference to making a "sacrifice" or to the efficacy of a "medicine" for protecting a human being from misfortune, to the Western mind something more than the "natural" is becoming involved. And the same is often the case with the Yoruba. Although this narrative is deliberately cast so as to highlight the empirical and objective elements of certain forms and fields of Yoruba discourse, it would be inexcusable to ignore the contributions believed to be made to the making of sacrifices and the preparation of medicines by supernatural powers.

The whole point of making a sacrifice may be to persuade a deity (òrìsà) to come to the petitioner's assistance, and in some cases the 'deity' might even be that person's own destiny (orí inú)! Similarly the curative powers of a medicine prepared by an onísègùn might well be attributed, by that onísègùn, to the spiritual input of a particular deity (òrìsà). To repeat, it would be absurd to deny the existence of this dimension to Yoruba discourse, or of the fact that a significant number of members of that culture are devout when it comes to such fundamentally important spiritual or supernatural beliefs. However, I am also concerned to point out that overemphasizing this supernatural dimension to the Yoruba form of life to a point where it excludes the contributions of the onísègùn as human beings who are also coming to terms with the concerns of their fellow human beings on the level of a predominantly *natural* world with

70. As is indicated by quotation (214), the definition of "medicine" (òògùn) is much broader than in the conventional Western context.

natural medicines and *sensible* advice would be to do them a gross injustice. This is the imbalance I am seeking to redress, rather than to create another equally unfair imbalance that totally ignores the spiritual or extraphysical. My overriding concern again is to underline or to highlight the *intelligence* that also distinguishes their professionalism. As this point was expressed to me by one of their number some years ago:

(218) It is the power of medicine. When you prepare your medicine and you say it is your deity (*òrìṣà*) which told you to give it to people, if the medicine should cure the type of illness to which it is applied, they [people] will regard your deity (*òrìṣà*) as powerful and will think that it is its [the deity's] power that you use to do whatever you do, not knowing that [really it] is your medicine.

For example, there are people [*oníṣègùn*] who may have prepared a medicine [and then put it] inside a container. When they open the container it will cause people around [it] to sneeze. If this person [the *oníṣègùn* who placed the medicine inside the container] is the worshiper of a particular deity (*òrìṣà*), they [people] will say it is the power of the deity which made the power of that person [the herbalist] displayed there. There are some people who ingest very strong medicines which will make them light [in terms of body weight], and then they will be enabled to perform many acrobatic dances [as in a masquerade]. If the person is attached to a certain deity, people will believe it is the power of the deity that he uses to perform his acrobatic dances.

For example, if there is a person who is an expert at a certain thing, if he should come to boast that he could do the thing without the power of the supreme deity (*Ọlọ́run*), if other people should know of his boast, they will not allow the thing to be possible. This is because they are not pleased by his pride in disconnecting the supreme deity from his power. For people would not respect the power [of the *oníṣègùn* as only human] and they [also] might [then come to] regard the deities as nothing.

One [*oníṣègùn*] can tie a white cloth in the corner of his room, put a stone there, and put oil on it [thereby creating an altar or a shrine]. He will put medicine inside this place which he will be giving to people who complain of headache or any kind of disease. If a person comes and complains of a certain disease, he will enter into the shrine and remove some medicine and tell the patient, "My deity (*òrìṣà*) asked me to give you this medicine." He may also give the medicine to all the people around. Since the medicine can cure the kind of disease to which he applied it, they will agree that the deity is powerful [i.e., the giving of the medicine to the patient and to "all the people around" are not simultaneous; once the patient has been cured and reported back, then the *onísègùn* may dispense it generally as a proven remedy].

Among those who are learned there are many titles which they use to honor themselves. These are with regards to the knowledge a person has got from academic pursuits. People who are called "B.A.," "Ph.D.," and those who reach the stage of elementary schools generally will be referred to as people who "know book" [are literate]. When we [*onísègùn*] ask someone to go and worship a certain deity so that a disease should leave him,[71] the person will know inside himself that there has been some bad behavior which he indulged in. For example, if they [*onísègùn*] ask a barren woman to make sacrifice to a certain deity, people [the *onísègùn*] will advise her privately to desist from having sexual relations with many people. After she has made the sacrifice to the deity, there are certain medicines which they will give to her. They will advise the lady that the deity will not listen to her prayer if she does not behave well toward her husband. If they are trying to cure a disease in a person, they may ask him to worship a certain deity, and tell him that the deity asks him not to go to the farm for seven days. They might [do so by] say[ing] the deity has asked him not to cross a river. [All] this would be to keep him at home for a rest.

I should first say that the *onísègùn* who provided me with this explanation of their approach to sacrifice and to medicine said explicitly that it should be taken as *generally* representative of his colleagues' attitude toward their profession. That said, there are several noteworthy points which arise from this statement. First is the unmistakable element of objectivity with which he assesses the role and importance of òrìsà (deity) worship with regards to his profession and the community. He does not even deal with the question of whether the deities *really* exist. It is somehow not relevant. What is important is that *honoring* these deities—attributing one's skill and success to a divine agency rather than only oneself—helps to mitigate and deflect the jealousy and envy that would otherwise very definitely be the response of the rest of the community. So, although the *onísègùn* is convinced that it is his own ability that is responsible for the accuracy of a diagnosis, the potency of a medicine, and thereby the

---

71. For the remainder of this paragraph the *onísègùn* aims to characterize the level or kind of erudition (analogous to the "B.A." or "Ph.D.") that distinguishes those who practice his profession.

patient's recovery, the *onísègùn* is careful to relate all these things to a deity.

Particularly relevant here is the last paragraph of the *onísègùn's* remarks, where he explains that a further advantage to using the deities as a screen for his talents is that it also helps to inflate the importance of the commonsense element that is part of his remedies. Rather than telling the barren woman to sleep with her husband on a more regular basis, he tells her that only by *beginning* to do so will the deity consider listening to her petition. The sick farmer is told that in order to worship the relevant deity properly, he will not have time to work on his farm. Or, if a stream happens to lie between his house and farm, he is forbidden by the deity to cross water—all in order to keep him quiet in his house so that he can get sufficient rest!

An unfortunate stereotype with which Africa has been saddled, as has been previously mentioned, is that the forces with which professionals like the *onísègùn* are most concerned to contend are spiritual—in other words, that the causal agents responsible for human problems and successes are preeminently *supra*natural. The spiritual or extra-physical (or religious) is certainly another important dimension to the Yoruba lifeworld, but it should never be exaggerated to a point where it overshadows the contributions made by the intellects of individual human beings. For it appears that at least one essential element to the power of the *onísègùn* and a key to their moral prominence in the community is the stabilizing, balancing, calming, healthy, and positive influence they exert by convincing clients that the "medicines" prescribed will be sufficient to enable them in future to cope with whatever may be the problems involved. In other words, the *onísègùn* are also the arbiters of the personalized causal model.

That someone is an *onísègùn* is no guarantee that they are a morally good person. As with all the other categories of persons, *onísègùn* too can be immoral human beings (*èniyàn burúkú*):

(219) There are some [*onísègùn* who are *èniyàn burúkú*]. These are the people who make bad medicine (*òògùn*) to harm others.

(220) Yes, there are some *babaláwo* who prepare bad medicines (*òògùn*) to kill other persons.

(221) Before a person can be regarded as the holder of bad medicine (*olóògùn burúkú*), they [other people] will have seen two or three places where he has used the bad medicine. Everybody who learns medicine also can learn bad ones [medicines]. The person teaching you would say that if you do it this way, the person will be in trouble [i.e., when you are learning the skill; your teacher will caution you about making medicines in such ways that their

results will be negative]. And if you turn [control] it to the other side, it will be good [if you do it the original way the medicine will be beneficial]. But there are some who know the bad ones [medicines] more than the good ones. If someone has offended you, he [the *oníṣègùn* with bad moral character (*ìwà*)] can say to you, "No one could do the kinds of things he or she does to you to me. I would not take that from anybody. I would punish him." Then, if you make the mistake of saying that the man [the immoral *oníṣègùn*] should help you [since, after all, he's just been deliberately rebuking you in the hope that you will ask him to], he will not take anything [remuneration] from you, and he will execute his artful deception (*idón;* etm 274: "conjuring," "sleight of hand").[72] You may not be able to thank him because he has helped you to do bad to somebody. But you know in your own mind that he [i.e., the immoral *oníṣègùn* who helped you] is a bad person (*ènìyàn burúkú*). It is you who will tell the others that they should beware of him. That is how we know whether a person is immoral (*burúkú*) or not. Then people will begin to call him a bad person (*ènìyàn burúkú*). They will say that he doesn't take time [hesitate] to kill a person. They will say good words never come out of his mouth.

Here again the basic pattern is repeated. When an *oníṣègùn* is known to be involved in an isolated incident of malpractice that has ethical implications, his behavior may be attributed to an error in judgment and his reputation for good moral character (*ìwà*) preserved. But if he is thereafter seen to be involved with further cases in which similar malpractice is evidenced, his moral character would be downgraded to that of *ènìyàn burúkú*, a person with an immoral character (*ìwà*).

Inborn or "native" intelligence is again the most important source of the skills of the superior *oníṣègùn*. Clients must beware of incompetents, and ordinary persons (*òní èmí* or *inú*) who become *oníṣègùn* can pretend to no more than ordinary success:

(222) There are many types of *babaláwo,* and many of them pretend to know (*mò*) what [in fact] they don't know.

(223) Yes, there are some people who have got this gift from 'heaven' (*òrun*). If anyone tries to be a *babaláwo* who has not been des-

---

72. Causing unwarranted misfortune to another person with the intention of not being held responsible. As was the case with the most vicious level of immoral persons, such *oníṣègùn* may not care about remuneration for their 'services' because the suffering of their victims is reward enough.

tined to do so, his "medicine" will not cure any illness. There are some people who can prepare only a single herb which will cure many people of certain diseases. This is destiny (*bí ó tì pín:* "this is how he chooses"). Not every person can prepare medicine which will cure a disease.

(224) It is possible, but his [the ordinary person's] medicine will not be as effective as that of those who have been 'given by the supreme deity' (*Olǫrun;* those destined to have exceptional intelligence and ability]. Such people, those 'given by *Olǫrun*', don't forget the prescriptions. They will understand [what is wrong] as soon as you begin to complain to them. They will not bother to write anything down. Those who are not 'given by *Olǫrun*' write all things down. They have to learn [them] by heart so that they will not forget. This is because they are not 'given'. People like us don't write medicine down, but we know it.

Those who are 'given by *Olǫrun*' are the most powerful (read "talented" or "skilled") of the *onísègùn.* Such individuals are frequently said to have selves (*èmí* or *inú*) that are a composite of a plurality of the special personality types:

(225) There are some who are *àjé.*

(226) There are some *babaláwo*[73] who are . . . *àjé* or *àlùjànún.* These people will be able to see what goes on in the night and in daylight. They are the strongest *babaláwo,* whose medicines are the most effective.

(227) There are some *babaláwo* who are *àjé.* . . . They will be very strong.

(228) They [the best *onísègùn*] are these types of people with two selves (*inú méjì;* [from the preceding remark it is clear that he has *àjé* in mind here]). If someone with one self (*inú*) becomes an *onísègùn,* he will know very few medicines. But these [with *inú méjì*] will be 'true' ones.

(229) These types of *babaláwo* [who are *àjé*] are the strongest. We regard them as having from two to three [superior] intellects (*ogbón*).

(230) The *babaláwo* who has *àlùjànún* and *àjé,* their medicine will always answer (*jé*) [work well]. He should have 'seen' the root of the problem (*ìdí:* the reason behind or the "bottom" of the matter) that he wants to use the medicine (*òògùn*) for. If you come to ask

---

73. Once again in these quotations the *onísègùn* are using the word for "diviner" to refer to themselves.

something from me now, I can tell you to go and come back. I will put that thing in mind (ọkàn). And when I foresee (rírón; "sight," "vision") it, if it is something that will not be possible, I will say so [i.e., in the interim he will use the àlùjànún to look into it (rírón here has the sense of assessing something's future feasibility and efficacy)] and be able to tell the person the answer—whether it is possible or not—when they return. If it is good, I will tell you to go ahead—that there is nothing [no problem]. It means that I've used my [cognitive powers of] understanding and insight (ojú inú) to see (wò) it. As àjé and àlùjànún, any medicine which I put my hands on must be good.[74]

(231) Yes (bέèni), there is (ó wà) [babaláwo who are àlùjànún, àjé]. . . . Everything will be correct in his hand [one of the best].

Having 'seven selves' may mean that one is a composite of all the other varieties.[75] But the underlying sense to the most talented onísègùn's 'being' all of these things is that they are then also in an optimal state to contend with them, if, as, and when encountered in other persons, in a successful manner.[76] For if my suggestions that being àjé and being àlùjà-nún mean that a person's intellect and abilities are of the highest caliber, then such individuals are better qualified to come to terms with life's problems and provide relief to the individual as well as to benefit humankind generally.

---

74. A repetition of quotation (203).

75. As quotation (144) implies.

76. In the case of a reputedly highly skilled onísègùn whose medicine fails to help a client, here too predestination may be invoked: "There are ways through which we can know that our medicines are effective. When we prepare a certain kind of medicine for a person, the medicine will heal him if he himself is a good person. There are some people who are the cause of their own bad fortune. No 'medicine' can cure such people."

5
THE BEAUTIFUL

AFRICAN "ART" AND YORUBA VALUES

Use of the word "values" to describe normative beliefs in a culture is less fashionable these days. Perhaps it is because this term suggests the subjective and the relative, a 'loose' collection of qualities that are preferred on other than objective grounds, that it has been replaced by terminology that places a pronounced emphasis upon reasoning and evidence: "principles," "criteria," "standards," "prescriptive judgments," and so forth. I have not chosen to resurrect the expression "value theory" because I find Yoruba discourse to be short on consistency or coherence. As should be evident from the preceding chapters, the epistemic criteria underlie and inform the ethical in an impressively systematic and coherent manner. I have chosen the term because it is a way to avoid the arbitrary division that has been introduced into English-language discourse by the use of the separate terms "ethics" (as arising from morality) and "aesthetics" (as arising from art) as if naming two different intellectual realms. For in the discussions with the *oníṣègùn,* the transition from the "good" to the "beautiful" was as systematic and coherent as was the case with that between the epistemological and the moral.

Any exegesis that has to do with the aesthetic in relation to an African culture must come to terms with the substantial corpus of publications that has arisen from the study and collection of African "art." Yoruba Studies is no exception in this regard. Vastly more has been published on Yoruba "art" than on other aspects of the culture. And it is a further commonplace generalization that more studies have been published about Yoruba "art" than that of any other sub-Saharan African people. If this narrative did not already have a *non*-aesthetic starting point, arising from the previous discussion of epistemic and moral values, it would be prudent to begin this discussion by turning to such recognized authorities on Yoruba aesthetics as Rowland Abiodun (1990, 1994; Abiodun et al. 1994), Robert Plant Armstrong (1971),[1] Babatunde Lawal (1974, 1996), and Robert Farris Thompson (1973, 1974).

But in the present circumstances that need not be the case. The disproportionate importance that has been assigned to a Yoruba aesthetic as a result of the influence of African "art collection" does not fairly represent the bulk of ordinary discourse about values in that culture. Scholarly publications that attempt to site that aesthetic in a broader cultural context continue to analyze that context *in terms of how* it relates to whatever happen to be the specific "art" objects of particular interest. This is neither to underrate such work nor to say it is misled. But I do think the effect of the disproportionate number of such studies has been to skew the scholarly presentation and popular perception of Yoruba culture so that it becomes overly art-historically aesthetic in nature. In the past a disproportionate emphasis on the aesthetic in an African culture has led to a similar emphasis on the "poetic-symbolic" and the (emotionally) "expressive" as core elements to the African mentality. Speaking again as an analytic philosopher, I would suggest that developing the rational analysis of aesthetic values in Yoruba culture may prove to be an alternative possibility worth exploring.

THE AESTHETIC OF THE PERSON

In discussions with the *onísègùn* the term most frequently mentioned that would appear to be relevant to an aesthetic was "*ewà*," which is normally translated into English as "beauty" (etm 199). But rather than being attributed to arts or crafts, its most common usage was emphatically with regard to persons, to human beings:

> (232) It ["*ewà*"] has more than one type (*orísi*). A person (*ènìyàn*) can be liked by others because of the color (*àwò*) of his or her body. This concerns the beauty (*ewà*) of the body (*ara*). When he or she wears cloth, the cloth will fit him as if it was sewn onto his or her body [perfectly].

In virtually every account of the term, however, *ewà* or beauty as a physical attribute was rated superficial and unimportant by comparison with

---

1. Still significant as a seminal, if not topical, figure who wrote on African aesthetics principally with the Yoruba in mind.

good moral character (ìwà rere) as a (metaphorical?) form of 'inner' beauty. The speaker in quotation (232) continued as follows:

(233) But he or she may not have a [good] moral character (ìwà). The absence of [good] moral character (ìwà) will spoil his or her beauty (ẹwà). People will say he or she has beauty (ẹwà), but not character (ìwà). There are some people who are very rough [not particularly good looking, rhetorically eloquent, or socially adept] but will have the character (ìwà) of a good person. Character (ìwà) and beauty (ẹwà) are mixed together (papò).

There were numerous other remarks in the same vein:

(234) Some people have an oddly shaped (l'àngo; etm?, but perhaps as òngò, etm 475: "stupid," "foolish looking") head, but they are still good or moral persons (ènìyàn rere). Other people have a head which is well shaped (rubutu; etm 579: "spherical") but are immoral (ènìyàn burúkú).

(235) There are some people with good faces (dára l'ójú), but they are bad persons (ènìyàn burúkú). And there are some with ugly faces (ojú rẹ̀ kò ní dára) who are good persons (ènìyàn rere).

The bad moral character (ìwà burúkú) of a physically attractive person was still attributed to the self (ẹ̀mí or inú):

(236) If the person (ènìyàn) is good looking (dára dára), but his or her innermost self (inú) is bad, they will still call him or her an immoral person (ènìyàn burúkú). Whenever anybody does bad things, it means his or her inside self may be bad.

(237) This is just like the yam that we plant. Though the bark of the yam looks fresh, it has become rotten inside. There are some persons like this. When we see them, though they look like a [normal] person (ènìyàn), we don't know that their self (inú) has decayed [that the ẹ̀mí is in some sense immoral].

The point here is that beauty may only be 'skin deep', and it is only by observing a person's (verbal and nonverbal) behavior that one is in a relatively secure position to be a judge of their character (ìwà). Having an immoral character, and self, continued to be linked to a person's being irresponsible and unreliable from an epistemological point of view:

(238) If a person (ènìyàn) is beautiful (ẹwà), and if he or she is not good (dára) 'inside' (inú; but as "self"), they will say he or she has beauty (ẹwà), but he or she has no [good] moral character (ìwà). This means that he or she uses his or her 'inside' self to create

darkness (òòkùn) for people (ènìyàn). He or she will not say the truth (òótọ́) to people (ènìyàn).

(239) We know (mọ̀) something is good (dára) by watching (wò) it. It is possible for something to be [appear] good externally but not [actually be so] inside (inú).

On the other hand, a person's *not* being physically beautiful was considered relatively *un*important if they were of good moral character:

(240) A person may not be beautiful (ẹwà) but can have a [good] moral character (ìwà). They will say that his or her character (ìwà) is very good.

(241) If someone [a woman getting married] is going to the husband's house in the olden days, they would say, "Go with character (ìwà) and not beauty (ẹwà)." We used to sing a song: "There are deceptive plantains [fruit that looks good on the outside but proves to be rotten on the inside]. A beautiful woman without a [good] moral character (ìwà) is of no real value." If she has beauty (ẹwà) of the face and has no character (ìwà)—it [her beauty] is of no real value.

This notion of 'inner' beauty becomes more than metaphorical and itself takes on the character of a moral attribute. In such cases it would be appropriate to speak of a *beauty of character* or of a *beautiful character*:

(242) But [good] moral character (ìwà) is the most important. It is the head (l'orí) [highest form] of beauty (ẹwà) for the person (ènìyàn). Somebody whose color (àwọ̀) is good (dára), but who has no character (ìwà), he or she is not completely good (kò dára tán).

(243) It is the behavior of the person that we look at before we say he or she has [good] moral character (ìwà). Character (ìwà) is the head [highest form] of beauty (ẹwà).

(244) Beauty really is character (ìwà l'ẹwà). If somebody has good character (ìwà rere)—character (ìwà), beauty (ẹwà)—that is how we explain it [the relationship].

(245) If we are talking of human beings (ènìyàn), if the person is not there, if we say good (dára) words about him or her—that is his or her beauty (ẹwà). Everyone that has beauty (ẹwà)—we always refer to them with good words.

Character (ìwà) as the beautiful is still defined as arising from what a person 'does' and 'says', from the combination of verbal and nonverbal behavior:

(246) "Àdìn"[2] has the same meaning as character (ìwà), and this is determined by the way people behave (ìṣesí).

But it is the further linkage of moral character (ìwà) to a thing's being
good (dára) that will later also become of consequence for judgments
about *natural or man-made objects'* (rather than merely human beings')
beauty (ẹwà):

(247) We shall point [to explain "ẹwà"] to somebody who is good
(dára). . . . And we shall point to another person who is bad. We
use them as examples for him. We can do this in respect of a palm
tree, a farm, a man, or a woman. Beauty (ẹwà) is very important.

(248) The same thing ["it has ẹwà, but it is not good (dára)"] applies to
people (èniyàn). If he or she has no moral character (àdìn), people
will say he or she is not good (dára).

(249) It is character (ìwà) that should make us decide that something is
good (dára) [this is with regards to human beings].

(250) It [what makes one person better than another] is the one who has
moral character (ìwà).

(251) It is the beauty of moral character (ìwà) that should make us decide that something is good (dára).

THE AESTHETIC OF THE NATURAL

By 'natural' is meant the "world of" nature, of all those things that are
neither human nor (hu)man-made. In a sense, "human" being also is a
part of nature, of course, but what sets it apart from all other things in the
world is the kind of self, the kind of èmí or inú[3] it has. As a species it is
this that gives us our own distinctive intelligence (ọpọlọ),[4] ability to speak
(sọ̀rọ̀),[5] and moral character (ìwà).[6] It is all of these things combined that
make it possible for us to communicate, to interact, and to hold one another responsible—in a reasonable manner—for what we 'do' or 'say'.

Stones, trees, and animals do not have the same types of selves (èmí
or inú) as human beings. Consequently they do not have the same kinds
of intelligence, speech, or moral characters. Precisely what these differ-

---

2. This should be read in conjunction with quotation (248).

3. See pages 44–45.

4. See pages 47–48.

5. See page 69.

6. See pages 44–45.

ences may amount to will be the subject of a further study. For the moment the important point is that human beings may value a natural object or phenomenon purely on the basis of its physical (i.e., external) beauty (ẹwà):

> (252) There can be things which have beauty (ẹwà) but are not useful (wúlò) to a person.
>
> (253) One can prefer a fowl just because it has many colors (adíkálà; etm?: speckled).
>
> (254) The trees, for example, the African teak (ìrókò), can stand in the 'bush'—four of them in one area. We can point to one as better (dára jù) than the others. The same thing with palm trees—that this palm tree is better than the others. Some trees are better in body (ara). . . . So also animals. Like goats—if there are six standing in a place, only two among them might be good.

In other contexts a thing's beauty (ẹwà) may be expressed as a measure of its utility:

> (255) We talk of beauty (ẹwà) about all things. Stones, water—there is some water which is better than others. One soil can be better than another.
>
> (256) The animals have beauty (ẹwà). The animals which do not fight human beings, people will bring them home. We bring it home because it has [a form of] beauty (ẹwà).
>
> (257) Many things which cannot talk have beauty (ẹwà)—palm wine, if good (dára), calabashes, and other things.
>
> (258) One thing can have more beauty (ẹwà) than another because that is the way the supreme deity (Ọlọ́run) created things. [Gives example of a tree that is on the farm and is not useful (lọ).]
>
> (259) There are some trees which have beauty (ẹwà)—people will like (fẹ́) the tree, and they will want to plant it in the center of the town. This means that it is useful (wúlò) and good (dára).[7]

In such contexts the oníṣẹ̀gùn could also refer to the character (ìwà) of a natural object, but when this occurred there was an interesting change in the criteria governing the use of this term. The character (ìwà) of the "natural" was measured or valued on the basis of its utility, its usefulness to human beings:

---

7. This passage could be interpreted as meaning that in certain settings or contexts a thing's physical beauty itself becomes the index of its utility—as in the case of planting certain types of trees in the midst of a town because of their aesthetic properties.

(260) Beauty (ẹwà) and not character (ìwà)? It is possible. [Gives the example of a beautiful goat with a nasty temper.] Such a thing has no character (ìwà).

(261) Beauty (ẹwà) . . . It is possible for something that is not a human being (ènìyàn) to have [it] but not have character (ìwà). [Gives negative examples of a beautiful tree on the farm that does not burn well in the fire, and of the python (òjòlá)—beautiful to look at, but the inside (sónú) is cruel (ìkà).]

I suppose this could be characterized as a *homo*-centric basis on which to assign values to the natural world. Or, since gendered rhetoric is now passé, perhaps *humano*-centric can serve as an acceptable alternative.

In other words, character (ìwà) is assigned by transposing the natural object into the human community and valuing it on the basis of its usefulness to that community. The word "ìwà" is, therefore, no longer being used in the sense of a thing's *moral* character, as has been conventional in discourse about human beings (ènìyàn). Ìwà still has something to do with a thing's character, but it is character as defined and measured on the basis of a pragmatic criterion—of the thing's utility to human society in general or to the individuals dealing with a specific situation. Such utility is regularly associated with the word "*dára*" (etm 127: "good"):

(262) One forest can be better (*dára*) than another because we can get logs from it.

(263) Dangerous animals are not good (*dára;* not ewa = not *dára*).

(264) If you make a farm in which you plant yams, there are some trees inside which you climb and of which you can cut down the branches [to use as stakes, trelliswork], so that the yams can climb up them. But there will be some trees which you cannot climb to cut the branches of. If you set fire to them, they will fall down and destroy your yams. Those trees are not good (*dára*).

THE AESTHETIC OF THE (HU)MAN-MADE

When beauty is attributed to the (hu)manufactured,[8] it becomes the product of human effort and creation. In the rural domains of Ekiti, the example to which most frequent reference was made (and upon which the onísègùn themselves labored daily) was a person's farm (*oko;* etm 466) and its produce:

8. For those who tend to associate this term exclusively with 'modern' industry, the *Concise Oxford Dictionary* still defines it as the "making of articles by physical labour" (p. 742).

(265) There can be beauty (ẹwà) on the farm because it is created by someone's hand.

(266) Some people's farms can have more beauty (ẹwà) than others.

(267) If they (wọn) make for you the walls of a house [the builders], the one which is good (dára)—we say that it has beauty (ẹwà). The same applies to the farm we make. If there is one without any weeds, and another with weeds, the one without weeds can be said to have beauty (ẹwà).

(268) There is beauty (ẹwà) in the farm (oko) we create. It is in the yam. There are some yams which you can just eat, like that, and there are some which you can use to make pounded yam—that yam is good (dára). Everybody will want to plant it.

When sequestered with the oníṣègùn in their sitting rooms, it became appropriate to discuss the furnishings in a similar regard:

(269) It [the ẹwà of a man-made thing] is the beauty (ẹwà) that we see in its body (ara). These tables, there are four different types. The one in that place is better than this one. We can look at the "color" [in English]—it makes us say that this one is better than that. These shoes, if you are asked to pick one, which one would you take [the newer looking pair, obviously]? Beauty (ẹwà) is important.

(270) The better "finished" [in English] something is . . .

(271) If they make (ṣe) it better than the other one [it will have more beauty (ẹwà)]. Or if this one has 'fat in the face' [is shiny, polished]. And if they "polish" [in English] it very well.

(272) If you add color (àwọ̀) to something, you increase its beauty (ẹwà).

There is nothing new about Yoruba informants saying that finishing, polishing, and the addition of color may serve to increase a thing's beauty. Similar remarks have been reported by anthropologists and art historians in the past. But aesthetic references to plebeian 'objects' like a person's farm have not. Their pointed inclusion here may help to right the aesthetic imbalance referred to above that has resulted from collectors' and art historians' disproportionate concerns with figurative carvings and sculpture.

Another human-made product to which frequent reference was made is the woven cloth for which the Yoruba are justly famous. The following passages make reference to an expensive and elegant fabric that is known as aṣọ òkè (etm 464), and then to cloth in general:

(273) Aṣọ has beauty (ẹwà). The one that is more beautiful *could* have more ẹwà. A cloth you can wear for one week and does not show dirt has character (ìwà). It is useful (ó ṣe é ṣe). There is some

cloth that you can only wear for one day [and so it has no character (ìwà)].

(274) There are some cloths that are very good. We can say that it has
character (ìwà). Among the things we are using, some may be
good (dára) but may not last. People will say it is beautiful (ẹwà),
but it is not good (dára).

I include them here because of their reference to character (ìwà). In both
cases, again, the sense of "character" conveyed is of a human-made thing
found to be better because of its better quality when judged on the basis
of utility and durability.

The onísẹ̀gùn did volunteer a limited number of observations about
sculpture in their culture. Before I introduce them I think I should also put
on record that none of these men were carvers or, to my knowledge, had
a history of carving in their families:

(275) You know (mò), there are some images (awòrọn; etm 80) [carved]
as persons (èniyàn)—there are some that resemble (dabi; etm
121) persons (èniyàn) [with bodily parts]. But people who make
them are unable to make the self (èmí). . . . Because the supreme
deity (Ọlọ́run) can create the self (èmí), he is greater than us.

Too much can easily be read into such a remark. But when reviewed on
the basis of the broader perspectives heretofore suggested, several points
come to mind. Carvings are human-made, usually from pieces of wood.
While it is true that trees may have their own kind of 'self' (èmí), that èmí
remains with the tree only so long as it is alive—with its roots in the
ground, 'drinking' water, and growing. When the tree is cut down the
'self' (èmí) departs and the 'body' is clinically dead. Whatever form with
which a sculpted piece of wood is thereafter endowed becomes a product
of its carver:

(276) The àlùjànún is regarded as someone capable of doing extraordinary things (ńṣe iṣẹ́ iyanu). You know (mò), not everyone can
make carvings or images (ère gbígbẹ́; etm 243: "carved idol").
Those who know (mò) [how to do this] use their 'inner' self (inú)
to 'look at' it, just as the àlùjànún use theirs [i.e., they can compose a piece, which also means to 'picture' or 'foresee' the finished carving].[9]

---

9. A topic that invites further investigation is to what extent Yoruba discourse replicates
precisely the same varieties of "knowing," based upon usage, as English, for example,
"knowledge by acquaintance," "knowledge how," and "knowledge that." Certainly the expression "Mò mò pé . . . " ("I know that . . . ") is not uncommon in Yoruba discourse. Analo-

(277) If we do something and it is not good, we shall say it is not good (*dára*). If it is good, we shall say "He has the knowledge (*ìmọ̀*) [of it]."

Are talented carvers regarded as *àlùjànún*[10] in a straightforward manner, or are they only said to resemble *àlùjànún,* to be 'like' *àlùjànún,* in certain limited respects? The ability the speaker in quotation (276) has in mind is clearly that of the *ojú inú,*[11] that faculty of imaginative insight that allows the artist to compose mentally the form with which he wants to end up.

To resume the process of synthesis with some relevant points previously introduced, a sculpture of a human being is not a human being. This is because it does not contain the *èmí* or *inú,* the self, of the human being. As such, a carving cannot behave (*ṣe*) in the conventional human sense. It cannot 'say', and it cannot 'do'. As such, it cannot have character (*ìwà*), in the conventional sense of a *moral* character, because this arises from verbal and nonverbal behavior. If the stance or posture of a sculpture[12] is said to have a form that re-presents certain limited forms of behavior that may symbolize certain moral attributes, this would have to be reconciled with the emphasis placed upon the insight that appearances may be deceptive, and that "rectitude" and "beauty" may only be 'skin-deep'. Perhaps indicative of this caution about whether appearance really does conform to (inner) reality is the phrase expressing aesthetic appreciation that occurs in quotations (232), (254), and (269): "the beauty (*ewà*) of the body (*ara;* etm 60)." I do not mean to suggest that any of these points present insurmountable problems, or perhaps even problems at all. But they do serve to reintegrate the values associated with carvings of human being with the values associated with real-life human being.

A NARRATIVE FOOTNOTE ABOUT TASTE

The vocabulary associated with the attribution of beauty (*ewà*) to the human, the natural, and the human-made is of interest too for its subjective

---

gously, exercising a nonverbal skill, such as carving, might involve comparable elements of "knowing how." However, in the discourse of the *onísẹ̀gùn* such knowledge, when related to carving of the highest caliber, seems to be grounded upon a form of "intuitive insight" (*ojú inú*) that exceeds merely exercising a skill.

10. See pages 97–101.

11. See pages 49–50.

12. As might be implied by the following: "The reason why the supreme deity (*Olọ́run*) gives us eyes: for example, when it is dark and we put on our lights—the eyes are just like when we use light in the darkness."

dimensions. As a term indicative of the attribution of subjective value, our old friend "dára" (etm 127: "good") becomes almost commonplace. In some of their remarks the onísègùn demonstrated their facility for articulating how the same word may be governed by different criteria when predicated of different classes of things:

> (278) [The meaning of] "Good" (dára)—[a] there are things that are good (dára) but have no beauty (ewà): the calabash that is mature but has no beauty (ewà). [b] There can be things which are beautiful (ewà) but are not ripe or mature (gbó). [c] There can be people who are good (dára) but are not [physically] beautiful (ewà). [d] There can be people who are beautiful (ewà) but have no [good] moral character (ìwà)—who are not "good" (kò dára).

From a perspective that is exclusively value-oriented, perhaps the lowest form of human being would be a person who was hideously ugly in the physical sense and quintessentially iniquitous in the moral sense. Conversely, the highest form would be a person who was incomparably beautiful in the physical sense and preeminently good in the moral sense. But these things were not said by the onísègùn in an explicit manner, and so it is advisable to beware of their becoming further examples of those 'logical consequences', possibilities of which armchair philosophers must beware when interpolating the rhetoric of ordinary language.

What does appear to amount to a safe generalization is that the guidelines or criteria for the assessment of 'inner' or moral human beauty (ewà), as the deepest expression of the self (èmí or inú), can be articulated and applied in a fairly determinate manner. Even if allowance—without any moral or aesthetic judgment implied—is always made for a certain degree of the subjective, for my preferred taste in friends, associates, or the 'other' sex not being the same as yours:[13]

> (279) One will say a thing is good [dára=ewà], another not, because that is the way their minds (opolo) work. Not everyone knows (mò) [is able to recognize] what is good (dára).
>
> (280) A—To be good (dára) is—among ten people, if nine will say it is good, and one person will say it is not good, it is the one [opinion] of more people that will come up [prevail].
> B—Ten persons can tell lies, while one can say the truth.
> A—His truth (òótó) would not be accepted.

---

13. This is also implied by quotations (119) and (120).

B—Truth is dead in our country (orílè èdè). We refer to those who say the truth as bad persons (èniyàn burúkú).[14]

But this was because they appreciated that tastes may differ, and that this is a normal, noncontroversial feature to everyday life:

(281) It is the one whose face draws you to it [that attracts you]. They can place three pieces of cloth side by side. They can ask which one is best (dára jù). The first person can say that "this one" is better. The second person can say another is the one he likes (wù). It is the one that your eyes strike, that you will like most among the cloths.

(282) Different people like different cloths because different people like different things.

(283) Different people like different colors.[15]

YORUBA ART HISTORY

In the early days of my career in the Nigerian university system, when I was just beginning to think about what could be involved in contributing to academic philosophy from an African point of view, I was privileged to make the acquaintance of a number of Nigerian, British, and American scholars who all happened to be involved somehow with defining the "meanings" conveyed by the "arts" in Nigerian cultures.[16] If they could come to terms with objects and verse, I wondered, why should not philosophers try their hands with concepts?

Many were involved with doing some form of what they referred to explicitly as "fieldwork." As a methodological element, that form of endeavor may now have become conventional to most of the disciplines involved with African studies. But in those days the very idea of academic

---

14. A reflection on national politics, included here for, if nothing else, its eloquence. "A" and "B" correspond to two different onísègùn who were in the room at the same time. The final remark in this exchange should be distinguished from what was said before, which does reflect upon the diversities of taste.

15. Other examples of terminology whose use was associated with subjective taste were sunwòn (etm 602: "it is good") and wù (etm 672: as "pleased").

16. In alphabetical order those I can recall included Rowland Abiodun, 'Biodun Adetugbo, 'Titi Akinyemi, Akinsola Akiwowo, David and Susan Aradeon, S. A. Babalola, Karin Barber, J. P. and Ebun Clark, Adrian Edwards, Perkins Foss, Peggy Harper, Robin Horton, R. I. Ibigbami, Sidney Kasfir, 'Tunde Kuboye, Ade Kukoyi, Deirdre La Pín, Babatunde Lawal, 'Femi Morakinyo, Pat and Bob Morgan, Nancy Neaher, Keith Nicklin, 'Femi Ojo, Alfred Opubor, J. D. Y. Peel, Jill Salmons, Frank Speed, 'Tayo Williams, and Richard York.

philosophers undertaking any form of empirical data collection and analysis outside the confines of their armchairs amounted literally to forsaking the discipline, to a vocational "category mistake."[17] The analytic philosopher's 'meat' is words, either individually as concepts or when strung together to constitute statements or reasons. Some of these colleagues concerned with the arts were involved with the exegesis of meanings as expressed by African myths. But this seemed to me at the time too metaphorical, too deliberately creative a form of thought to serve as a basis for an African analytic philosophy that would warrant comparison with its Western counterpart.

An art historian specially interested in the Yoruba, whose work these colleagues brought to my attention as representing a qualitatively new initiative in the field that might be of interest to me, was Robert Farris Thompson (1971, 1973). He had identified and analyzed, at some length, a list of Yoruba aesthetic criteria that were said to be indigenous to the thought of a variety of people in that culture. I received this discovery as a 'great leap' forward, as precisely the form of conceptual research and analysis that would provide a model for comparable work by philosophers of language on indigenous African cultures. If Thompson could succeed in so notoriously subjective and difficult to articulate a realm as the aesthetic, more pedestrian fields of discourse involving the moral and the social-political would beckon enticingly. I scrutinized as much of Thompson's published work as I could. Although his approach to the discovery of these criteria also incorporated material from myth and song, it was his apparent claim that the criteria were articulated in conceptual form that particularly attracted my attention. But the more I studied Thompson's exposition, in particular the linguistic evidence he presented for the derivation of the criteria, the less certain I became about the semantic basis for a number of them. Some did appear to relate in a straightforward manner to a term in the Yoruba language. But others seemed to have been inferred by Thompson from his own studies (formal, empirical) of preferred Yoruba sculptural forms and his own readings of the oral literature. For these there were in fact no clearly defined or articulated Yoruba concepts in the sense conventional to linguistic philosophy. In other words, the Yoruba did not really 'talk' in some of these terms.

Shortly thereafter I expressed these reservations in a paper suggesting

---

17. Working in an area for which one is not professionally qualified. See Bodunrin (1981) for a skeptical assessment of the very idea of the philosopher doing something like fieldwork.

that, given the evidence presented, some of Thompson's claims appeared excessive (Hallen 1979). I was later made to understand that this paper was not received in a positive manner by some specialists in the field of African art. The tenor of my criticisms, in particular, was taken to be excessively destructive rather than constructive—counterproductive to what was emerging as a fruitful innovation in the methodology of African art historical studies. For the record, I reiterate that my criticisms were not aimed at the methodology generally so much as at specific instances of its application. As for the paper's tenor or tone, Anthony Appiah once remarked to me that the level of criticism taken for granted in (academic) philosophy is exceptional among disciplines. I expect this is because severe critical exchange is one of the fundamental means by which our discipline evolves.[18]

Another prominent contemporary figure concerned with identifying the concepts with which a Yoruba aesthetic may be articulated is Rowland Abiodun. Abiodun too has set out to specify a determinate vocabulary that underlies artistic conception, interpretation, and criticism. Since this work is premised explicitly on the Yoruba aphorism "Character is beauty" (ìwà l'ewà), and his definition of "character" (ìwà) differs fundamentally from that articulated by the oníṣègùn, those who are conversant with his work may anticipate that the disagreements between us are fundamental—because the meanings I associate with the same term, "ìwà," seem very different.

Here I shall be more concerned to explore points of coincidence and similarity between Abiodun's interpretation of this aphorism and my own. Nevertheless at least one other rendering of its meaning deserves explicit, if brief, mention.[19] If, when given full expression, the aphorism[20] should read as "ìwà ní l'ewà" (the "ní" making explicit the verb "is" in its English-language translation as "Character is beauty"), the significance, the import, of the statement as a rhetorical whole could change. For in Yoruba discourse it can happen that when two nouns are joined by the verb "is"

18. "Only are very few studies [of African art history] attempted to reflect upon the methods of others (Hallen 1979)" (Drewal 1990, p. 50).

19. I am particularly grateful to Karin Barber for the discussion underlying this suggestion.

20. A further problem with aphorisms is that their meanings are context dependent. Given linguistic and social conventions, it may be appropriate to recite an aphorism in certain circumstances but inappropriate to introduce it in others. This means that they cannot be treated as if universal truths. Detailing the unspoken conventions that make a specific aphorism appropriate to a certain situation could become a very difficult task. This point will be discussed further in the final chapter.

in such phrasing, the class named by the word succeeding the verb is meant to be included in or subsumed by the class preceding the verb. In this case the meaning of the aphorism would in fact be that "Beauty is [actually, really] character" rather than that "Character is beauty." Such an interpretation would heighten this aphorism's moral import and make its independently aesthetic relevance of less consequence.

In this study I interpret the English-language "character" in a moral or valued-behavioral sense, whereas Abiodun defines its meaning as "being" or "essence." He therefore renders the aphorism "ìwà l'ewà" (for the onísègùn, "[good] moral character is beauty") as "Beauty arises from the expression of a thing's unique (ontological) essence," whether via sculptural form or divination verse. But I do not foresee any serious problems arising from our different renderings of "ìwà." There are several reasons for this. One is that our methodologies are different. The meaning for "ìwà" that the onísègùn elaborate arises from ordinary language, from everyday discourse. The meaning that Abiodun elaborates arises from the relatively abstruse and esoteric rhetoric of Ifá divination literature and the technical, professional terminology of artists in traditional Yoruba society. Abiodun does not deny that "ìwà" may in certain contexts refer to moral character (1990). His point is that in others the same term may be used to name whatever ontological factor it is in Yoruba metaphysics that gives each different individual thing in the world its unique thing-ness (something like the philosophical sense of individuated "being").

Other etymological analyses of "ìwà" by distinguished Yoruba scholars support the idea that it may have these two different meanings, depending upon the context in which it occurs. For example I. O. Delano, in his monumental two-volume A Dictionary of Yoruba Monosyllabic Verbs, defines "ìwà," the nominalization of the verb "wà" ("to be"), in precisely these two different senses:

ìwà n.   (a) existence:
                 as in "Eni tí ó fún ó ní ìwà rè" ("He who created
                 you.")

            (b) character:
                 as in "Ìwà rere ní èsó ènìà" ("Good character is
                 one's ornament and beauty.") (vol. 2, p. 365)

Abiodun's own exegesis arises from 'Wande Abimbola's derivation of ìwà (as "character") from what he interprets to be the more semantically primordial meaning of ìwà ("as the fact of being, living or existing") (1975, p. 393). How in more precise terms the one meaning relates to the other may be a subject inviting further elaboration,[21] but what is relevant here is that recognized experts on the Yoruba language attest to the fact that the term may be used in these *two* different senses. The *appreciation* of a thing's *ìwà*, when conceived in Abiodun's sense, as its "unique character-istics . . . , as totally distinct from the generalized kind of which it is a part" (1990, p. 70), defines the talent of the artist in Yoruba culture. This is what sets the artist apart, what makes the "aesthetic consciousness" distinctive, and what also distinguishes the "artist's *ìwà*" (p. 71). If I read Abiodun correctly, another foundational element to this aesthetic con-sciousness is a sense of good character (*ìwà rere*) in the moral sense that has been elaborated via the remarks of the *oníṣègùn*.[22]

To continue the discussion of what is especially distinctive about the consciousness of the Yoruba artist and, by extension, about objects pro-duced by that consciousness, some of its features are explicitly said by Abiodun to overlap with Thompson's original criteria, and some are origi-nal to his exposition. Several are of special interest to this study because of their direct relevance to my previous analyses of epistemological and moral discourse. First and foremost is the importance assigned to "insight" (*ojú inú*) as a faculty of the artistic consciousness. It is said to be respon-sible for "insight, a special kind of understanding of a person, thing, or situation, and is not usually derived from an obvious [I take this as another way of referring to the special talent or genius as 'inborn' in a person] source" (1990, p. 75).

When Abiodun shortly thereafter also identifies this "insight" (*ojú inú*) with the intellect, I think it becomes safe to conclude that his analysis of this important intellectual faculty parallels my own. The most obvious difference I find in Abiodun's analysis is that he concentrates upon its

---

21. See, for example, the following passage from a forthcoming paper by O. Taiwo and O. B. Lawuyi entitled "'*Ìwà*': Towards a Naturalistic Ethics": "However, as Abimbola points out, the ethical-evaluative meaning [*ìwà* as moral character] is closely connected to the ontological-descriptive meaning [*ìwà* as nature or essence]. He suggests that the ethical-evaluative meaning of *ìwà* 'originates from an idiomatic usage of (the) original lexical (onto-logical-descriptive) meaning.' Apparently it does not occur to Abimbola that the connection he affirms is problematic" (p. 13).

22. In his comments on this book as a draft manuscript Rowland Abiodun agreed with this point. However, since he understandably wants Yoruba society to be moral overall, Abio-dun immediately goes on to say, "The artist's *ìwà*, incidentally, is also the type that Yoruba culture demands of chiefs, kings, diviners, and family heads for their works or activities to be considered beautiful" (1990, p. 71). In Abiodun's exposition *ìwà rere* is as often rendered as "*ìwàpèlé*," arising from Abimbola's (1975) expression for "'gentle character', or *sùúrù* (patience)" (ibid.).

effects, perfectly understandably, with special reference to artistic or aesthetic abilities. Other features of a Yoruba aesthetic consciousness that are relevant involve the importance of being calm, controlled, and reasonable[23] and of listening 'well' (perhaps now as a metaphor for artistic "sensitivity").[24] But as the Yoruba terminology introduced by Abiodun is different from the *oníṣègùn*'s own, and as it is to be expected that generalized expressions of the epistemological virtues may underlie any variety of cognitive processes detailed by Yoruba discourse, there is no need here to consider their consequences in further detail.

In some of his publications Thompson treats the criteria in a straightforward manner as technical points, as norms which the form and finishing of a piece of sculpture must evidence if it is to be judged beautiful (1973). In others he links the values emphasized by the aesthetic criteria to the values emphasized by Yoruba morality and then to the principles or forces emphasized by Yoruba philosophy and ontology (1971). The aestheticized ontology of the worldview thereby arrived at is meant to be encapsulated by his well-known phrase "the aesthetic of the cool." Although Abiodun also incorporates elements of the ontological, his approach seems more narrowly focused on its specifically aesthetic ramifications. The narrative structures of these two scholars reflect this difference in emphasis. Thompson begins from a list of formal aesthetic criteria and out of these eventually adduces generalized values and the principles said to underlie a Yoruba ontology. Abiodun begins from a limited ontological analysis of *ìwà* (as "being"). From his elaboration of the values that certain authorized sources in Yoruba culture consider important for being sensitive to this "being," he arrives at the aesthetic values exemplified by the talented artist.

My analyses of Yoruba discourse arising from the discussions with the *oníṣègùn* have not addressed the subject of ontology, which may here be defined as the study of the most fundamental elements ("being") or principles (the "cool") believed to order the world. In philosophical terms my analyses have not extended beyond the epistemological, which may here be defined as the cognitive faculties and the kinds of evidence human beings have at their disposal for understanding their experience—including whatever may be relevant to the study of the most fundamental elements or principles believed to order the world. Nevertheless in both

---

23. Said to arise from a deliberate emphasis on being *ìfarabalẹ̀* (Abiodun 1990, p. 77; etm 95: "composure of mind").

24. Said to arise from a deliberate emphasis on *ìlutí* (Abiodun 1990, p. 78).

Thompson's and Abiodun's expositions of aesthetic-ontological values, there is a substantial class of terms that are held in common and that have epistemological implications. I am thinking here of the class constituted by, in Thompson's case, balance, composure, control, cool (*tútù*), equilibrium, mean, patience (*sùúrù*), and restraint, and in Abiodun's, calmness (*ìfarabalè*), composure (*ìfarabalè*), control, patience (*sùúrù*), poise, reason rather than emotion (*ìfarabalè*), and thoroughness.

According to both authors these terms are said to express forms of behavior that are valued in Yoruba culture because of their intrinsically aesthetic properties and because their instantiation is a necessary prerequisite to artistic creation and appreciation. There is also an old-fashioned functionalist undercurrent to all of these values when combined—a sense of keeping the social 'ship of culture'—whether aesthetically, morally, or ontologically—on an even keel. But my inclination is to remind readers that they reaffirm many of the epistemological virtues and moral values enunciated by the *onísègùn:* because these are the values that support optimal cognition (understanding) and thereby (in principle) responsible 'words' and 'actions'. Saying this need not involve a claim that epistemological concerns are more fundamental than aesthetic ones (even if my philosophical self might tend to favor that line of thinking). Aesthetic "sensitivity" is a form of knowing—even if so introspectively experienced that it becomes, comparatively, a very difficult one to define in explicit verbal (behavioral) form.

If, given their respective approaches to the study of the Yoruba arts, Thompson may be said to be educing aesthetic criteria from a (multimedia) variety of sources, and Abiodun to be elaborating a theoretical aesthetic on the basis of a refined terminology, the frequently cited article on Yoruba aesthetics and aesthetic terminology by Babatunde Lawal (1974) appears to be based upon ordinary language, everyday usage. I say this because of the numerous points of agreement between his exposition and my analyses. Let me detail some of them here because, in addition to reinforcing the meanings outlined by the *onísègùn,* in some cases Lawal's own analyses deepen one's appreciation of the semantic contexts in which they may occur.

Lawal says very little about beauty (*ewà*) in relation to the natural world,[25] and a great deal about beauty in relation to persons:

---

25. Apart from the following noteworthy passage: "while in objects it [*ewà*] is implied in the word *wíwúlò,* or functional utility" (p. 239). This would appear to parallel my suggestion that natural or man-made objects' beauty (*ewà*) and sometimes character (*ìwà*) may be rated on the basis of their utility (*wúlò*) to human society.

The person who is outwardly beautiful but inwardly ugly. . . . The physical beauty of such a person may at first be admired, but as soon as his inner ugliness surfaces he becomes repulsive (p. 241).

The ugliness or beauty of the 'inner' person is attributed to the nature of one's character (ìwà):

Therefore the most important element in the Yoruba conception of human beauty is ẹwà inú, or character (ìwà). (p. 240)

In man ẹwà inú is frequently implied in the word ìwà, or character. (p. 239)

Lawal's analysis does not make explicit mention of the hypocrite or liar whose external *behavior,* rather than external physical *beauty,* is meant to seem that of the morally good person until recognized by others as 'masking' an immoral character (ènìyàn burúkú). But adding this as a further dimension to the "ugly" does nothing to vitiate his narrative. This also would be consistent with his rendering of the aphorism ìwà l'ẹwà, which is the same as that of the onísègùn:

the possession of ìwà is universally [I take his use of this last term to be a sign that his analysis arises from convention, something related to ordinary usage or everyday language] accepted as a sine qua non of beauty. Hence the saying "ìwà l'ẹwà" (character is beauty). (p. 240)

His agreement about the meaning of other, less significant details also is reassuring: the association of a person's being "good" (dára) with their being beautiful,[26] and the use of the appellation ọmọlúàbí (in his spelling "ọmọlúwàbí") as a positive commentary on a person's moral character.[27] Lawal also places greater emphasis on the social dimension to a Yoruba aesthetic—as arising from, most obviously, persons—the sphere of human being. This is what one would expect of ordinary language in any case, since it is employed in the overwhelming majority of cases to refer to the human rather than to the arts:

---

26. "Thus in Yoruba culture ẹwà is synonymous with 'good' or dára" (p. 239).

27. See quotation (28), where ọmọlúàbí is defined as the "good person" in a context where this means knowing how to 'do' and to 'say' the right thing at the right time. Lawal's rendering of the meaning is as follows: "A man's [or woman's] character is either good or bad. If it is good, he [or she] is called ọmọlúwàbí (the well-born)" (p. 240). "The ọmọlúwàbí . . . is a beloved person. Even if he [or she] is ugly, his [or her] character (ìwà) is so pleasing that people are usually blind to his [or her] ugliness" (p. 241).

> In essence Yoruba aesthetics is a quest for happiness in life. Ẹwà is pleas-
> ant to behold and experience; Ìwà fosters social harmony among men,
> thereby generating law and order in society. Since more premium is put
> "on the mean" than on extreme or facial beauty—which in any case is
> given only to a few—Yoruba aesthetics affords almost every individual
> the opportunity for being admired once he has ìwà [good moral charac-
> ter]. For to possess ìwà is to be beautiful. (p. 247)

With regards to the aesthetics of the (hu)man-made, Lawal equates the
beauty (ẹwà) of most things with their usefulness, their functional utility to
human being in a decidedly instrumental or pragmatic sense:

> Ẹwà is the manifestation of the "well-made" or the "well-done." (p. 239)

But it is when he approaches the subject of sculpture or figurative carving
that the quoted opinion of an informant replicates, in a most reassuring
fashion, one perspective upon carved rather than human being that has
been suggested by this narrative:

> By and large sculpture is judged in terms of its visual appeal rather than
> character [ìwà] because, as one informant remarked, "*it can neither
> speak nor act*" (p. 245, my italics).

In other words, since a carved sculpture of a human being cannot behave
in any conventional human sense, the ordinary person to whom it bears
no special relationship has no other basis on which to evaluate it than its
"visual appeal."[28]

I do not find any explicit contradictions between the accounts of
Thompson, Abiodun, and Lawal, as here outlined, when compared on a
methodological basis. Their methodologies are diverse, and this seems
sufficient, in each case, to account for any discrepancies between their
overall findings. To concentrate on the positive results of all this research
when viewed as cumulative, perhaps the happiest form of resolution
would be to suggest that Yoruba studies may now be in a position to
demonstrate that (1) when the culture is approached on the basis of plural
subject matters—whether aesthetic, epistemological, moral, or ontological, or (2) when the culture is analyzed on the basis of different methodologies—whether anthropological, art historical, or philosophical—select

---

28. Also of interest is the recurrence of the same metaphor for the eyes as in note 12 above:
"the eyes (ojú)—the lamps with which man wades through the dark jungle of life" (p. 244).

values and concerns become prominent and may therefore be hypothe-sized as fundamental.

FORMS OF THE EPISTEMIC, FORMS
OF THE AESTHETIC

"Form" is being used here in the sense of a formative principle, and the question to be asked is, Now that we have dealt with several prominent art historians' assessments of Yoruba aesthetic values, do any possible additional or supplementary theoretical perspectives on the subject arise from our own prior analyses of the epistemic and the moral? So attenuated a process of cross-topical theoretical extrapolation is fraught with peril. Its theses may seem either so obvious as to be completely banal, or so rarified as to have lost whatever sense they originally derived from the study's analytic foundations.

The portraits drawn of Yoruba artistic values consistently link them with moral values. My first concern, then, should be whether it is possible to carry the linkage exercise one step further and involve the epistemolog-ical dimension to this study in a meaningful way. For example, another prominent African art historian, Suzanne Blier, has made the intriguing suggestion that the Yoruba distinction between "knowledge" and "belief," between what one experiences firsthand and what one 'hears about' only on the basis of secondhand reports, may help to account for certain gen-eral characteristics of the culture's sculptural corpus. The comparative uniformity of human figurative sculpture, for example, could relate to the fact that artists experience the human form in a firsthand manner that cannot be denied; whereas the comparative lack of uniformity, indeed, the wild variety of sculptural styles, associated with masks and masquer-ades involving supra-human beings arises from the fact that the spirits and forces they are said to represent are not observable firsthand, in conven-tional empirical terms. By comparison they are experienced secondhand, as the consequences of 'beliefs', and this greater cognitive 'distance' be-tween the artist and his subject matter allows for greater diversity of figu-rative representation.

The problem with a challengingly syncretic, and perhaps even bril-liant, hypothesis such as this is with what sort of evidence could it be proved, or disproved? Let me add an adjective to the word "evidence," so that it becomes *empirical* evidence. What sort of material evidence, what sort of test could be arranged, what manner of etymological or con-ceptual analysis could be introduced, that would be sufficient to settle the question of its truth or falsity? The answer seems to be—none. In such a case it must be labeled and remain a speculation, a speculative hypothesis, whose truth status will remain indeterminate. This does not make it any less interesting as a speculation, but the analytic philosopher would therefore caution against continuing to apply the hypothesis *as if* it did provide empirical guidelines, definitive empirical consequences.

The same seems to be true of any number of aesthetic values that are attributed to the Yoruba "consciousness." If the art historian observes that most carvings of human figures stand upright, that certainly is a safe empirical generalization. But to impute or infer therefrom that standing upright *represents* a definable moral or aesthetic value is not.[29] A good deal more becomes involved than, for example, attributing the prevalence of standing figures to the possibility that it may be an easier physical task for artists to carve a figure that is upright out of a cylindrical piece of wood. For one is hazarding to say what the original 'safe' generalization "means," why it happens to be the case—and on the basis of what evidence?

I do not mean to single out the work of any one African art historian as particularly 'guilty' of such inferences. It seems to be a general characteristic of certain forms of interpretation normally undertaken by the discipline. It will even be evidenced by this study when I endeavor to 'link' certain properties of masquerade to Yoruba epistemological priorities. But in the absence of reliable empirical guidelines to test (prove or disprove) such speculative interpretations, perhaps it is best to be forthright about them for what they are, and to embrace some form of theoretical and limited empirical *coherence* as an alternative criterion for identifying the more compelling interpretation of whatever interpretative task is being undertaken. Arriving at criteria to determine the "more compelling" may also present a problem, but I suppose it could arise from a consensus on the part of informed professionals in the field. In the opinion of this philosophical observer, this seems to be one way African art history as a discipline functions at the present time.

The aesthetic consciousness is also, relatively, a very introspective form of consciousness. Whatever part of it may be shared in conventional empirically observable terms still does not allow for firsthand experience

---

29. "Standing is a task. Constant muscular adjustment to the pull of gravity is required. To stand is to intervene in a decisive way, attesting the power to compensate for perturbation, to maintain balance. It is a form of strength which engages the whole of the person" (Thompson 1974, p. 49).

of its inspiring, motivating genius. If the African art historian finds a talented artist who mentions a concept as referring to something he or she believes in part responsible for the quality of his or her work, should that artist be regarded as speaking for himself or herself or for the 'culture'? The analytic philosopher would incline to the former, unless it can be established that the same term is conventional to a plurality of talented artists and that the sense attributed by them to it is substantially the same. Establishing this with straightforwardly empirical terminology can be a tiresome task. With relatively introspective, aesthetic terms it would seem even more so.

This is one reason why ordinary usage, everyday language, seems so sane an alternative. Ordinary language philosophy does derive from the British empirical tradition. It embraces usage because it is relatively easily demonstrable (how people who speak a language really do use a word) and because it therefore must treat any single term on the basis of the semantic contexts in which it actually occurs—no more, no less. Although art historians may not regard this as the best way of arriving at the specialized and talented artist's own understanding of his or her work, it is lamentable that more attention has not been paid to the aesthetic terminology associated with ordinary, everyday usage in Yoruba culture.

Yoruba epistemological discourse—claims about what one is entitled to know (ìmọ̀) and to believe (ìgbàgbọ́)—targets human behavior (ìṣesí) as one of its principal concerns. Human behavior is composed of what people 'say' (verbal) and what people 'do' (nonverbal). If we carry this behavioral bifurcation over to forms of artistic expression, does it add anything to existent theoretical analyses to suggest this may help to explain why, in Yoruba culture, the verbal arts have been assigned so high a priority? Suggesting this is somehow different from the bare-faced, empirical observation that one is dealing with a culture that is or was 'oral'. It is to say that, in addition to the "fact" of its being oral, the verbal has been singled out and elaborated by the culture itself as a valued form of expression. I confess that, given my own professional limitations, I am not able to carry this line of thought much further. But I suspect there might be a happy confluence at this point with scholars like Olabiyi Yai and Karin Barber. The conventional Western philosophical text views human verbal behavior as a means of "communication," and the emphasis therefrom is to make one's meanings "determinate," "fixed," "clearly defined." But this rather colorless portrayal misses entirely the senses of action and creation conveyed by the adjectival vocabulary Yai and Barber associate with certain forms of the verbal in Yoruba culture: "unfinished," "generative," "endless," "spread," "reach," "open up," "illuminate," "shine,"

"shed light on," "fluidity," "boundarilessness," and "centrelessness" (Barber 1994; Yai 1994).[30] The emphasis falls upon the verbal as a creative
force that is very much able to 'behave' in its own right.

Of course, the verbal and the nonverbal aspects to behavior (ìsesí)
should not be sundered in an absolute manner—"compartmentalized"
after the Western fashion, as Soyinka puts it. There are artistic forms in
Yoruba culture where the two are interwoven in an inspired manner. I
am thinking here principally of the masquerades. One popular but false
Western impression of African masquerades is that they are *not* verbal in
any significant manner. The masquerader is essentially a costumed figure
that moves (via dance or otherwise), frequently to music. For purposes of
our analysis of the meaning of "behavior" (ìsesí) in Yoruba discourse,
which also has distinguished what is 'said' (via words) from what is 'done'
(via actions), it would be structurally neater if it were possible to point to
certain forms of masquerade that do not depend upon any verbal content.
In Yoruba culture there certainly are some masquerade performances
where this is the case. For it then becomes possible to suggest that using
nothing more than physical movement to 'talk' justifies concluding that
this other extreme of the behavioral spectrum also may become a valued
art form. Movements could then be collated and graded for epistemic
content on the basis of how they convey moral values, for example.[31] But
most Yoruba masquerades do involve more than nonverbal behavior.[32]
Masqueraders talk and sing, their accompanying ensembles of musicians
do so as well, and frequently the audience also becomes involved. It is
the "meaning of" all these forms of behavior that attracts the interest of
the philosopher. To assert this adds absolutely nothing new to this field,
which has now been designated as "performance studies"—except perhaps to indicate how a common link might be created between the two
disciplines.

Henry and Margaret Drewal's schematic exposition and analysis of

---

30. Yai and Barber are referring specifically to *oríkì*, a special genre of so-called "praise"
poetry. But let us not forget that it was not so long ago that this genre was regarded as a
ritualistic, polyglot collection of rote-memorized, archaic formulae, whose meanings were
lost to the mists of time—as the apotheosis of the vital, ongoing, and creative.

31. "Criticism of visual traditions has been identified in Africa, but the canons of motion
remain to be established" (Thompson 1974, p. 1).

32. Concerning masquerades among the Kalabari, Robin Horton at one point wonders: "If
sculptures [masks] are thought of as names of the spirits, one may well ask what it is they
can do which verbal names can not" (1965, p. 10). One thing they can 'do' is to give the
spirit another behavioral dimension (the nonverbal) through which to 'be'.

Yoruba *Gèlèdé* masquerade(s)[33] provides an optimal example with inter-disciplinary potential. Rather than "behavior" as the more general cate-gory, they speak of "performance," which makes good sense for a deliber-ately enacted artistic form that is at the same time a good deal more than an artistic form. Their general approach to the exegesis of this masquer-ade is compatible with the foundational perspectives outlined by this study:

> By examining the content of the various art forms that constitute *Gèlèdé* performance, it is possible to understand its social concerns and the way these concerns are expressed both *verbally* and *nonverbally*. It is also possible to perceive how Yoruba spectacle operates, communi-cating discrete bits of information simultaneously through the use of multimedia. (1983, p. 37, my italics)

A narrative structure that focuses, independently and conjointly, on the verbal and nonverbal aspects of behavior or performance makes sense from the wider (Yoruba) epistemological context. This is what the Drewals proceed to do via chapters devoted to the songs (verbal), masks, cos-tumes, and dance (nonverbal).

Masquerades may involve much more than "art," of course (Horton 1963, 1965). There are moral (what one should 'do') and epistemological (what one should 'know') dimensions to them as well. (This is also true of the previously referred to "purely" verbal arts.) But that is all well and good for a study, such as this one, which also is seeking to reintegrate or rerelate diverse lots of values. The Drewals do detail the moral dimension to *Gèlèdé* behavior or performance, via both verbal and nonverbal means, linking them to forms of behavior considered to be moral and immoral, and to *ìwà* as moral character (1983, pp. 56, 73):

> *Gèlèdé* spectacle thus exhibits social concerns and brings society's desires into actual existence through lavish visual and musical asser-tions. With the mothers' concurrence, it comments on male and female roles in society, on traditional and contemporary fashions, and on inno-

---

33. *Gèlèdé* performances "represent a highly visible, artistic expression of a pan-Yoruba belief: that women, primarily elder women, possess certain extraordinary power equal to or greater than that of the gods and ancestors, a view that is reflected in praises acknowledging them as 'our mothers', 'the gods of society', and 'the owners of the world'. With this power, the 'mothers' can be either beneficent or destructive. They can bring health, wealth, and fertility to the land and its people, or they can bring disaster—epidemic, drought, pesti-lence" (Drewal 1990, p. xv).

vations and achievements. It likewise criticizes antisocial individuals and deeds. The art forms that constitute *Gèlèdé* comment on society both independently and collectively to produce a complex multifaceted phenomenon. A performance involves space as well as time, and seeing as well as hearing, in addition to the other senses. To understand the content of *Gèlèdé* performance, that is, the ideas it affirms, is to understand its creative capacity to shape the world in which it periodically exists. (1990, p. xvi)

When one reflects on the wealth of Yoruba art forms, as represented by the (oral) literature in all of its variety and splendor and by the force of performance as represented by the masquerade, the state of the diverse 'bits and pieces' of sculpture that have been severed from their epistemic, moral, and aesthetic contexts and revalued and reconstituted as African "art" in Western collections seems comparatively forlorn. This too is a point that has been expressed in an eloquent and forceful manner by other scholars (Clifford 1988; Thompson 1974; Vogel 1988), but reiterating it here enables one to appreciate how difficult the task of the art historian becomes when called upon to breathe both life and meaning 'back into' figurative carvings demoted to static and isolated museum-like display.

RATIONALITY,
INDIVIDUALITY,
SECULARITY, AND
THE PROVERBIAL

African philosophy has now become established on a secure and dynamic foundation. The genre accommodates a wide variety of approaches to the subject: Afrocentric (Eboussi-Boulaga 1997), analytical (Appiah 1992; Hallen and Sodpio 1986/1997; Wiredu 1996a), deconstructive (Mudimbe 1988), ethnophilosophical (Kagame 1956; Tempels 1959; Hegba 1982), hermeneutical (Serequeberhan 1994), Marxist (Towa 1971; Fashina 1989; Taiwo 1996), phenomenological (Kinyongo 1982), postmodern (Appiah 1992; Eze 1997b; Mudimbe 1988), and those committed to fashioning a methodology specially suited to what they see as the subcontinent's distinctive cultural heritage (Makinde 1988b; Oruka 1990; Sogolo 1993). The genre is also writing its own history (Masolo 1994). A number of African entries are included in the latest *Encyclopedia of Philosophy* (1998). New 'mainstream' journals in the subject are being funded. African, African American, and philosophers of the diaspora are interrelating and interacting on concerns they have in common (Pittman 1997). Both in Africa and overseas, more conferences, either specifically on or including African philosophy, are taking place than ever before. This is as it should be if the substance of academic philosophy is to be both profitably applied to and enriched by the relatively neglected intellectual heritage of this remarkable subcontinent. If this book appears to harp excessively on the value of an analytic and linguistic approach to the subject, it is hoped readers will appreciate that such special pleading is taking place in the much wider and richer African philosophical context outlined above.

This concluding chapter is devoted to discussing one fairly standard approach to the exegesis of indigenous African philosophy, and two widely discussed contemporary themes from moral philosophy in Africa. The approach concerns the use of *proverbs* as a source of African philosophy. The themes concern the importance of the *community* to the moral life of the individual, and the importance of the *religious* or *spiritual* to African systems of morality. The discussions of these topics are not meant to be comprehensive or even broadly representative of the varieties of argumentation and research that have been and are being devoted to them. Rather, it is incumbent upon a narrative such as this to offer the viewpoints it might have upon such relevant topics that have not been discussed in the main body of the text.

THE PROVERBIAL

With regards to the indigenous cultures of sub-Saharan Africa generally, proverbs have long been treated by anthropological and philosophical researchers as a legitimate source of African philosophy. Africanists caution us against unceremoniously and unjustifiably transferring the banality and triviality now associated with the proverb as a form of expression in Western culture to the African context (Yai 1989, 1994). For in Africa they are said to have both a different function and level of theoretical meaning that make them key components as well as expressions of a culture's viewpoints on a variety of important topics and problems. The literature that has been devoted to their cataloging and interpolation is therefore substantial (Biebuyck 1973; Dalfovo 1985; English and Hamme 1996; Gyekye 1987/1995, 1997; Wiredu 1996b).

Proverbs have not featured in this narrative in an important or prominent manner. They do occur in some of the quotations (22, 67, 130), but these are contexts in which a speaker also uses ordinary language and prose to portray and analyze a type of situation or problem and then 'adds on' the proverb as a more abbreviated way to epitomize an inductive generalization, sometimes involving a value judgment, that might be relevant to that type of situation or problem.

My motive for raising this topic is that I have several rather standard reservations about texts which presume to articulate African philosophy *solely* on the basis of the exegesis of a culture's proverbs. By comparison with ordinary language analysis, which concentrates on comparatively explicitly expressed, explicitly defined, and explicitly assessed values, a preponderant reliance upon professional academics as the agents who choose *which* proverbs should be considered 'keys to the kingdom's' cultural values, who determine how diverse proverbs should be *interrelated* to constitute some sort of system, network, or "worldview,"[1] and who dictate which *interpretations of the meanings* of those proverbs should be considered *most* accurate and essential could from a methodological viewpoint become a perilously subjective exercise.[2]

Generally proverbs do not introduce themselves to us as universal truths, as generalizations that always apply. Their pith, their point, their punch is situational or context-dependent to an essential degree. It is these extra-proverbial constraints—these nonverbal, semi-intuitive assessments of a situation's distinctive character—that make it appropriate to relate specific proverbs to it rather than others. And to identify these constraints in an authoritative manner—this would seem to involve nothing less than doing a conventional social anthropological study of the relevant culture.

I acknowledge that these reservations arising from the situational nature of proverbs are nothing new. They have been raised and discussed in the relevant literature many times (Bascom 1965, p. 483; Finnegan 1970, p. 399; Gyekye 1987/1995, pp. 16–24; Mbiti 1970, p. 2). Let me take, as an example, my own exposition of "*ìwà l'ẹwà*" in chapter 5. Is it reasonable, is it justifiable, to treat this 'simple' expression as *so* important a generalization, as such a Yoruba moral or aesthetic 'gem', without also taking into account the kinds of social circumstances in which it is *actually* used? In any case, as that analysis also indicated, which rendering of this aphorism is to be preferred when it is translated into the English language: "character is beauty," "beauty [really, actually] is character," or

---

1. "Nor has there been any real attempt to weave appropriate proverbs together in order to construct a coherent ethics or moral philosophy of the Akans" (Gyekye 1987/1995, p. 16). Gyekye's methodological ruminations throughout are healthily and disarmingly candid.

2. From a personal conversation I know that it was considerations such as these that persuaded Peggy and Anthony Appiah to catalog their collection of seven thousand Akan proverbs alphabetically (on the basis of the first letter of the noun with which a proverb begins) rather than thematically (according to subject matter). In my opinion the most philosophically sophisticated exponent of proverbs as components of a culture's philosophical thought is Kwame Gyekye (1987/1995). Himself an analytic philosopher, Gyekye explicitly acknowledges these same problems for the exegesis of proverbs and then proposes to come to terms with them by acknowledging that proverbs can be used only as "*a* source of knowledge of African traditional philosophy" (p. 24) rather than the only or major source, and that their "topical" nature can be utilized in a positive manner if they are treated as distillations of a culture's knowledge about specific themes (pp. 16–19).

"beauty arises from the expression of a thing's unique [ontological] essence"? Otherwise its meaning, as well as its significance, might be blown totally out of proportion to the importance actually attributed to it in real-life Yoruba discourse. Note, I am not saying that such distortions have actually occurred with reference to this particular aphorism. But I am suggesting (even if this involves shooting myself in the foot) that there may be need for further research and analysis before this expression can be convincingly cited and sited as so key a generalization.

THE COMMUNAL: "I AM BECAUSE WE ARE"

The place of the community in African morality can become an equally controversial topic. It is virtually commonplace that texts on African moral systems place primary emphasis on the role of the community in creating, defining, and sustaining a culture's moral values. The contribution made to an African community's moral 'life' by the individual consciousness, by a sense of truly *personal* obligation and responsibility, is therefore said to be of less significance than in some other cultures:

> What then is the individual and where is his place in the community? In traditional life, the individual does not and cannot exist alone except corporately. He owes his existence to other people, including those of past generations and his contemporaries. He is simply part of the whole. The community must therefore make, create or produce the individual; for the individual depends on the corporate group. (Mbiti 1970, p. 141)

This aspect of African moral systems became so stereotypical that some more recent accounts seek to redress the impression that African society has no place for the moral status of the individual vis-à-vis the community:

> that the individual in traditional African societies is crushed by the almighty presence of the community is not the whole truth. . . . There need not be any tension between individuality and community since it is possible for an individual to freely give up his/her own perceived interest for the survival of the community. But in giving up one's interest thus, one is also sure that the community will not disown one and that one's well-being will be its concern. It is a life of give and take. (Gbadegesin 1991, pp. 64, 66–67)

Is this supposed importance of the community to the sustenance of moral virtues reflected by the present study? This is more than a rhetorical question and becomes a query that deserves to be made explicit because readers may at this point be under the impression that the central thrust of this narrative is on the individual, with society at large functioning as an implicit and tacit moral background. For this book has not really directly addressed any notion of "community" in an explicit manner. Perhaps the first point to make is that this study does not set out to discuss *all* of the values embraced, either explicitly or implicitly, by Yoruba discourse. It concentrates deliberately upon apparent semantic *interrelations* between *select* aspects of epistemic, moral, and aesthetic values.

One reason to be concerned now with this issue of the importance of the African community with reference to the moral life of the individual is that the apparent relative imbalance between individual and community in the maintenance of moral values has been used to assign African moral systems a relatively lower status on the scale of comparative value systems. If the contribution made by an *individual's* moral consciousness is said to be *relatively* insignificant, in effect such critics claim that we retrogress to an "earlier" (the evolutionary implication of the term is deliberate) form of *pre*-reflective moral consciousness on the part of the individual. Moral values have the status of *fixed* rules and regulations ("traditions") that govern individual and communal life in a more or less mechanical manner. The input to morality made by the individual moral consciousness, reflecting on what it should or should not do in a given situation, therefore becomes comparatively insignificant.

This kind of appraisal is evidenced by Alasdair MacIntyre's portrayal of what he sometimes refers to as "traditional" societies (1967, pp. 91–92)—cultures in which the criteria used to define the moral are essentially communal and dispositional. MacIntyre's point is that a culture that manifests this form of the moral life has yet to make an individually self-reflective distinction between the "is" and the "ought"—between what a person *does* or *does not* do and between what a person *should* or *should not* do, because behavior is rigorously rule-governed by conventions. If an individual's (verbal and nonverbal) behavior adheres to whatever conventions apply to the role he or she happens to be playing in the community, that individual is good. If not, he or she is bad. There really is no middle ground. "You cannot avoid blame and penalty by pointing out that you could not help doing what you did, that failure was unavoidable" (p. 7).

A passage from John Mbiti's *African Religions and Philosophy* makes essentially the same point, in this case specifically with reference to the dispositional status of moral values in sub-Saharan Africa's indigenous cultures:

> Therefore the essence of African morality is that it is more "societary" than "spiritual"; it is a morality of "conduct" rather than a morality of "being" . . . for it defines what a person *does* rather than what he *is.*

Conversely, a person is what he is because of what he does, rather than that he does what he does because of what he is. . . . Man is not by nature either "good" or "bad" ("evil") except in terms of what he does and does not do. This, it seems to me, is a necessary distinction to draw in discussing African concept[s] of morality and ethics. (1970, pp. 279–80)

The most important *reflective* transition that MacIntyre finds moral thought to have undergone, following this pre-reflective period of rule-governed values, is when human beings consciously began to reflect upon what the "right" was independently of whatever might be the factual consequences of their actions, for themselves or others: "What ought I to do if I am to do right? Modern ethics asks this question in such a way that doing right is made quite independent of faring well" (p. 84).

My portrayal of Yoruba moral values as attaching primarily to a person's (verbal and nonverbal) behavior, in some passages in an indisputably dispositional manner, might suggest that the culture meets this pre-reflective criterion that MacIntyre and Mbiti prescribe for a "traditional" or "customary" society. But I do not think this need be the case, and I would like to refer to a now older article by Peter Laslett (1970) to assist me in developing this point. In relatively 'thought experimental' terms, Laslett imagines what sorts of human relationships generally might obtain in a society that operated socially and politically on what he describes as a "face-to-face" basis. Although his favored paradigm for this type of society is the Greek *polis* (city-state), and although in passing he makes several allusions to "tribal" societies as constituting less intellectually developed (again in a clearly evolutionary sense) forms of human communities (p. 162), I believe several speculative implications can be drawn from his thought experiment that can be used to counter the portrayal of 'traditional' African society as an example of the 'herd mentality'. Most simply put, a face-to-face community is one whose members have the opportunity to be more or less acquainted (Laslett uses the French verb *connaître*) with one another in a *firsthand* manner. He discusses several other attributes of such societies that are more specifically politically related (as that is his primary area of interest), but I think we can find this single defining criterion of value for further insight into the moral contexts discussed by the *onísègùn*. For the importance they attach to *firsthand* knowledge of another person's moral character certainly is compatible with a face-to-face community.

Obviously a community in which one would have a realistic opportunity to interact with everyone else on a firsthand basis would have to be comparatively small. Laslett does not characterize such a community's attitude toward its values as dispositional or pre-reflective. He prefers the word "intuitive," by which he seems to mean that by being born and bred in a face-to-face community one would absorb many of its values and norms of behavior semiconsciously, through a process of cultural osmosis. This provides a different kind of intellectual foundation for such a culture's values than having recourse to a pre-reflective paradigm of consciousness (even if Laslett himself might have reservations about my saying so). I do agree that the criteria defining (verbal and nonverbal) moral behavior enunciated by the *oníṣègùn* evidence strong influence of a dispositional viewpoint—"handsome is as handsome does," to invoke the old Western adage. But it would be unfair to concentrate exclusively on this dispositional dimension to their discourse about morality and *not grant equal weight to the underlying, articulated epistemological virtues that are explicitly said to be the prerogative of the individual moral agent*—the emphasis placed by the *oníṣègùn* upon the ordinary person's *reflecting deeply* upon difficult moral decisions with which they find themselves confronted;[3] the definitions of someone's being a good "listener" and "speaker" as meaning being perceptive and thoughtful rather than merely behaviorally "correct"; or the appreciation and respect paid to the *àlùjànún* for their intellectual insight, rectitude, and consciously creative genius. It is difficult to reconcile, taken in concert, such specifically enunciated epistemic and moral priorities for the *self*-conscious individual with a 'traditional' culture that is supposedly by definition quintessentially pre-reflective. Granted there may be an intuitive basis to behavior in many everyday Yoruba epistemic, moral, or aesthetic contexts (as there certainly is in Western cultures as well). But that intuitive aspect to behavior may be made the object of explicit and deliberate conscious reflection and discussion when and if a specific situation warrants (as is also the case in Western cultures).

Individuals in Yoruba culture are not described as "living up" to their moral responsibilities on the basis of nonreflective rule- or rote-governed behavior. They are emphatically encouraged to develop a degree of empirical and intellectual (here in the sense of "reflective") awareness that is designed to make them perceptive and objective agents in the social contexts that constitute shared communal life. If the word "agent" may be said to have a specifically moral significance, then a Yoruba "face-to-face" community is better regarded as a composite of agents who, as a group, do share common moral values that in many situations are evidenced by common forms of behavior. But that is the case in any society

---

3. See the discussion of *ronúpìwàdà* ("thinks deeply and changes behavior") in chapter 4.

worthy of the name. The importance of the word "composite" is that such shared forms of behavior are made flexible and meaningful by the consti- tutive, individual, moral agents who can *self*-consciously deliberate upon how, when, why, and where such values may best be enacted and en- hanced.

SACRED OR SECULAR?

In the literature dealing with the nature of morality and moral thought in Yoruba culture, a dispute has arisen about the nature of the relationship between morality and religion in that culture. The point of disagreement is the influence religion is said to have upon moral values and conven- tions. There are those who argue that religious beliefs are so fundamental and so formative of values generally that to speak of morality in secular terms, as something that may be understood or assessed independently of the religion, is impossible (Kayode and Adelowo 1985; Makinde 1988a).

There are those who argue that "Far from having a religious founda- tion . . . we have here a system of morality which, while it makes use of religion as a motivating factor, is clearly pragmatic and this-worldly to the core" (Gbadegesin 1991, p. 78). This comparatively secular interpretation argues that certain religious beliefs in Yoruba culture may serve to "sup- port" certain moral values. But what Gbadegesin seems to mean by this is that the values of one social institution (whether religion or morality) serve to *confirm* or to *reaffirm* those of the other (whether religion or morality). The alternative "foundation" for which he argues involves the comparatively profane considerations that an individual will *benefit* from being a moral person because of the positive "pragmatic" and "this- worldly" consequences that will follow, such as respect, trust, responsi- bility, and (social) success.

The deliberative and rational character of Yoruba thought as pre- sented by this narrative aligns it with this second, comparatively secular alternative. The emphasis placed by the *onísègùn* upon the importance of an individual's deliberating upon a secularly "good" course of action, the painstaking detail with which the morally deliberating self is por- trayed, and the decidedly positive or negative *social* consequences of be- ing a moral or immoral person make this evident. Nevertheless, Soyinka's point about the analytic propensity to "compartmentalize" deserves con- sideration one final time. For his portrait of the Yoruba viewpoint or "worldview" insists that it would be wrong, indeed false, for scholars to present it *as if* the sacred may be sundered from the profane.

Is there a middle way here—a further alternative by means of which these two apparently opposing interpretations might be reconciled? I think there might be, if one was willing to acknowledge that the 'job' of ordinary, everyday discourse *is* essentially "pragmatic" and "this-worldly." This *is* the realm of the prosaic, after all. But to say that is neither to denigrate nor to underrate the thoughtful sophistication that realm may exhibit in its own right. When there is a need to go 'beyond' the everyday because of exceptional circumstances, then the religious or metaphysical may become involved as well.[4] But must this make the latter foundational of the former? That would seem too strong a term to use, as it implies that in some sense the profane itself becomes a (logical?) consequence of the sacred. Yet given the, admittedly limited, selection of epistemic, moral, and aesthetic values enumerated by this study and, more importantly, the nature of their interrelations, their rational, coherent, and consistent qualities, purely on secular grounds, appear indisputable.

THE STRAW CULTURE ARGUMENT

To conclude: the most distinguishing characteristic of a study such as this is its attempt to interrelate the epistemic, the moral, and the aesthetic in a systematic manner. Yet what may attract the attention of critics even more is the preponderant emphasis it places upon a rational basis for the values it claims to find intrinsic to Yoruba discourse and culture. Could it be that what was characterized at the beginning as a "rationalist's rendering" of Yoruba values is no more and no less than what one should expect of a *philosophical* approach to the topic? Rationality is philosophy's primary concern, indeed, its defining interest. Just as the ubiquitous paradigm of the pre-reflective, symbolic character of traditional cultures channels anthropological approaches to Africa, analytic Western philosophers' favored paradigm of the reflective, critical consciousness must analogously inform (or should the verb be "distort"?) their rendering of the same subject matter. In other words, every academic discipline has its own distinctive and defining methodological approaches to (or should the phrase be "biases toward"?) its subject matter, and it should therefore come as no surprise that those approaches must inevitably structure whatever studies are the consequences of their application. It would be diplomatic and certainly deconstructive to say "yes" to this, and that the truth

---

4. This would not be imposing an artificial analytic distinction so much as acknowledging that, in certain types of circumstances, a 'rough' one may exist or be observed.

APPENDIX OF YORUBA-LANGUAGE QUOTATIONS

Translation between languages whose meanings may vary in a fundamental manner is both a difficult and delicate enterprise. For that reason, and for readers who are fluent in Yoruba, I thought it helpful to include this appendix of the numbered passages in my text in the original Yoruba. Unfortunately, some of the tapes and Yoruba-language transcriptions relating to aesthetics are in storage in Nigeria and could not be accessed. However, the accuracy of the English-language renderings, which I did fortunately have with me, should be no better (or worse) than those for which both the English-language and Yoruba-language versions were available.

(1) Èyí tí o fi ojú ara rẹ tí ọkọ̀n rẹ jẹ́ ọ lẹrí pé o ṣe òótọ́ yẹn ni ó dára jù.

(2) Ó dá mi lójú. Èyí ni pé mo rí ẹ̀rí òótọ́ ni o ṣe kín ni yí . . . Ó ti dá ẹ lójú.

(3) Tí a bá ń ṣe ǹkan nisiyi, òmíràn lé jà sí òfò, òmíràn lè já sí òótọ́ ni ọ̀rọ̀ tí à ń sọ yí, oníkálùkùn ni ó ní ẹ̀bùn ọ̀rọ̀ síso, ẹlòmíràn irọ̀ pípa, ẹlòmíràn òtítọ́ síse. Nígbàtí o bá ti ńṣe, ó ṣee kó jẹ́ pé o purọ́, ó ṣeéṣe kí o jẹ pé o sọ́ọ́tọ́ èyí jẹ́ ǹkan tì a kò ri.

(4) Èrò ọkàn, òun ńaà ni a ńpè ní ògínrínrínginrìn gbogbo ǹkan kékékèé bàyí náà ni àwọn ènìyàn ńrí tí wọ́n máa ńpè àwọn kan ní àjẹ́. Wọ́n a sọ pé ọ̀rọ̀ rẹ̀ kankan kò kí ńṣelẹ̀ (tà sé) wọn a sọ pé kò kín sọ kí ó má ṣe. Ó ti parí rẹ̀ kí ó tó wá sọ̀rọ̀, bẹ̀ẹ̀ ni àlá ni ó ńlá.

Ìkan tí wọ́n bá ti se lóru ló wá ńsọ níbi tí yíò sì máa sọ pé òun kì
ńse àjẹ, bẹ́ẹ̀ alá ni ẹni béyẹnń lá.

(5) Èyí tí o fí ojú ara rẹ rí tí ọkàn rẹ jẹ́ ọ lèrí pé o se òótọ́ yen ni ó dára
jù. Nwọ́n sọ ìyen fún ni, bóyá o puró tàbí o kò puró o kò mò.
Bóyá lágbájá yìí bóyá kò le puró ni o fi gbà. Tí nbá ní pé olòótọ́
ènìyàn ni ẹ́ máa gbògbọ́ pé òótọ́ ni o se. Ṣùgbọ́n bí o bá ti ńse
élèké, ẹníkẹni kò ní gbàgbọ́, wáá a sọ pé o puro wọn kò ní
dáhùn síi.

(6) Ṣùgbọ́n ènìyàn tí o mò, tí o ti ńse òótọ́ tí wọn bá sọ wípé ó sèkè
wọn kò ní ńfi agbára gbà gbọ́. Nítorí pé a ti ní gbàgbọ́ sí olóòtọ́
ènìyàn, bẹ́ẹ̀ ńaà ni tí ènìyàn bá ńse búburú tí a bá gbọ́ pé ó se
rere a kò le fi agbára gbàgbọ́.

(7) O ti mọ̀ pé 'cupboard' ni eléyìí, bí ènìyàn nsọ́ pé kò kí ńse
'cupboard', èmí yìí ó tẹnu mọ́ pé 'cupboard' nì nkan tí mo mọ̀
dáadáa, èrí ọkàn ti jẹ́ o pé òun ni; ìgò funfun yì, bí wọ́n sọ́ pe
dúdú ni, o ti mọ̀ dáadáa pé funfun ni. Ìwọ yì ó sọ wípé funfun ni,
ó ti dámilójú pé funfun ni, mo mọ̀, mó mọ̀ pé funfun ni.

(8) Òótọ́ ni sí orísìrísì, kí èmi rẹ jìjọ sọ ǹkan kí o ló sọọ́ níwájú, kí
wọ́n sì wá bèèrè lọ́wọ́ mi, èmi yíò sọ wípé òótọ́ ni, pé o kò puró
pé bẹ́ẹ̀ ló rí.

(9) Ìyàtọ̀ tí ó wà láàrín ǹkan tí mo mọ àti èyí tí mo gbà ni pé, ǹkan tí
o jẹ́ kí ó gbà ni ó jẹ́ wípé o ti rí ǹkan ńaà . . .

(10) Ìwà rẹ nipé bí ó bá ti ńse dáadáa wọn á sọ wípé ìwà rè mà dára ò.
Tí o bá ti ńse burúkú wọ́n a sọ pé ìwà rẹ mà burú o. Síse eni ni
wọ́n fi ńmo ìwà eni.

(11) Ìṣesí.

(12) A máa ńfi ojú rí ọ̀pọ̀lọpọ̀ ǹkan, a sì máa ńwo ìwà ènìyàn.

(13) Bí ènìyàn ṣe ńhùwà sí ara wọ ni a ṣe ńmo èyí.

(14) Èyí dà gégé bí ǹkan gbígbé ṣe tí mo sọ léèkan. . . . Ìwà tí ènìyàn
ńhù ni á npè ní orí inú, kò kí ńse wípé ó ní òpó kan gédégbé bí
kò se wípé ó jẹ́ ìwà tàbí ọ̀rọ̀ ẹnu láti sọ.

(15) Kí á tó mò ọ̀tá eni a ó rí iṣe tí ó ńse sí ènìyàn, tí ènìyàn kò bá rí iṣe
yen tí ènìyàn kò sí rí ṣé ọwọ́ rè olúwa rè kò ní mọ ǹkankan ni.

(16) Ẹnirere ni ó ńsọ̀rọ̀ rere, ẹniburúkú a máa sọ̀rọ̀ burúkú.

(17) Wọn a sọ wípé ènìyàn burúkú ni, wèrè ló máa pe olúwa rẹ̀ dànù; wọn á ní ọ̀rọ̀ rere kìnjáde lẹ́nu rẹ̀.

(18) Ǹkan tí o ńse kò dára.

(19) À fi ìrírí yẹn.

(20) Ẹni tí kò bá fẹ́ jẹ́ elékè ǹkan tí wọ́n kò bá ṣe lójú rẹ̀ kò gbọdọ̀ sọ wípé òun gbàgbọ́. Kí o tọ́ so pé o gbà, o yé kí o ti rí ẹni tí ó ti se rí lójú rẹ̀ ǹkan tí ẹni bá ti rí rí ni ó yẹ kí o mọ̀.

(21) Mo gbà ọ́ gbọ́ nígbà tí mo rí ìwà rẹ̀, èyí tí o rí yẹn ni ó jù, mo rí dájúdájú. Mo gbà ọ́ gbọ́ sùgbọ́n èmí kò rí ǹkan ńaà, sùgbọ́n èyí tí mo rí kedere yẹn ni ó dájú.

(22) Ǹkan tí ó ńjẹ́ orí lásán yẹ̀ẹ kò lágbára léhìn ǹkan tí ó ńbẹ nínú ẹni. Èmí yẹ̀ẹ náà ni a ńpè ní orí, ibi tí ọkàn ènìyàn bá sọ ni ènìyàn ńlọ orí ni ó máá a fi ńsọ wípe ibi tíorí bá ti ńgbe ni lo kí ẹsẹ̀ máa sin ènìyàn lọ. Kí á tó ṣe ǹkankan inú ni a ti mọ ọ̀rọ̀ kò kí ńse orí ni a fi mọ̀. Ṣùgbọ́n, inú ni.

(23) Ohúnkohun tí a bá ti [sic] rò kí á tó ṣe òun ni èrò ọkàn.

(24) [Wọ́n] sòro mọ̀, . . . nítorí a kò mọ èrò ọkọ̀n wọn.

(25) Ṣọọ̀sì tí à ńlọ ọ́ jẹ́ ǹkan tí ńwọ́n dá kalẹ̀ bí ìgbà tí ńwọ́n sọ wípé a fé wá ṣe ẹgbẹ́. Tàbí kí a wá má se ìpàdé, sùgbọ́n ní ìpàdé yìí èmi kò mọ inú rẹ ìwọ kò si mọ inú tèmi.

(26) Àwa èdá a wá sáá ni, èmi kò mọ inú rẹ, ìwọ kò sì mọ tèmi.

(27) Ènìyàn fún ra rẹ̀ ló mọ̀ wípé òun ṣe ọ̀tá ènìyàn.

(28) Tí a bá sọ pé ènìyàn nínú, tí o bá sọ̀rọ̀ létí rẹ̀ kò le dé ọ̀dọ̀ ẹlòmíràn kí ó lọ máa wíi. Èyí já sí wípé ó rí inú fi ọ̀rọ̀ sí.

(29) Ẹni tí inú rẹ̀ bá ti dáa búburú kò ní rí ibi dúró sí bí inú ènìyàn bá dáa bí o bá ńkọ ní búburú kò ní gbà. Ẹni tí nwọ́n bá sì kọ̀ ní búburu tí ó gbà òun náà fẹ́ ṣe ìkà tẹ́lẹ̀ ni.

(30) Wọn a sọ wípé inú ènìyàn náà dára . . . Ìwà náà nì yẹn.

(31) Gbogbo ìwà àti ìṣe inú yìí ni wọ́n diisi.

(32) Èmí yẹn ńaà ni, ẹni tí ẹmí búrukú bá wà lára rẹ̀ àti àwọn tí èmí rere bá wà ní ara rẹ̀. Inú ni ǹkan búburú ti máa ńjáde.

(33) Èmí ni ó máa ńjé kí ènìyàn ó hu ìwà rere. Òun ná ni ó sì máa ńmú kí ènìyàn kí ó hu ìwà búburú, bí e se wà yí èmi kan ni ó mú yín ronú tí e fi wá. Òhun náà ni ó sì ńmú kí ènìyàn [jalè].

(34) Òkan soso ni, nínú èmí ni èrò rere àti búburú ti ńjáde.

(35) Eni tí èmí búburú bá ti wà nínú rè àwon ló máa ńse ìkà.

(36) Eni tí ó bá ní èmí rere yíò máa hùwà rere. Èmí búburú yóò máa hu ìwà búburú.

(37) Bí ayé ènìyàn bá máa bà je òun fúnrarè ni yóò fi owó ara rè fá, bí ó sì máa dára òun ni ó mò. Inú ènìyàn ni èmí ti ńtúńayé ènìyàn se èyí ni èmí.

(38) Sé o mò wípé okàn ni ìgbòran wà. Gbogbo ohun tí o bá ńkó ní báyìí tí o bá ti ńfi etí gbó ó ńlo sókan. Tí okàn re bá ti lo síbè o gbódò mo kíni yen. Tí okàn re kò bá lo síbè o kò ní mo, a jé wípé o wò lásán ni.

(39) Bí isé tí agogo ńse ní sìnsìn yí náà ni inú wa se ńsise. Sé o rí mò wípé kò séni tí ó lè dúró lâì ro ǹkankan. Kó o dúró lásán kí wón bi é e pe níbo ni inú re wà, kí o so wípé òun kò ro ǹkankan, kí ó dúró lásán. Bí a se ńsòrò yí bà yí, èmí wa ńsise míran sílè fún wa.

(40) Ó ye kí èmi mò. Nítorípé bí o ti jòkó nísìsiyí lâì jé wípé òrò tí ò ńso yí, okàn re yíò wà ní ibi tí ó tó mérìnlá, méjìlá tàbí jùbéè lo. A sì dà bí eni wipé ibè gan ni ó wà. Lâì sí òrò tí ènìyàn ńso kí ó dúró géé lâì se kànkan okàn yíò lo sí ibi gbogbo. Bí o se wà nísisìyí okàn re lè wà ní Èkó, nítorípé o jé pé ibi tí o tí ńgbé télè. Gbogbo ǹkan tí o mò níbè tí èmí re yíò máa wò.

(41) Nwon kò ní gbàgbó, nwón lè ní kí ó lo ronú sí.

(42) Tí ènìyàn bá bí omo re a máa kó lógbón, tí bàbá yen bá dàgbà a má a so wípé báyìí báyìí ni wón ti se ńsoó fún mi. Ǹkan tí ó ti rírí a máa so fún omo rè. Sé omo rè kò rí kinní yen rí. Ǹkan tí a kò bá rírí tí wón so fún o, ni ó ńjé pé bàyíbàyí ni wón ńso fún wa.

(43) Bí ènìyàn bá wà tí ó bá ńsòrò nípa ìlúyí pé o yé kí á ní omi tàbí 'bank' tàbí kí 'hospital' wa yì dí 'General'. Ònà tí ó ye kí á gbà láti mú kí gbogbo èyí se ni kí okùnrin ati obìnrin kí ó sanwó kí gbogbo ìlú kí wón parapò kí wón ro òrò yen. Won a ní tani eni tí ó ro òrò yí? Won a ní lágbájá bàyì ní ó mú ìmòran yen wá. Wón á so wípé bàbá yen ní opolo tàbí omo yen mà ní opolo o. Èyí jé ònà tí à ńgbà ńlo òrò yen.

(44) Ohúnkohún tí o bá ti ṣe tí kò sí ènìyàn kankan tí ó rí ọ, tí kò sí ènìyàn kankan tí ó mọ̀. Ọkàn rẹ á wá jẹ́ ọ lèrí wípé o ti ṣe kinní yẹn. Ǹkan tí o ṣe tí ẹnikéni kò rí sùgbọ́n tí ìwọ gaan wá jẹrí sí oun ni a ńpè ní ẹ̀rí ọkàn. Ó lè jẹ́ rere ó sì le jẹ́ búburú.

(45) Bí o bá ṣe ènìyàn gidigidi yío mọ́ pé ǹkan tí o sọ nígbà yẹn kò dára.

(46) Èyí pín sí orísirísi, òmíràn wà tí wọ́n lè pè ní àjé. Tí o bá rorí sí ǹkan pé kíni ó yẹ kí o ṣe, tí ò ńṣe tí ó sì ńbósi làì sí ẹnì kọọkan tí ó sọ fún ọ èrí ọkàn rẹ ni ó ń bá ẹ ṣe yẹn. Wọ́n lè pè é kí o jẹ́ kí á lọ sóde, "tí o bá ṣe ilé èmi bàyí niemi kò lọ." Ẹ̀rí ọkàn rẹ ni o mú ọ sọ fún mi pé o kò lọ yen. Tí wọ́n bá fá ẹ́ lọ kí ẹ dé bẹ́ kí ìjà ṣẹlẹ̀, wà á sọ́ pé ǹje o ò ti sọ pé o kò lọ? Pé ẹ̀rí ọkàn rẹ ti sọ fún ẹ pé kò ye kí o lọ. Ẹ̀rí ọkàn ẹni ni o má ńsọ pé bóyá ǹkan kò dára. Èyí sì sé pàtàkì jù àmòràn ẹnikéni. Bí ẹ̀rí ọkàn rẹ bá bá ẹ sòrò ẹmí tí ó wá yío lórí padà yen kí o yìo pé. Ẹ̀rí ọkàn gangan ni èmí ẹni. Òun ni ó gbé ènìyàn ronújù, ẹnití kò bá ní èrò ọkàn ara rẹ̀ òun ni ó ńṣe.

(47) A lè wo ènìyàn tàbí ǹkan ògbin, tí o bá ńwo ǹkan ògbìn tí kò bá dára wáà sọ pé ilẹ̀ ibí yí kò dára tí o bá wo ọmọ tí ó ńbá siṣé sùnùkùn wàá sọ pé aláìsàn ni. Tí ó bá ńse gánnagànagànà wà sọ́ pé ọmọ ibi ni ọmọ yí kò kí ńse alálùbáríkà ọmọ. Ojú inú ni a fi ńwò yẹn. Orísirísi ọ̀nà ni a ńfi ójú inú wò.

(48) 'Key' oníkáluku ọ̀tọ̀ọ̀tọ̀ tí ó ńsí, tí o bá fẹ́ lo ogbọ́n nísísìyí inú yí ni o máa ti mú jáde. Tí o bá fẹ́ ní ẹ̀mí sùùrù inú yí ni ó wáà tí mú jáde, oníkálùkù ni ó ní àyè tirẹ̀. . . . Gbogbo 'key' tí ó ńsiṣé lára inú kan soso yì ní ó wà.

Ibi tí kọ́kọ́rọ́ yen wà ibẹ̀ ni iyè yen wà. Iyè yen ni ó má n júwe ǹkan sínú ènìyàn. Tí ó bá ṣe ǹkan iyè ọkàn rẹ á sọ síi. Ọ̀tọ̀ ni inú, ọ̀tọ̀ ni ẹ̀mí, sùgbọ́n inú ikùn kan ni ọ́ńgbé.

(49) Láíláí ni wọ́n ti ń pá ló we wípé à kún lè yàn ni à dá yé bá. Èyí fi hàn wá pé bí ó ti wù kí ó rí ẹ má ni ìpìn tí ó pín. A kìí dáyé nkò ìse ìpín ẹni.

(50) Ìpín gan ni ó ńjẹ́ orí, èyí tí a pín lorí wa. Wọ́n má ńsọ wípé orí yí ni ó bá ni ṣe ìpín yí kí ènìyàn tó wá sí ayé. Wọ́n lè sọ wípé orí búburu ni orí rẹ̀, ìpín yí tí ó mú ti ọ̀run wá ni.

(51) Ìpín tí a tí yàn yí ná ni à ńpè ní orí. Wọ́n máa ńsọ wípé ìpín buruku ni ìpín, pé orí búrukú ni ó wà ní orí rẹ̀. Wọ́n lè sọ wípé ìpín rere ni ó pín orí ni orí rẹ̀ yen. Orí àti ìpín jẹ́ ǹkankan.

(52)   Èyí tí à ńpè ní ìpín yí kádàrá ni.

(53)   Gbogbo ǹkan tí a bá ti ṣe ní ayé ìpín rẹ ni, bí ènìyàn ńse búburú tàbí rere èyí tí ó pín nìyí.

(54)   Ènìyàn ni ó ńfi ọwọ́ ara rẹ̀ yan ǹkan tí ó wá ńse láyé. Ṣùgbọ́n ènìyàn má ńsábà máa sọ wípé Ọlọ́run ni ó fún wọn ní èyí tàbí tọ̀hún. . . . Ṣùgbọ́n òun fún ra rẹ̀ ni ó fí ọwọ́ ará rẹ yan tí Ọlọ́run fi àṣẹ sí pé kí ó rí bẹ́ẹ̀.

(55)   Ìgbésí ayé ènìyàn ní ayé yí òun ni ó ńsiṣẹ. Oun ló darí ènìyàn ìgbésí ayé ẹni lâì ku ǹkankan.

(56)   Òun ni ó ṣe pàtàkì jù, òun ni ẹléda tó yàn sí wa sáyé.

(57)   Kò sí ẹni tí ó lè mọ bí ò nse pín, bí ó bá jẹ́ bẹ́ẹ̀ ni ènìyàn ìbá máa tọ ọ̀nà yẹn kooro. . . . Ṣùgbọ́n ẹnìkéni kò le sọ wípé bí lágbájá tí ṣe yàn gan nìyen.

(58)   Ẹnikéni kò le mọ́ ǹkan tí ó yàn. Ènìyàn kò le yàn ǹkan lọ́run kí ó dé ayé kí ó mọ̀, bí ó bá jẹ́ bẹ́ẹ ibẹ̀ ni ìbá máa tẹ̀ sí.

(59)   Ènìyàn kò le dáyé mọ ǹkan tí òun ti pín láti ọrun wá.

(60)   Nígbàtí a dá ènìyàn ní wọ́n ti dá ìpín yẹn pèlú rẹ. Ṣùgbọ́n ènìyàn ni ó ńse gbogbo ǹkan tí à ń ṣe.

(61)   Èyí dà gẹ́gẹ́bí ǹkan gbígbése tí mo sọ léèkan. Orí inú ni ọ̀rọ̀ ẹnu eni, nígbàtí ǹkan bá ti délẹ̀ tí ènìyàn ńso ìsokúso, bí a sé ṣe ètò gbogbo ibí ní ìsiyí, kí ndé bí kí nmáa dàrú. Èyí ni à ń pè ní orí inú, kí ndédé wọlé nísisìyí kí nsá déédé má na àlejò kí àlejò yí sì dídé lọ mú ọlọ́pàá mú mi pé mo bá òun jà. Nígbàtí kò sí ǹkan tí ó ṣe fún mi tí wọn bá mú mí tí a sì ri wípé kò sí èṣẹ̀ kan pàtàkì tí ó ṣe fún mi, àwọn ènìyàn á sọ pé orí inú ba ti òde jé nìyen. Ìwà tí ènìyàn ńhu ni à ńpè ní orí inú. Kò kí ńse wípé ó ní òpó kan gédégbé bí kò ṣe wípé ó jẹ ìwà tàbí ọ̀rọ̀ ẹnu láti sọ.

(62)   Èyí dà gẹ́gẹ́ bí ǹkan gbígbése tí mo sọ léèkan. Orí inú ni ọ̀rọ̀ ẹnu ẹni, nígbàtí ǹkan bá ti délẹ̀ tí ènìyàn ńso ìsokúso, bí a sé ṣe ètò gbogbo ibí ní isinyí. Kí ndébí kí nmáa dàárú èyí ni à ńpè ní orí inú. . . . Àwọn ènìyàn á sọ pé orí inú ba ti òde jé nìyẹn. Ìwà tí ènìyàn ńhu ni à ńpè ní orí inú. Kò kí nse wípé ó ní òpó kan gédégbé bí kò ṣe wípé ó jẹ ìwà tàbí ọ̀rọ̀ ẹnu láti sọ.

(63)   Èyí ni wípé orí eni ni ó ti ènìyàn lọ. Orí ènìyàn ni ó sin ènìyàn lọ sí ibi tí ó bá ńlọ. Òhun tí a ti yàn tí ọrun wá ni ìpín a kò le yí tí a

bá dé ayé. Èyí jé ǹkan tí yíò selè tí o bá jé wípé isé ńlá ni yí ò jé tirè orí re ni yíò gbé e lo sí ibé.

(64) Tí a bá dé inú ayé tí a rí ǹkan tí ó té wa lórun a ó so wípé ìgbà tí mo ti ń bò ni mo ti yàn láti òrun.

(65) Gégébí enití ó ńlo sí ilé ìwé èyí tí ó jé wípé ó ti mú òkè jù ni yío jé ònà fún nwon.

(66) Elòmíràn tí ó ńse ìkà ó lè wùú láti máa se rere. Sùgbón síbèsíbè bí ó ti wù kí ó gbìyànjú tò yíò máa hu ìwà ìkà ní okàn rè. Nítorípé ǹkan tí ó ti yàn ǹiyen lati òde òrun wá.

(67) But 'ire àti ibi ni ó ńtèle ara won'. Kò sí eni tí ó lè ní ire kí ó ma ní ibi.

(68) Búburú àti rere ní o ńrìn pò. A kò le pín rere fún enìkan kí ó má si ibi kokan nínú rè.

(69) Eni tí ó dá bí eni wípé rere sáà ni ó ńrí ní ayé won rí ibi tí o tí jé wípé bàtà ti ńtaá lésè. Ènìyàn tí ó dàbí eni wípé búburú ni ó ńrí, ó ní ibi tí ó ti jé wípé ó ti tura fún. Orí ènìyàn máa ńburú sùgbón kò kí ńse ní gbogbo ònà wón a sáà ní ibìkan tí yíò ti dára fún.

(70) Sùgbón ó sìnà. . . . Gégébí mo ti so ní ìjósí òun ni ó fá kí ènìyàn máa lo sí ilé babaláwo láti lo wàdí báwo ni ònà òun se rí láyé. Babaláwo tí ó bá ríran yíò sí so fún un wípé ó ti fi ònà rè sílè. Ìgbà náà ni yíò sè wa padà sí ònà. Ònà sísì ni wípé bí títì ti pò tó, kí ènìyàn kan tí kò mó ìbì kakan rí máa lo sí ibè. Tí kò bá rí eni tóo sí ònà, ó lè sìnà. Kí enìkan nísisìyí kí ó máa bò láti ònà tí ó jìnà wá sí Ìjàn sùgbón kí ófi orí lé ònà Enúgu. Tí ó bá sì dé ibè tí ó bèrè wón á sì so fún un wípé ó ti sìnà wón á sì to sí ònà ìyen dúró gégébí babaláwo.

(71) Orí yen gan ni ó ńpín ǹkan yìí, ó dàbí eni tí wón sì lónà tí ó sì bá ònà pàdé. Yíò so wípé orí ni òun fi sé kí ni ó se tí òun kò fibá ènìyàn béè pàdé kí ó júwe òótó fún òun, sùgbón tí Olórun bá fé kí ònà rè se kooro gbogbo òdò eni tí ó bá ti dé ni yíò máa so wípé bàyí ni ó se sé bàyí ni ò bá rín tí yíò dáa rìn sí ònà. Bàyí yíò má so wípé orí òun bá òun sé tí ó gbé òun pàdé ènìyàn rere.

(72) Kò sí ǹkan pàtàkì tí babaláwo yen se, ǹkan tí ó tilè selè ni wípé ìdàmú tí eni yen má rí nínú ayé ni ó ti rí yen tí ó bá dára fún léhìn ìgbàtí ó ti rí babaláwo tán. Òun fún ra rè ti fi owó ara rè yàn ní òrun wípé òun yíò jé ìyà dìè kí ó tó dára fún òun. Lóòtó a lè gba isé babaláwo míràn sí bí wípé eni tí ó sì ònà tí wón wá rí ènìyàn

júwe ọ̀nà fún. Sé o mọ̀ wípé ǹwón rí ọmọ tí ó lówó tí o ńyan olòsì bí baba irú ẹni bẹ́ẹ̀ tilẹ̀ ràn lọ́wọ́ títí tí kò ní sí àyípadà fún irú ẹni bẹ́ẹ̀ ṣùgbọ́n àwọn ènìyàn á sọ wípé ìpín tí ó pín ti ọ̀run wá ni.

(73) Tí ẹnì kan bá ńsìnà ìpín ènìyàn míràn yíò wá tí kò ní jẹ́ kí ó sìnà tàbí tí yíò tọ̀ sí ọ̀nà. Ọlọ́run yíò ti yan èyí tìí, yíò sọ fún wípé kí ó yà sí ibi bàyí. Ó sì le pín ìpín wípé yíò sìnà gba iye ọjọ́ mèló kan kí ó tó bọ́ sí ọ̀nà gan.

(74) Ó ṣe é ṣe kí ènìyàn kan fí ọwọ́ ara rẹ̀ yàn pé òun fẹ́ wá se búburú ní ayé, tí ó jẹ́ wípé ti nwọ́n bá ńfi rere wá sùgbọ́n tí ó jẹ́ pé ibi ni yíò fi ọkàn sí. Yíò sì máa se búburú, àwọn ará ayé a sì má sọ wípé ènìyàn búburú ni irú ẹni bẹ̀. Irú àwọn ènìyàn báyí ni a sọ wípé ó pín ìpín búburú tàbí a lè pe nwọ́n ní Olórí búburú.

(75) Bẹ́ẹ̀ni. Nwọ́n ní tí a bá fẹ́ sé òògùn fún ènìyàn, tí ó bá ti se ènìyàn dáadáa ni ẹnì yẹn òògùn ńaa yíò jẹ́, ìwọ yíò mà. Elòmíràn yíò sì máa se ara rẹ̀ òògùn kò ní jẹ́ fún un.

(76) A máa ńsọ wípé orí rẹ ni ò padà ní ẹ̀hìn rẹ. . . . Èrò rẹ̀ dópin. Òní nìkan torí nìkan ló rò. Kò ro ǹkan tí ó tùn lè sẹlẹ̀ lọ́la èrò rẹ̀ kúrú.

(77) Bẹ́ẹ̀ni a dá ara rẹ ni ìmí pé kò burú ó di ọjọ́ míràn tí òun bá wá sí ayé.

(78) Tí ènìyàn kò bá dè ibí tí ó fẹ́ dé tí ó bá mọ̀ wípé isé ọ̀tá ni. Yíò ní àmìn tí yíò rí, tí ẹ bá ńse isé tí isé nà kò bá dára yíò mọ̀ wípé isé ọ̀tá ni. Tí o lọ fẹ́ ìyàwó ní ìta tí ẹlòmíran gbàá lọ́wọ́ rẹ yíò mọ̀ wípé isé ọ̀tá ni. Ẹni tí ó bí ọmọ sí ilé tí àjẹ́ pa ọmọ yen jẹ ó mọ̀ wípé isé ọ̀tá ni.

(79) Àwọn aráyé lè dàrú mọ́ ní ọwọ́ gégébí ènìyàn tí kọ́ ilé yí, tí kò bá sí ẹni tí ó ní ilé yí nílé àwọn olè lè wá koo nwón sì ko lọ. Ṣé onísé ti se isé rẹ̀, kí ẹnìkan wá bàá jẹ́.

(80) Igi rígi lè wà, ńlá àti kékeré èyí ńlá yẹn lè wó lé orí kékere bí ogúnọdún ó lè wà ní orí rẹ̀ kí kékeré má lè gbérí. Bẹ́ẹ̀ náà ni àwọn ènìyàn tí ọ̀tá ńbò mọ́lẹ̀.

(81) Díẹ̀ ènìyàn ló lè sọ wípé òun yan búburú láti òde ọ̀run. Sùgbọ́n yíò sọ wípé àwọn aráyé ló ńbá òun jà.

(82) Ìdí ni wípé bí a se dé inú ayé yìí a rí ara wa a kò mọ̀ bóya àyípadà lè wà. A kò mọ̀ ìpín tí a pín láti ọ̀run wá. Kí á mọ́ wípé bóya búburú ni ọmọ kan wá mú sùgbọ́n àwa kò mọ̀ à bá lè sọ wípé ọmọdé yìí má se èyí tóhun mú kí o se tí a básì mú ọmọ kan kí á pé kí a pèè sí wípé búburú ni ó yàn ó lè jẹ́ ǹkan tí Ẹlédá lè jẹ

èníyàn ní ìyà sí ni. Èyí ni ó jẹ́ kí á máa kọ́ wọ́n. Sùgbọ́n bí a bá kọ́ wọn tí nwọn kò bá gbọ́ kò sí ǹkan tí a lè se.

(83) Ẹlòmíran a má hu ìwà rere lójú tí ó bá ti dé àárín agbo, sùgbọ́n tí ó bá ti de ẹ̀hìn, ǹkan búrukú ni yío se àwon tí ó bá ti rí àsírí rẹ̀ yío má sọ wípé ó wulẹ̀ ńsọ̀rọ̀ tó dára ni. Sùgbọ́n èníyàn búrukú ni.

(84) Tí wọ́n bá sọ wípé ẹnìkan se ǹkan tí ó sì dá ẹnìkejì lójú pé kò le se irú ǹkan bẹ́ẹ̀ a lè sọ pé mo gbàgbọ́ tàbí mo gbà ẹni yen gbọ́ kò le se irú ǹkan bẹ́ẹ. Tàbí kí o sọ wípé mo gbàgbọ́ pé ó lè sé é, èyí ni pé o tí mọ àdìn rẹ̀.

(85) Tí a bá ti ńwo ìwà èníyàn, a lè sọ wípé a gbà pé ó lè sé. Tí kò bá tîî sé ǹkan yẹn lójú rẹ rí yío sọ wípé òun gbàgbọ́ sùgbọ́n bí o bá ti sé ǹkan yẹn lójú rẹ yío wá sọ wípé òun mọ èyí ni pé èyí ti dá lójú. Tí o bá sọ wípé òun gbàgbọ́ tí wọ́n bá si bèèrè pé kíni ó jẹ kí o lè gbàgbọ́ ọ́ lè sọ wípé ìsesí rẹ̀ jẹ́ kí òun mọ̀.

(86) Wọ́n sọ ìyẹ fún ni bóyá ó purọ́ tàbí kò purọ́ o kò mọ̀. Bóyá lágbájá yi bóyá kò le purọ́ ni o fi gbà. Tí nbá ri pé olóotọ́ èníyàn ni ẹ́ màá gbàgbọ́ pé òótọ́ ni o se, sùgbọ́n bí o bá ti ńse eléké ẹnikẹ́nì kó ní gbàgbọ́ wọ́n á sọ pé ò pùrọ́ wọn kò ní dáhùn sí.

(87) But èníyàn tí ó mọ̀, tí o tí ńse òótọ́ tí wọ́n bá sọ wípé ó sèké wọn kò kí ńfi agbára gbà gbọ́. Nitorípé a ti ní gbàgbọ́ sí olóotọ́ èníyàn, bẹ́ẹ̀ náa ni ti èníyàn bá ńse búburú tí a bá gbọ́ pé ó se rere a kò le fi agbára gbàá gbo.

(88) Tí mọ bá ńbá èníyàn ńrìn, mà mọ́ gbogbo ìwà rẹ̀, èyí tí ó lè ṣe àtí èyí tí ò kò lese. Tí ẹnìkan wá sọ fún mi pé ó ṣe kinní kan báyìí, níwọ̀n ìgbàtí ó jẹ́ pé mo ti mọ ìwà rẹ, tí o bá se pé o kò sé, èmi yí ò gbà ọ́ gbọ́ pé o kò sé, sùgbọ́n bí ìwà rẹ kò bá yé mi, tí ó nse sẹ́gẹsẹ̀gẹ, mà á sọ wípé èmi kò mọ ìwà rẹ pé èmi kò gbàgbọ́ pé o kò le sé.

(89) Mo gbà ó gbọ̀ nígbà tí mo rí ìwà rẹ, èyí tí o rí yẹn ni ó jù, mó ri dájúdájú. Mo gbà ó gbọ̀ sùgbọ́n èmi kò rí ǹkan náà, ṣugbọ́n èyí tí mo rí kedere yen ni ó dájú.

(90) A kò le gbà wọ́n sí èníyàn búrukú tàbí èníyàn rere nítorípé a kò bá wọ́n gbé. A kò sì mọ irú èníyàn tí wọ́n jẹ́ tẹ́lẹ̀.

(91) Ẹni tí kò bá ńgbọ́ fọ̀, óní wà búrukú ni. Eni tí ó bá ti ńgbọ fọ̀ oní wa rere ni. Ẹni rere ni ó ń sọ̀rọ̀ rere eni búrukú a máa sọ̀rọ̀ búrukú.

(92)   Tí a bá sọ pé ènìyàn nínú, tí ó bá sòrò létí rè kò le dé òdò
       ẹlòmíran kí ó lọ máa wíi. Èyí já sí wípé ó rí inú mú òrò síí. Ó sì le
       jásí wípé eni tí a fí ọ̀rọ̀ lọ tí o sì kó ènìyàn bí yío ti sé se tí ènìyàn
       se tí ó sì bọ́ ọ́ si. Ènìyàn tí ó fi ọ̀rọ̀ lọ̀ yẹn yío má sọ pé ènìyàn nínú
       ó se fi ọ̀rọ̀ lọ̀. Tí ó bá jẹ́ pé tí ìyá ni, ènìyàn nínú já sí wípé ó ní
       àjẹ́. Nípàtàkì tí a bá sọ wípé ènìyàn nínú, a gbà sí ọmọlúàbí. Pé
       kò kí ńfo ra. Ẹni tí ó bá ti gbọ́n tí ó mo ojú tí ó mò ra.

(93)   Èyí ni ǹkan tí ènìyàn kò se tí wọ́n sọ wípé ó se. A sọ wípé iró ni
       wọ́n pa.

(94)   À fi awọn kan ti ńpurọ́, ǹkan tí wọ́n kò mò tí wọ́n yío sọ wípé
       wọ́n mò o. Èyí jẹ́ òpùrọ́.

(95)   Ẹni tí kò bá fẹ́ jẹ eléké ǹkan tí wọ́n kò bá se lójú rẹ kò gbọdọ̀ sọ
       wípé òun gbàgbọ́. Kí ó tó sọ pé o gbà ó yè kí o ti ri ẹni tí o ti se rí
       lójú rẹ. Ǹkan tí ẹni bá ti rírí ni ó yẹ kí ó mò.

(96)   Wọ́n sọ ìyẹn fún ni bóyá ó purọ́ tàbí kò purọ́ o kò mò. Bóyá
       lágbájá yí bóyá kò le purọ́ ni o fi gbà. Tí nbá ní pé olóòtọ́ ènìyàn
       ni ẹ̀ màá gbàgbọ́ pé òótọ́ ni o se. Sùgbọ́n bí o bá ti ńse eléké
       ẹnikẹ́ni kò ní gbàgbọ́, wọ́n á sọ pé ó purọ́ wọn kò ní dáhun si.

(97)   Ìwà sùúrù. Èyí ni olórí ìwà tí ó dára jù.

(98)   Àwọn ẹlòmíràn lè wà láàrín agbo títí kí wọ́n má sòrò. Ẹlòmíran
       wà tí ó lè má dìde ní ìgbà mẹ́ta mẹ́rin kí ó má sòrò a ní èmí sùúrù
       ju ara wa.

(99)   Ìgbésí ayé ènìyàn ní ayé yí òun ni ó ńseé. Òun ló ńyàn ìgbésí ayé
       eni láî kù ǹkankan, tí ó bá fẹ́ ṣe ìjòngbòn tí gbogbo èèyàn wulè
       ńbẹ́ ó, tí inú rẹ kò bá gbà dandan ni iwọ yío ṣe ǹkan ná sùgbọ́n ó
       lè jẹ kí ènìyàn tí ó wà ní ibẹ̀ lọ. Sùgbọ́n tí ó bá ti lọ fi ìnú rẹ rò pé,
       o dúpé pé o rí ẹnití ó tù ẹ́ nínú, sé o rí tí inú bá bí ènìyàn tí inú
       eni kò bá gbà sùgbọ́n kí ńwọ́n má fi ọwọ́ ra orí ènìyàn ǹjẹ́ ó lè
       gbọ́ bí inú kò bá gbọ́n. Inú ni yío ti gbọ́ wá. Ìgbà náà ni a ó máa
       sọ wípé orí rẹ̀ dára pé kò sí ǹkan tí ńwọ́n lè sọ sí kí ó má gbà.

(100) Bẹ́ẹni, tí ó bá ti rí ènìyàn rere bá rìn. Ti ńgbà ní ìyọ̀njú. Ó lè yí
       padà a jẹ wípé ó ronúpìwàdà. Sùgbọn iyípadà wà, nítorí wọ́n rí
       ẹni tí ó jẹ wípé ó fẹ́ má se búburú tí ó bá jẹ wípé tí wọ́n bá rí ẹni
       sòrò fun yío yí padà. Tí kò ní sée mọ́. Èyí ní pé ó ronúpìwàdà.

(101) Èṣù ló máa ń múnú bíni bẹ́ẹ yen. Sé o rí mọ̀ wípé inú máa ńdédé
       ńbí ni láî jẹ pé ẹní sẹ̀ ó? Tí ó jẹ́ pé inú ńdédé ńbí. Tí èmí Èṣù yẹn

bá ti kúro lókàn ẹni, a sọ wípé òun kò mọ ìgbà tí irú ìyen se òun, pé òun ti ronú jù lòní yìí.

(102) Ẹ̀mí Èṣù ni. Tí kò bá ńse ẹ̀mí Èṣù a wá la ohun tí ó ń bí ẹ nínú. "Lágbájá bàyí ǹkan tí ó ṣe pẹ̀lú mi ni èyí." Tí wọ́n bá bẹ̀ẹ̀ à gbébẹ̀. A sọ́ ìdí nkan tí ó jẹ́ kí inú máa bí ẹ yẹn.

(103) Ṣé o mọ̀ wípé ẹlòmíràn wà tí ó jẹ́ wípé ó gbóná. Tí wọ́n bá bá siré yíò sọ́ di ìjà, ibẹ̀ ni ẹlòmíràn wà tí wọ́n máá bá se eré tí kò ní bínú. Wọ́n á sọ̀ wípé inú ènìyen má dára o. Ẹlòmíràn á rorò ìwà náà nì yẹn. Ìwà pín sí orísirísi ọ̀nà.

(104) Èrò rẹ̀ ni ó dópin. Ó ti ro ọ̀rọ̀ náa dé òpin.

(105) Wọ́n rí eni tí kò jalè rí tí ó padà wá ńjalè. Tí ó bá ń kégbe olè. Ó di olè nìyẹn.

(106) Tí ó bá jẹ́ wípé o ti ńse ǹkan dáadáa tẹ́lẹ̀tẹ́lẹ̀ ni a lè gbà wípé ǹkankan ni ó dé si tí ó fí se èyí. Ó lè jẹ́ wípé àwọn àjẹ tàbí àlùjànún burúkú ni ó tìí se èyí.

(107) Kò sí eni tí ó ńsisé tí kò nímọ irú isé tí òun ńse. Ẹni tí ó bá pa ènìyàn yíò mọ̀ wípé òun se búburú. Ẹni tí ó bá pa iró mò ènìyàn ńmọ̀ ǹkan tí òun ńse. Àwọn olè yẹn mọ̀ wípé ǹkan tí wọ́n ńse kò dára.

(108) Nwọn kò ní gbàgbọ́, nwọ́n lè ní kí ó lọ ronú si.

(109) Tí ọ̀rọ̀ rẹ̀ bá ti já sí iró, wọ́n á jẹ́ é ní ìyà pé ó mọ̀ọ́mọ̀ se bẹ́ẹ̀ [ni].

(110) Tí wọ́n bá ti rí tí ó ńṣe kò yẹ kí wọ́n gbà pé kò mọ̀.

(111) Tí ọ̀rọ̀ rẹ̀ bá ti já sí iró, wọ́n á jẹ́ é ní ìyà pé ó mọ̀ọ́mọ̀ se bẹ́ẹ̀ [ni].

(112) Wọ́n kò ní gbàgbọ́, wọ́n lè ní kì ó lọ̀ ronú síi. Bóyá ó mu ẹmu ni tàbí orí rẹ̀ ni ó dàrú. Tí orí rẹ̀ kò bá dàrú tí ẹmu kò sì pàá wọ́n á gbà wípé ó puró.

(113) Tí wọ́n bá ti rí tí ó ńṣe kò yẹ kí wọ́n gbà pé kò mọ̀.

(114) Ẹni rere yen ni ńwọn lè bá wí ni òhun ẹnu kí nwọ́n sì kìní ílò̀. Sùgbọ́n eni búrukú yẹn nwọn yíò fi ìyà tí ó pọ̀ jéẹ́.

(115) Ẹnití ó ti ńse ǹkan láti ilẹ̀ wá ni a ó jẹ ní ìyà jù. Sùgbọ́n eni tí kò kí ńse èyí tẹ́lẹ̀ nwọn yío kíi ní ìlò̀ lásán ni. Tàbí kí ìyà ̀rẹ kéré sí ti ẹni búburú yẹn.

(116) Ìjìyà ẹni búrukú yẹn yíò pọ̀ lọ́pọ̀ tí ẹni rere yen, nítorípé wọ́n ti mọ̀ọ́ sí ènìyàn búburú tẹ́lẹ̀. Nwọ́n sì máa sọ wípé aráyé ni ó bá ẹni rere yen jẹ́ kí nwọ́n ma se fi ìyà jẹ́ wípé kò kí ńse bẹ́ẹ.

(117) Ẹlòmíràn a má hu ìwà rere lójú tí ó bá ti dé àárín agbo, ṣúgbọ́n tí ó bá ti dé ẹ̀hìn, ǹkan búrukú ni yíò ṣe. Àwọn tí ó bá ti rí àsírí rẹ̀ yíò má sọ wípé ó wulẹ̀ ńsọ̀rọ̀ tó dára ni, sùgbọ́n ènìyàn búrukú ni.

(118) Àwọn tí à pè ní ọ̀tá yí lè jẹ́ ènìyàn rere lọ́wọ́ ẹlòmíràn.

(119) Wọ́n rí eni tí ó ńse eni rere lọ́wọ́ enìkan tí ó jẹ́ eni búburú lọ́wọ́ enìkejì.

(120) Ọlọ́run kò ńse ọ̀tá ènìyàn. Àwa ènìyàn ni ọ̀tá ara wa. . . . Ọ̀tá kan kò sí láti ọ̀dọ̀ Ọlọ́run wá, àwọn ènìyàn ni ọ̀tá ara nwọn.

(121) Ẹnikẹ́ni lè jẹ́ ọ̀tá. . . .Ènìyàn lásán ńaà lé jẹ̀ ọ̀tá ènìyàn míràn.

(122) Tí irú ọ̀tá bẹ́ẹ̀ bá wà nwọ́n lè yọ ènìyàn lénu ni fún ìgbà díẹ̀ kí Olúwa rẹ̀ sì bọ́ lọ́wọ́ wọn tí òun ńaà kò bá ní ìpín nínú ìwà búburú.

(123) Àwọn ènìyàn nà ni ọ̀tá ara nwọn, ọ̀tá kan kan kò sí ní ibì kan jù àwọn tí ó bá ńbínú enìkejì nwọn. Ọlọ́run sọ wípé kí á féràn ara wa. Àwọn tí kò bá fẹ́ran ènìyàn ni ọ̀tá ẹni.

(124) Kò ní enìkan lọ́tọ̀ sùgbọ́n àwọn tí ó bá ti ńbínún sí àwọn tí ó bá ńse dáada ó lè jẹ́ wípé iṣẹ́ rè dára ju ti ènìyàn lọ ni.

(125) Ẹnikẹ́ni tí ó bá ti ńhùwà ibi, tàbí ìwà búburú, sí enìkejì rẹ̀, tí ó ṣe ní ìkà òun ni ọ̀tá ẹni. Ọ̀tá enikẹ́ni ni kò kí ńse ọ̀tá enìkan. Ó lè máa ṣe ọ̀tá bí àádọ̀ta ènìyàn, nítorípé inú ènìyàn búburú kò kí ńdùn sí ènìyàn ní ìgbàkígbà, kò kí ín dunú sí ẹrankò ní dunú sí ènìyàn. Ẹni búburú ọ̀tá ẹni ni.

(126) Àwọn ńaà tí yàn láti ṣe búburú láti ọrun.

(127) Ẹlòmíran yío mọ̀ ó mọ̀ ṣe ǹkan búrukú, àwọn yí jẹ́ ìkà. Tí ńwọ́n kò kí ńwo ojú ènìyàn. Àwon nwọ̀nyí ti yan búburú yí láti ọrun wá.

(128) Ènìyàn ni àwọn nwọ̀nyí, àwọn tí nwọ́n ńṣe ìkà, tí ó ń gbèrò búburú sí àwọn ènìyàn, tí kò fẹ́ kí ènìyàn ṣe àǹfàní.

(129) Ọlọ́run ti dá abanijẹ tẹ́lẹ̀tẹ́lẹ̀ ńaà ní ìbẹ̀rẹ̀ ayé.

(130) Ewu wà nílé ara ẹni. Nwọ́n ní "ẹ̀hìnkùlé ni ọ̀tá wà, ilé ni aseni ńgbé." Nwọ́n tún ńsọ wípé, "ènìyàn ni ọ̀tá ara rẹ̀," "ará ilé eni ni

òta eni. . . . Ilé ni ǹkan ti ṣe ènìyàn jù. Lọ́rọ̀kan, tí o bá gbọ́ pé
ǹkan ṣẹlẹ̀ sí ènìyàn kan níbì kan, ilé ni nwọ́n ti báa lọ.

(131) Òun fún ara rẹ̀ lè mọ́ wípé òunse ọ̀tá ènìyàn tí ènìyàn bá mọ ọ̀tá
ara rẹ̀ yíò má sá fún un. Àwọn ọ̀tá sókùnkùn, ènìyàn ni nwọ́n
ṣugbọ́n nwón yàtọ̀.

(132) Kí á tó mọ́ ọ̀tá eni a ó rí iṣẹ́ tí ọ́ńse.

(133) Tí o kò bá ṣe ènìyàn, tí ó bá ńbí inú rẹ, tí ó ńro òrọ eni ní búburú
tí ó bá pa irọ́ mọ́ ènìyàn. Tí ó bá ńbínú sí ènìyàn tí ó sí ńse ìkà sí
ènìyàn ọ̀tá wa ni.

(134) Tí ènìyàn kò bá dè ibi tí ó fẹ́ dé tí ó bá mò wípé iṣẹ́ ọ̀tá ni. Yíò rí
àmìn tí yíò rí, tí ẹ bá ńse iṣẹ́ tí iṣẹ́ nà kò bá dára yíò mò wípé iṣẹ́
ọ̀tá ni. Tí ó lè fẹ́ ìyàwó ní ìta tí ẹlòmíràn gbàà lọ́wọ́ rẹ̀ yíò mò
wípé iṣẹ́ ọ̀tá ni. Ẹni tí ó bí ọmọ sí ilẹ̀ tí àjẹ pa ọmọ yen jẹ ó mọ̀
wípé iṣẹ́ ọ̀tá ni.

(135) Nwọ́n lè so wípé ọ̀tá ni ó tì, ńwọn sì le so wípé èrò inú rẹ̀,
ńmejèèjì ni nwọ́n lè sọ́.

(136) Díẹ̀ ènìyàn ló lè sọ wípé òun yàn búburú láti òde ọ̀run. Ṣúgbọ́n
yíò sọ wípé àwon aráyé ló ńbá òun jà.

(137) Kò sí ǹkankan tí ènìyàn ńṣe tí àwọn tí ó kù kò kí ńsọ wípé àwọn
aráyé ni ó tì ṣé.

(138) Kò sí èyí tí ó borí ènìyàn rere lọ. Ó dà bí aṣọ funfun tí a ńgba dúrà
wípé kí á má ṣe rí eni tí yío wá ta epo sí.

(139) Kò sí àwọn tí mo mò ju àwọn rere. Àwọn ǹwonyí jẹ́ ènìyàn tí ó
ńran ènìyàn lọ́wọ́ tí kò ńlépa ibi ní ìgbọ̀ kankan.

(140) Orísirísi èdá ni Ọlọrun dá, elòmíran wà tí ó jẹ́ wípé ó jẹ aláfọ̀ṣẹ tí
kò mọ̀ ara rẹ, ṣugbọ́n tí ó jẹ́ wípé Ọlọ́run ǹikan ni ó mọ̀.

(141) Orísirísi ènìyàn ni àwọn ǹwonyí, ènìyàn dúdú, ènìyàn pupa àti
àwọn tí ó mọ́ díẹ̀.

(142) . . . oní inú kan, náá nì . . .

(143) Ẹ̀mí ni ó máa ńjẹ́ kí ènìyàn ó hu ìwà rere. Òun nà ni ó sì ńmú kí
ènìyàn kí ó hu ìwà búburú.

(144) Ẹlòmíràn wà tí ó jẹ́ wípé ó ní ẹmí méjì àjẹ ní ẹ̀mí méjì, àwọn osó
ní ẹ̀mí méta, àwọn ọ̀jọ̀gbón ní ẹ̀mí mẹ́rin, àwọn tí ó bá jẹ́ wípé ó
ní ẹ̀mí méje ni àwọn ọgbólògbó àlùjànún gidi. Nwọ́n ní onímọ̀
nkan tí nwọ́n ńfi àwọn èmí nwọn yí se. Ṣé o mò wípé eniti ó bá ní

èmí méje yen lágbára ju àwọn tí ó bá ní èmí kan. Ó dàbí enití ó ńdánìkan ńsisẹ́ òun eni tí ó bá ní ọmọ ọ̀dọ̀ púpà.

(145) Orísirísi èmí ní ńbẹ, àwọn Awólọ́wọ̀ yen, èmí kan ni ó ńlo wọ̀n àti àwọn bẹ́ẹ̀bẹ́ẹ̀, àńgbọ́ pé èmí ẹlòmíràn pé méjì, à ńgbọ́ pé ó ju bẹ́ẹ̀ lo.

(146) Ènìyàn lè ní inú méjì tàbí mẹ́ta.

(147) Agbára ni, ènìyàn lè ní inú méjì tàbí mẹ́ta. . . . Ibi tí ó lo agbára tirẹ̀ sí nìyẹn.

(148) Ibi tí Ọlọ́run fún wa lágbára mọ yen, ibi tí ẹlẹ́dá fún ẹ lágbára dé nìyẹn. Òun nà ni ó mú àwọn tí ńwọ́n ní gbogbo rẹ̀ yen, sùgbọ́n ó tún mò ọkàn síti àwọn nwònyí. Ó jẹ́ kí ó lè sí ju ti àwọn tí ó kù. Tí ó mú kún tirẹ̀ ó sì ní ìlópo méjì. Gẹ́gẹ́bí aṣọ òmíràn á jẹ̀ ọ̀pá kan Náírà méjì òmíràn á sì jẹ́ iye tí ó jù yen lọ púpọ̀. A lè rí àwọn kan míràn bí kéké tí ó dára ju àwọn egbẹ́ rè tí ó tún wá, bẹ́ẹ̀ni tí àwọn yen ò lágbára jù ti àwọn tí ó kú lọ.

(149) Èrò ọkàn wọn ni, ọgbọ́n àti èrò ni wọ́n fí ṣe gbogbo ìyen.

(150) Èmi kò mò, sùgbọ́n awon tó gbón lè ṣé. Tí nwọ́n mọ́ èyí mọ ohun.

(151) Àwọn tí ó lè ṣe kìí pọ̀, nítorípé àwọn tí ó gbón dáadáa ló lèsé irú èyí.

(152) Tí òyìnbó nwọ́n ńfí tiwọn ńse agbára, ńwọn ńfi ńsisẹ́ ohun ìyanu. Ṣùgbọ́n ti àwa ènìyàn dúdú, dúdú ni. Inú wa dúdú, ẹni tí ó ní ǹkan sí ikùn tí ó fí lọ sí oko ọmọnìkejì tí ó lọ fi dàrú. Ibi tí ó lo agbára tirẹ̀ sí nìyẹn. Ẹnití ó ní òògùn tí ó fí ńfa òjò sé ó mọ́ wípé nígbàtí ńwọn rí òògùn tí wán ńfi mójò kí ó má ṣe rọ̀. Nwọ́n sì le rí òmíràn tí nwọ́n lè fi mọ̀ kí ó máa rọ̀. Òògùn wà láyé tí nwọ́n fi ṣe ọ̀gbìn yẹn láílái ni ó sì ti dáyé.

(153) Tí o bá ṣe wípé ó ṣeéṣe ni, àwọn dókítà ìbá máa mú ti ènìyàn dáda tí ó fẹ́ kú sí ti ẹlòmíran tí ìbá sì di ènìyàn dáradára. Mo rí wípé èyí lè yí ìwà eni tí ó ti ńwù ìwà tí kò dára padà sí bí enití ó ńse dáadáa ṣé ńlo èmí rè tẹ́lẹ̀tẹ́lẹ̀.

(154) Ènìyàn gidi ní nwọn, bí o ṣe wà yí bí èmi ṣe wà yí bẹ́ẹ̀ nà ni àjẹ́ ṣe wà.

(155) I: Ǹjẹ òótọ́ ni wípé ààrín àwọn obìrin ni àwọn àjẹ́ pọ̀ sí jù?

O: Kò kí ńse òótọ́, ǹkan tí ó jé kí á máa pe àjẹ ní ìyá àwọn
ọmọdé nìwònyí. Òun wípé ìbẹ̀ru ni, a kò le sọ wípé àbá
àwọn ọmọ wònyí, tí a bá ti sọ wípé iye ọmọdé a ó ti mọ̀ wípé
àjẹ́ ni à ńpè bẹ́ẹ̀. Orúkọ ni nwọ́n gbà jẹ́.

(156) Àwọn ni ó máa ń ní àjẹ́ jù.

(157) Bákan bákan ni, ṣùgbọ́n (booti) okùnrin lè pọ̀ jù.

(158) Ọlọ́run ni ibẹ̀ yen yẹ.

(159) Àjẹ ńse ènìyàn dáadáa, ki i ṣe gbogbo àjẹ ni ènìyàn búrukú, àjẹ́
dáadáa wà. Aì kí sọ̀rọ̀ wọn ní kò jé kí á mọ̀ sóòtọ́ bóyá àjẹ́ àwọn
bàyí dára, àjẹ́ àwọn bàyí kò dára. Kí èmi àti èyin máá jìjọ lọ
sọ́de bàyí, kí á jìjọ wọ irú aṣọ kan Ọlómọwé ni wọn yíò pè wá,
nítorípé wọ́n rí wa lójú, wọn kò ní mọ̀ pé èmi kò mọ̀ wé bẹ́ẹ̀ni
àjẹ́ rí.

(160) Kí í ṣe gbogbo wọn ni ènìyàn burúkú. A rí àjẹ́ tí . . . kò le se ìkà
kọọkan tí ó bí rí àwọn tí ó bá fẹ́ lọ se ìkà tí yíò kìlọ̀ fún pé ǹkan tí
ó fẹ́ ṣe yen kò dára. Tí ó lè sọ fún ènìyàn wípé "ará ibẹ̀ yen kò
dára ò, má mà gba ti ibẹ̀." Àjẹ́ dáadáa wà. Tí ó tilẹ̀ máa ńsọ fún
ènìyàn, ṣùgbọ́n wọ́n á ní kí wọ́n má dáa lóhùn pé ó fẹ́ kí wọ́n fún
òun ní ẹmu mu ni, ẹmu ló ńpa, bí ó ti lè je wípé ó ti lè fẹ́ sọ òótọ́
ni. Sùgbọ́n yíò jẹ́ wípé ẹnì yẹn fún ra rẹ̀ kò ní lọ́wọ́ tàárà. Nwọ́n rí
ẹni tí ó ní lọ́wọ́ tí ó níláárí, tí ó sì ní àjẹ́, tí kò sí ǹkankínkan tí ó lè
bá ǹkan rẹ̀ jẹ́, tí ó lè sọ bí ọ̀rọ̀ ṣe rí ní òòjọ́ gaaan kí ò dẹ̀ ṣe.

(161) Nwọ́n ńse ǹkan rere, ó dà bí ìgbà tí a ra àdá ní ọjà, ǹkan tí a fẹ́ fi
se ọ̀tọ̀ ṣùgbọ́n enìkan ló lọ ra tirẹ̀ tí o fi bẹ́ ènìyàn. Kò kí ńse ǹkan
búrukú ni nwọ́n ní kí nwọ́n máa fí àjẹ́ ṣe. Ogbọ́n kí àjẹ́ lè dára ni
ńwọn wà fún. Àwọn tí nwọ́n ńse àdá nwọn kò ṣé fún ènìyàn pípa.

(162) Bí ẹ̀mí àjẹ́ bá se rí ni ó se ńhùwà kò kí ńse gbogbo nwọn ni ó
ńsìkà. Òmíràn wà tí ó jẹ́ wípé yíò má fi tirẹ̀ tún ayé se.

(163) Àjẹ́ tí ó bá ti jẹ́ àjẹ́ tí ó dára tí kò ńse àjẹ ìkà, pé ó lè máa pomoje
tí ó lè má da ọmọ ẹlòmíràn. . . . Àjẹ́ rere ni kò kí ńse ibi kọ̀ọkan.
Rere ló wà fún.

(164) Nwọ́n rí èyí rere nínú nwọn, tí ó bá jẹ́ wípé rere ni ó mú lọ̀hún
rere ni yíò máa ṣe. Kò dẹ̀ ní máa bá àwọn yẹn se búburú.

(165) . . . àwọn àjẹ́ kan wà tí ó jẹ́ wípé kò kí ńhun iwà búburú.

(166) Èyí ni ìgbà míràn lásán.

(167) Àwọn nwọ̀nyí nà ni a lè pè nì ẹlẹ́mí méjì.

(168) Àjẹ́ ní ẹ̀mí méjì.

(169) Ẹlòmíràn wà tí ó jẹ́ wípé ó jẹ́ aláfọ̀se tí kò mọ ara rẹ̀. Ṣùgbón tí ó jẹ́ wípé Ọlọ́run nikan ni ó mọ̀, ẹlòmíràn wà tí kò mọ́ ara rẹ̀. Ṣùgbọ́n tí ènìyàn mò, tí ó jẹ́ wípé ọ̀rọ̀ tí ó bá ti ṣo ni yíò máa ṣe. Àwọn aráyé lè pè ní . . . àjẹ́. Ó lè se é ṣe kí ó jẹ́ wípé kò kín se èyí. Ẹlòmíràn lè jẹ́ àjẹ́ kí ó mo ara rẹ̀, tí ènìyàn yíò sì mọ̀ tí Ọlọ́run yíò sì mọ̀ọ́. Ẹlòmíràn wà tí ó jẹ́ wípé ohúnkóhun tí ó bá tí ńse ní yíò máa dáaa fún un tí nwọ́n á sì má wípé àjẹ́ ni. A má ńpe èyí ní eléjẹ̀ funfun ènìyàn. Ọlọ́run ni ó mọ́ èyí bí nwọ́n ṣé òògùn sí kò lee mú, bí òun nà ṣe òògùn kò le jẹ́.

(170) Èrò ọkàn, òun náà ni a ńpè ní ògínrínringinrìn. Gbogbo ǹkan kékèkéè bàyí nà ni àwọn ènìyàn ńrí tí wọ́n má a ńpe àwon kan ní àjẹ́. Wọ́n á sọ pé ọ̀rọ̀ rẹ̀ kọ̀ọkan kò kí ńsélẹ̀ (tà sé) wọ́n á sọ pé kò kín sọ kí ó má ṣe.

(171) Ẹlòmíràn tí kò ní àjẹ́, yíò ńmáa hù wà àjẹ́. Ọlọ́run á fún ẹlòmíràn ní òye láti mọ ǹkankan ju ẹni tí ó jẹ́ àjẹ́ gan. Ẹlòmíràn kò ní àjẹ́ sùgbọ́n tí ó ní ènìyàn tí ó ní àjẹ́ séhìn. Irú àwọnwònyí ni kò jẹ́ kí nwọ́n mọ́ àjẹ́ sọ́tọ̀. Àjẹ́ má nsọ fún ènìyàn ǹkan tí ó yẹ kí ènìyàn ṣe. Àwọn àjẹ́ má nsọ ǹkan abàmì fún ènìyàn, nwọ́n sì ún nfini sùn pé ènìyàn kan ṣe ò oun pé òun yíò bá ọ jà tí àjẹ́ bá sì fẹ́ bá ènìyàn jà tí ó bá fẹ́ ṣe yíò ní ọ̀nà ṣe èyí. . . . Ọgbọ́n wọn pọ̀jù, àwọn fún ra nwọn kò mọ́ ara wọn tán, nwọ́n sì ju ara nwọn.

(172) Dáadáa, bí a ti lágbára ju ra lọ náà ni ojú inú wa ti lágbára jura wa lọ̀. Méjì á wà nínú méjọ á wà ní ìta, á máa ń pè yẹn ní àjẹ́. Sé o rí wípé yíò lágbára ju ẹni tí ó ní méjì péré. Ẹlòmíràn wà tí ó lè jòkó sí bí yí, kí ó má mọ ǹkan tí wọ́n ńse ní ìsàlẹ̀ lòhún. Ẹlòmíràn lè lajú bàyí kó tí lọ, ojú inú rẹ ti rí ibi tí ó lọ sí. A máa ńpe yẹn ní 'àjẹ́'.

(173) Ènìyàn nà ní nwọ́n, sùgbọ́n nígbàtí nwọ́n nbọ́ láti ọ̀run ni nwọ́n ti sè mọ́ wọn. Àwọn fúnra nwọn ni ó yan èyí ní ọ̀run nítorípé ó wùn wọ́n.

(174) Àwọn òtá àti àwọn àjẹ́ ni o má a ńbí inú sí àwọn tí ó ńse dáadáa.

(175) . . . àjẹ́ sì ńse búburú.

(176) Nwọ́n ńse búburú nítorípé nwọ́n kò ní ìfé ènìyàn . . .

(177) Ọ̀tá àjẹ́ yàtò sí ọ̀tá gbogbo, bí o ṣe àjẹ́ tàbí bí o kò sè, ó lè ṣe àjẹ́ sí ẹ kí ènìyàn sáà tó ṣe ọ̀tá sí ẹlòmíràn yíò jẹ́ wípé ǹkan wà tí ó jẹ́ pé o fi séé.

(178) Àjẹ́ dà gẹ́gẹ́bí olè, kò sí eniti ó lè jalè kí ó lọ máa sọ kiri. Bẹ́ẹ̀ na ni àwọn àjẹ́ títí yíò fí kú kò ní sọ wípé òun ni àjẹ́.

(179) Bẹ́ẹ̀ni, nwọ́n rí ènìyàn tí ó se ojú bí enipé ó gọ̀ sùgbọ́n tí yíò jẹ́ àjẹ́.

(180) Nwọn kìí mọ oní inú kan yàtò sí àjẹ́.

(181) Èyí ńba iṣẹ́ eni jẹ́. Sùgbọ́n ènìyàn kò le rí nítorípé ó ń gba ohun òkùnkùn.

(182) Àjẹ́ . . . sòro mò, nítorí a kò mọ èrò ọkàn nwọn.

(183) Sùgbọ́n àjẹ́ ni ó mó èyí tí kò dára.

(184) Àmìn wà tí ó lè fi mò̀. . . . Yíò máa wu ìwà àjẹ́ yen. Tí mo bá ńsọ̀rọ̀ ǹkan tí ó se mí, wọn yíò máa sọ wípé kò sí tirè̀ níbè̀.

(185) Tí ó bá rí àwọn tí ó bá fẹ́ lọ se ìkà tí yíò kìlò fún pé ǹkan tí ó fẹ́ se yẹn kò dára. Tí ó lè sọ fún ènìyàn wípé "ará ibè̀ yen kò dára ò, má má gba ti ibè̀." Àjẹ́ dáadáa wà. Tí ó tilè̀ máa ńsọ fún ènìyàn. . . .

(186) Ẹlòmíràn kò ní àjẹ́ sùgbọ́n tí ó ní ènìyàn tí ó ní àjẹ́ séhìn. Irú àwọnwọ̀nyí ni kò jẹ́ kí nwọ́n mọ àjẹ́ sọ́tò. Àjẹ́ má nsọ fún ènìyàn ǹkan tí ó yẹ kí ènìyàn se. Àwọn àjẹ́ má nsọ ǹkan abàmì fún ènìyàn, ńwọn sì ún nfini nsùn pé ènìyàn kan ṣe òun pé òun yío bá ọ jà tí àjẹ́ bá sì fẹ́ bá ènìyàn jà tí ó bá fẹ́ sé yíò ní ọ̀nà se èyí. . . .

(187) . . . àwọ̀ wọn kò yàtò̀ sí ti ènìyàn míràn, wọn kò lójú mẹ́rin. Kò sí ibi tí a fí yàtò̀ . . .

(188) Àlùjànún ènìyàn, àlùjànún burú jura búburú àti dídára rè̀ wà. Búburú wà rere rè̀ wà.

(189) Bẹ́ẹ̀ni, tí ǹkan búburú bá ti wà nínú enití ó jẹ́ àlùjànún yẹn yío ṣe ǹkan búburú.

(190) Ènìyàn rere wà nínú wọn bẹ́ẹ̀ni ènìyàn búburú sì wà. Àwọn míràn wà tí ó jẹ́ wípé wọn a máa fi ti wọn ṣe iṣẹ́ rere kiri. Ẹlòmíràn a sì má ṣe búburú.

(191) Nwọ́n ǹsìkà, kò sí enití ó ní inú méjì tí kò le se ìkà. . . . Nwọ́n lè ṣe ìkà nwọ́n sì le sè̀ rere onínúkan lè sè ìkà ó sì le se rere.

(192) Kò sí nínú èyí tí wọ́n kò tí rí èyí burúkú. Gbogbo àwọn yen. Èyí tí ó dáda nínú wọn ni ó pọ̀ jù.

(193) Ẹni tí à ńpè ní àlùjànún ni ènì tí ó bá ti ńse iṣẹ ìyanu àti ǹkan abàmì. Tí a bá rí ǹkan tí ó jẹ́ abàmì ní àtijọ́ a máa ńsọ wípé iṣẹ́ àwọn àlùjànún ni.

(194) Àlùjànún jẹ́ enití ó ńsisẹ́ ìyanu. Sé o mò wípé ara àlùjànún ni èmi?

(195) Àlùjànún àwọn ni ó ńṣe ayé.

(196) Àwọn tí ó tún lè mó ǹkan jù ni àwọn tí à ńpè ní àlùjànún, tí àwọn ènìyàn yíò máa wá sì ọ̀dọ̀ rẹ̀ láti wá bééré wípé sé ọ̀nà tí mo fẹ́ lọ sí yíò dára?

(197) Nwọ́n rí aláfọ̀ṣẹ ènìyàn. Tí ó bá wí tí yìo ṣe béè. Irú ènìyàn bẹ́ẹ̀ kò sọ ǹkan tì a kò ní pèé. Nwọn a sọ pé àlùjànún ni . . . Á ti rí gbogbo rẹ̀ kí ó tó wá sọ́. Tí ó bá pè wọn kò ní máa jà ní ìyàn. Tí wọ́n bá sọ̀rọ̀ títí nwọ́n á sọ wípé ó di ìgbà tí ó bá dé, wọ́n kò ní fi orí ọ̀rọ̀ tì sí ibì kan à fi bí ó bá dé. Nwọ́n á fí sílẹ̀ dé. Tí ó bá déé yíò máa sọ pé òun ló máa mọn èyí tí ó tọ́ níbẹ̀.

(198) Ṣùgbọ́n àwọn tí ó bá ní àlùjanùn ní òògùn nwọn máa ńje ju ni àwọn àlùjànún tí àwọn ènìyàn yíò sọ wípé kò kí ńse apojú ni ó ńfi ńse ǹkan tí ó ńse.

(199) Kí ènìyàn tó mọ pè àlùjànún ni ènìyàn kan yío máa sọ ǹkan tí yìo sí maa ṣe. Tí a o sì mò pé abàmì ènìyàn ni.

(200) Nwọn á ní 'àlùjànún' mà lọkùnrin yẹn tàbí obìrin yẹn. Ẹ ẹ̀ wó bí ó se ńsọ̀rọ̀ àti bí ó se ńhu ìwà. Nwọ́n ní àlùjànún ènìyàn ni. Àlùjànún rere ni.

(201) Nwọ́n ńsìkà, kò sí ẹnití ó ní inú méjì tí kò le ṣe ìkà, tí àlùjànún bá gbọ́ ǹkan tàbí kí nwọ́n sọ wípé kí ó lọ ṣe ǹkan tó yóò yọ ènìyàn ní ibì kan tó sì kọ̀ láti ṣe e, ó ṣe ìkà nìyen. Nwọ́n lè ṣe ìkà nwọ́n sì le ṣe rere. Onínúkan lè ṣe ìkà ó sì le ṣe rere.

(202) Nwọ́n ńgbọ ohùn ni kò kí ńse wípé nwọ́n ríi, nwọ́n ńgbọ́ sétí ni.

(203) Áti rí ìdí ǹkan tí ó fẹ́ ṣe òhun sí, tí ó bá wá bèèrè ǹkan lọ́wọ́ mi bàyí, mo lè sọ wípé kí o lọ kí ẹ padà dé. Ọ̀rọ̀ yín yẹn ni mà gbé sí ọkan, tí nbá fí ńrírọn bó bá ti rí, tí o bá ṣe ǹkan tí kò ní bọ́ si ni, èmi á sọ kò le bọ́ si. Tí ó bá ṣe wípé á dára ni, mo lè sọ wípé kí o má lọ sí ibẹ̀ pé kò sí ǹkankan. A jẹ́ wípé mo ti fi ojú inú wòò, gẹ́gẹ́ bí àjẹ́ àti àlùjànún, òògùn tí mo bá ti dà ọwọ́ lé ó gbọ́dọ̀ dára ni.

(204) Ńwọn ńtójú ènìyàn, ńwọ́n máa ńse òògùn tí a fí ńtójú ènìyàn. Ònà kejì nwọ́n ńran ènìyàn lọ́wọ́ kúrò lọ́wọ́ òtá kí ó má báa rí àyè se ènìyàn lése.

(205) Babaláwo lè se kí ènìyàn mọ̀ nwọ́n. Òun fúnrarè lè ṣé kí ó má mọ̀. Ó sì le ṣe òògùn kí nwọ́n má wá sí ọ̀dọ̀ eni yen mọ́.

(206) Sé o rí babaláwo yẹn, iṣẹ́ ẹ̀dà wọn ni. Kò sí ibi tí nwọ́n lè lọ sí kí ọkàn wọn máa balè. Nkankan kí ǹkan kí ó lè wù kí ó se lè, nítorínà ọkàn nwọn balè̩, lọ́ọ̀rọ́ lọ̀sán àti lálẹ́, Ọlọ́run dá wọn fún atúǹlúṣe.

(207) Àwọn nà ni ọ̀tá, àwọn oólògùn, òtá àwọn emèrè ni.

(208) Ó se é se kí ó jẹ́ ìdánwò ayé, bí ó bá jẹ́ bẹ́ẹ̀ ni Ọlọ́run yíò yọ́, inú rere yẹn yíò gbe pàdé eni tí yíò yọ́.

(209) Léhìn ìgbàtí ó ti rí babaláwo tán, òun fún ra rẹ̀ tí fí ọwọ́ ara rẹ̀ yan ní ọ̀run wípé òun yíò jẹ ìyà díẹ̀ kí ó tó dára fún òun.

(210) Bí nwọ́n tilẹ̀ máa gbà nwọ́n yíò mún lọ sí ọ̀dọ̀ oniṣègùn tí yío rí bóyá ó ńse wèrè.

(211) Ó lè gbàá là dáadáa, yío ṣe òògùn fún.

(212) Bẹ́ẹ̀ni nwọ́n lè ṣé. Yío ṣe òògun rẹ̀ sí ara yí ò sì mú kí ó mú kí ó mọ̀.

(213) Ṣùgbọ́n bí ènìyàn bá nínú tí ó bá sì fi ẹ̀mí ara rẹ̀ fún òrìṣà, kí ó máa fi ṣé orísirísi ǹkan ìyanu àwọn ènìyàn yíò ma sọ wípé òrìṣa yẹn ni ó ńgbé. Bẹ́ẹ̀na ni àwọn ẹlòmíràn ńfi òògùn sí ti nwọn láti pa idán òrìṣà. Àwọn òrìṣà yí kò jẹ́ ǹkankan lâì jẹ́ wípé ènìyàn fi ǹkan míran tí.

(214) Èyí ni ó fá kí ènìyàn má lọ sí oko babaláwo, nwọn á sọ fún ẹlòmíràn kí ó se ètùtù kí ó bá le dára fún. Sé o rí, kí ó se mí nísisìyí kí nsì tí kò sílé pé lágbájá sẹ̀ mí, sùgbọ́n kí èmi bẹ̀ẹ́ padà wá bẹ̀ mí, ẹ̀bẹ̀ yí ni a lè túmọ̀ sí ètùtù, sé tí ó bá bẹ̀ mí tí mo bá gbọ́ èmi á dárí jín ín. Ìyen ni wípé ètùtù yen gbà. Sé tí ètùtù yí bá gbà èni ná yío bọ́ sí ọ̀nà ayé rẹ yío sì dára.

(215) Ènìyàn búrukú ni èyí. . . . Ènìyàn ni ó ńse àwọn ǹkan búrukú nwòn yí. Ìdí rẹ̀ ni èyí tí ẹmá fi má mú ẹbọ láti rí wípé àwọn wọ̀nyí fi òun sílẹ̀.

(216) Olóògùn ni babaláwo, tí ó ńjá ewé tí ó sì ńtójú àwọn ènìyàn tí ara nwọn kò bá yá.

(217) Babaláwo ǹkan náà ni ó lè gbà ènìyàn sílẹ̀ lọ́wọ́ àwọn irú ènìyàn bàyí nwọ́n yío ṣe òògun tí yío mú kí nwọ́n ma lágbára mọ́.

(218) Òògùn nà ni, nígbàtí ó ṣe òògun sí agolo tí ó bá sì ti sí yí o sì mún kí gbogbo ènìyàn má sín, tí ó sì bọ́ síta tí gbogbo nwọn ńlu ìlù tẹ̀le ó tì ó si ńjó. Àwọn ènìyàn yío máa rò wípé agbára òrìsà rẹ̀ yẹn ni ó pọ̀ tóbẹ́ẹ̀. Ò sì le máa fí òògùn bẹ̀ léraléra lójú kan tí yío ya gbogbo ènìyàn lẹ́nu tí nwọ́n á sì gba wípé agbára òrìsa ẹ yẹn ni ó fi nṣé èyí ǹkan tí ó ṣe ni wípé ó ti jẹ òògùn ara ẹ ti fíye dáadáa.

Kí ènìyan kan wà kí ó mọ kiníkan dájúdájú, ṣùgbọ́n kí ó wá máa sọ fún gbogbo ènìyàn wípé òun fẹ́ ṣe kíni yí láì sí Ọlọ́run lẹ́hìn òun, tí awọ́n tówà níbẹ̀ bá ní òògùn, nwọn yío ní ẹnití yío bá ènìyí jà tí ó fí jẹ wípé ǹkan tí ó fẹ́ ṣe yí kò ní bọ́ sí rárá. Nítorípé bí ó se mú ti Ọlọ́run kúrò yẹn inú ènìyàn kò ní dùn si.

Kò ní ní ẹ̀pọ́n. Ènìyàn lè ta aṣo funfun sí ìkángun yàárá kí ó sì wá ò kúta kan kí ó má ta epo si, ẹnití orí ńfọ́ tàbí ibà bá ńse ó lè wọ ibẹ̀ yẹn kí ó mú òògun fún wípé kí ó lọ fún ọmọ rẹ̀ wípé ìmọ́lẹ̀ rẹ̀ yí ti sọ wípé yío wá ní àláfíà pé ara á má yá. Kí ó sì fún òògùn fún gbogbo àwọn tí ó bá wá kí í kí ó sọ fún nwọ́n wípé ìmọ́lẹ e yẹn ti sọ wípé ara nwọn yío máa yá. Ẹniti ara rẹ̀ bá yá yíò máa sọ wípé ìmọ̀lẹ̀ yẹn lágbára púpọ̀.

Ní èdè àwọn ọlọ́mọ̀wé wọn má ńfi orúkọ dá ara wọn lólá, tí nwọ́n bá fi ènìyàn kan jẹ 'B.A.', ìwé ni ó ńjẹ bẹ́ẹ̀ wípé ó ní èyí tí ó jẹ́ wípé ó ka 'Primary Six' ọ̀mọ wé ni, enìtí nwọ́n tún ńpè ní 'Ph.D.' náà wà níbẹ̀ tí ó jẹ́ ọ̀mọ̀wé. Tí a bá ti sọ wípé òun fẹ́ lọ bọ Ògún yẹn òun fúnra rẹ yío ti mọ àìdáa kan tí òun se. Lóbìrin tí ó se àgbèrè tí kò lóyún, tí òun àti ọkọ è ńtan ara nwọn jé, tí nwọ́n dá ẹbọ fún pé Ògún ilé nwọn yẹn ní kí ó lọ bọ kí ó jẹ aláàfèhìntì è. Tí ó bá ti jẹ wípé Ògún ilé bàbáre ẹ ni òun gan nà yí pa ara è mọ́, ẹnití ó lọ sọ fún kí ó lọ bọ Ògún yí, yío pèé séhìn àwọn á kì ìlọ ọ̀pọ̀lọpọ̀ ǹkan lẹ́hìn tí ó bá se wípé óńse àgbère ni yío dáwọ́ rẹ̀ dúró. Tí ó bá se wípé iṣẹ́ tí ó ńse ní àsejù tí kò jẹ́ kí ó gbádun, nwọ́n lè sọ fún wípé kí ó má lọ sí oko fún ọjọ méje. Nwọ́n lè sọ wípé ìmọ́lẹ̀ sọ wípé kí ó má se dá òrùn kojá lónà oko fún ọjọ́ méje. Èyí yíò jẹ́ kí ó má se lọ sí oko fún ọjọ́ méje.

(219) Ó wà. Àwọn tí ó bá ńse òògùn burúkú sí ènìyàn.

(220) Dáadáa, nwọ́n rí ọ̀pọ̀lọpọ̀ tí yío máa ṣe òògùn tí yío fi má pa ènìyàn.

(221) Kí wọ́n tó máa pe ènìyàn ní olóògun burúkú wọn á ti rí ibi méjì tàbí méta tí ó ti fi òògùn se ènìyàn ní jàmbá. Kò sí enití óńkọ́

òógùn tí kò kí ńkọ́ òògùn burúkú. Nwọ́n á sọ wípé tí ó bá se bàyí, á jé wípé ẹrù páá. Ṣùgbọ́n bàyí ni ó se lè yíi padà kí àlàáfíà dé. Sùgbọ́n eni tí ó bá ti se èyí búrúkú yẹn ló mọ̀ jù, tí ó bá rí ẹ ó lè sọ wípé, "Bẹ́ẹ̀ ìwọ ni èyí burúkú yen bú lẹ́ẹ̀kan, tí ó ṣe àtijọ́ ni ìbá jẹ ìyà sí." Tí o bá lè wá ṣè èsìsì sọ pé kí ó bò ọ́ ní àsírí kò ní gbà ǹkankan lọ́wọ́ rẹ tí yio fi pa idán. O kò ní lè dúpé ore tí ó se fún o. Sùgbọ́n wàá wá ti mọ̀ wípé ènìyàn búrukú ni. Ìwọ ni yíò máa sọ fún àwọn tí ó kù pé ẹ sọ́ra yín fún ọkùnrin yẹn. Oun ní ńse ǹkan búrukú máa ńtẹ̀te bá. Nwọ́n á sọ wípé ènìyàn búruku ni. Wéré ló máa pa Olúwa rè dànùn. Wọn á ní ọ̀rọ̀ rere kò kí ńjáde lẹ́nu rẹ̀.

(222) Orísirísi babaláwo ni ó wà èyí tí ẹlòmíràn kò mọ̀ ó lè sọ wípé òun màń.

(223) Bẹ́ẹ̀ni, ó ní enití Ọlọ́run ńfún ní èbùn à ti ṣe iṣé babaláwo. Tí Ọlọ́run kò bá fún tí o bá já ewé kò le jé, ẹlòmíràn yíò ṣe òògùn títí òògun rè kò kí ńjé. Ibẹ̀ ni ẹlòmíràn yíò jé ẹyọ kan soso tí yíò sì jé bí ó ti pín nìyí Ọlọ́run ni ó pín fun. Kì ńse gbogbo ọwọ́ ènìyàn ni òògùn ti lè jé.

(224) Ó lè mọ̀ sùgbọ́n kò ní jẹ gégébí ẹnití Ọlọ́run fi rán láti òrun. Yíò máa gbàgbé enití Ọlọ́run bá ti fún, kò kí ńgbèègbé òkankan, tí ó bá ti ńsọ fún náà ni yíò ti máa yée. Sé ó rí wípé kò sí ìwé kò ní kọ sílẹ̀, enití Ọlọ́run kò fún gbogbo nwọ́n ni nwọ́n ńkọ sílẹ̀ kí nwọ́n má báa gbàgbé. Nwọ́n ńfí agbára kọ̀ ni kì sé pé nwọ́n fún wọ́n. Irú àwa bàyí a kì ńkọ́ sílẹ̀ tí a fi mọ̀ọ́sè.

(225) Nwọ́n rí babaláwo tí ó ńse àjé . . .

(226) Nwọ́n rí babaláwo tí ó ńse àjé àti àlùjànún. Ṣùgbọ́n àwọn ni wọ́n rí gbogbo ǹkan tí ó ńkojá lòsán àti lóru, àwọn ni nwọ́n jé ògbójú òògùn wọ́n ní ó sì ńjé jù.

(227) Nwọ́n rí, tí ó bá jé wípé àjé. . . . Yíò lágbára púpọ̀.

(228) Àwọn onínú méjì yẹn nà ni. Tí onínú kan bá máa se awo, ìwọ̀n ìba ǹkan tí ó ba tì mọ̀ yíò jé òótọ́.

(229) Ó wà àwọn ní òògùn yẹn dá lójú jù ogbọ́n nwọn di méjì, méta.

(230) Babálawo tí ó ní àjé, tí ó ní àlùjànún, tí ọ́ mọ òògùn wón (jé) jù. Ati rí ìdí ǹkan tí ó fẹ́ se òhùn sì, tí ó bá wá bèèrè ǹkan lọ́wọ́ mi bàyí, mo lè sọ wípé kí o lọ kí ẹ padà dé. Ọ̀rọ̀ yín yẹn ni mà gbé sí ọkàn, tí nbá fi ńríron bó bá ti rí, tí o bá se ǹkan tí kò ní bọ́ si ni, èmi á sọ kò le bọ́ si. Tí ó bá se wípé á dára ni, mo lè sọ wípé kí ó

má lọ sí ibẹ̀ pé kò sí ǹkankan. A jẹ́ wípé mo ti fi ojú inú wò, gẹ̀gẹ̀ bí àjẹ́ àti àlùjànún, òògùn tí mo bá ti dá ọwọ́ lé ó gbọ́dọ̀ dára ni.

(231) Bẹ́ẹ̀ni, ó wà. Tí gbogbo rẹ̀ á pé pérépéré sí ọwọ́ rẹ̀.

(232) Ó ju orísi kan, ènìyàn lè máa wun ni ní àwọ̀ ara tí ó bá wọ aṣọ tí yíò dára bí ẹni pé wọ́n ran mọ́ ẹ̀gbẹ̀ rẹ̀.

(233) Sùgbọ́n kí ó má ní ìwà. Àì ní ìwà yẹn yíò bá ẹwà rẹ̀ jẹ́. Bí ènìyàn ní ẹwà bí kò ní ìwà, ó bá jẹ nìyẹn. Nwọ́n á sọ wípé ó léwà sùgbọ́n kò ní ìwà. Ẹlòmíràn wà tí yíò rí jáujàu sùgbọ́n tí ó ní ìwà ènìyàn. Ìwà àti ẹwà ó papọ̀ dáradára.

(234) Orí ẹlòmíran yío máa ní lọ̀ngọ sùgbọ́n tí yíò jẹ́ ènìyàn dáradára. Nwọ́n dẹ̀ le rí orí ẹlòmíran tí ó dá rubutu sùgbọ́n tí yío jẹ́ ènìyàn burúkú. Orí inú rẹ̀ ni ó burú.

(235) Ẹlòmíran wà tí ó jẹ́ wípé ó dára lójú, sùgbọ́n tí ó jẹ́ wípé ènìyàn búruku ni. Bẹ́ẹ̀nà ni òmíràn tí ó jẹ́ wípé ojú rẹ̀ kò ní dára sùgbọ́n tí yíò jẹ́ wípé ènìyàn rere ni.

(236) Bí ènìyàn dáradára bí inú rẹ̀ kò bá dára á sà a ní ǹkan búrukú èyí tí ó rí yì inú rẹ̀ ni ó gbé báa.

(237) Ó dàbí isu tí a gbìn sínú ilẹ̀, tí inú rẹ̀ ti bàjẹ́ kí ẹ̀hìn rẹ̀ sì dára, á ti bàjẹ́ ní inú, bẹ́ẹ̀ni àwọn ènìyàn kan rí. A ó máa wò sùgbọ́n a kò mọ pé kò ní inú pè inú rẹ̀ kò dára.

(238) Bí ènìyàn bá léwà tí kò bá dára nínú, wọ́n á sọ wípé bí ó ti ní ẹwà tó kò ní ìwà. Èyí ni pé ó fi inú sòòkùn sí ènìyàn kò ní se òótọ́ sí ènìyàn.

(239) [Yorùbá not accessible.]

(240) Ènìyàn jẹ́ ǹkan míràn, ó lè se kí ó má ní ẹwà, kí ó sì ní ìwà. Nwọ́n á sọ pé ìwà rẹ ti dára jù.

(241) Tí ènìyàn bá ńlọ sí ilé ọkọ ní à tijọ́, a má ńsọ pé ìwà ni kí ó bá lọ kí ó má bá ẹwà lọ, a máa ńkọ orin kan "Isu ńmú àlùmọ̀n, ògẹ̀dẹ̀ nlatùmò, obìrin tí ó dára tí kò níwà asán ló jẹ́, tí ó ní ẹwà lójú tí kò ní ìwà asán ni."

(242) Ìwà yẹn ló ṣe pàtàkì òun ni olórí ẹwà lára ènìyàn. Ẹnití àwọ̀ rẹ̀ dára tí kò ní ìwà kò dára tán.

(243) Ìṣesí ènìyàn ni a má ńwò kí á tó rò pé ó níwà ní olórí ẹwà.

(244) Ìwà lẹwà, tí ènìyàn bá ní ìwà rere. Ìwà, ẹwà, ǹkan tí a lè túmọ rè sí.

(245) Tí ó bá jẹ́ pé ènìyàn ni tí kò wá níbẹ̀ ọ̀rọ̀ dàa ní a ó máa sọ pèlú rẹ̀, ẹwà náà nìyẹn. Gbogbo ǹkan tí ó bá ti lẹ́wà ọ̀rọ̀ rere ni a máa ńsọ pèlú rẹ̀.

(246) [Yorùbá not accessible]

(247) A ó mú ènìyàn kan tí ó dára, a wò pé orúkọ enìkan aó tún mú ẹnìkejì tí kò dára a ó fi ṣe àkàwé. A lè ṣe èyí pẹ̀lú ọ̀pẹ, oko, ọkùnrin tàbí obìnrin. Ẹwà jẹ́ pàtàkì.

(248) Bẹ́ẹ́nà ni ènìyàn, bí kò bá ní àdin wọn á sọ wípé kò dára.

(249) [Yorùbá not accessible]

(250) Èyí tí o bá ti ní ìwà jù.

(251) [Yorùbá not accessible]

(252) [Yorùbá not accessible]

(253) [Yorùbá not accessible]

(254) Àwọn igi bí ìrókò yẹn lè dúró bí mẹ́rin a lè kà wọ́n wé ara wọn pé èyí dára tàrà jù, bẹ́ẹ̀na ni ọ̀pé, ó dára jù àwọn tí ó kù. Bẹ́ẹ̀na ni àwọn igi míràn dán lára. . . . bẹ́ẹ̀na ni ẹranko, bí ó bá jẹ́ pé ewúrẹ ni, nwọ́n lè ṣe méfà kí méjì dára ńibẹ.

(255) Gbogbo ǹkan ni a má ń sọ ẹwà nwọn, òkúta, omi, wọ́n dára ju ara wọn lọ. Òmí míràn á see mu, ilé náa dára ju ara wọn lọ.

(256) Eranko náa lẹ́wà. Eran tí kò bá lè bá ènìyàn jà, wọn á wá sín nílé, á mú wá ilé nítorípé ó lẹ́ wà.

(257) [Yorùbá not accessible]

(258) [Yorùbá not accessible]

(259) Igi míràn wà tí ó lẹ́wa tí àwọn ènìyàn á sọ wípé igi ná lẹ́wà, ìbá se ǹkan tí ó sée gbìn sí àárín ìgboro ni, èyí jẹ́ wípé ó wúlò ó dára.

(260) [Yorùbá not accessible]

(261) [Yorùbá not accessible]

(262) [Yorùbá not accessible]

(263) [Yorùbá not accessible]

(264) Bí a bá dá oko isu, igi míran wà tí ó jẹ́ wípé a lè gé kí ó ní ẹ̀ka tí isu lè fà mó, ṣùgbọn òmíràn wà tí kò wúlò bẹ́ẹ̀, tí ó bá gée kò le dára, tí ó bá pa míran yíò dà lu ǹkan ọ̀gbìn kò dára nìyen.

(265) [Yorùbá not accessible]

(266) [Yorùbá not accessible]

(267) Bí wọ́n bá bá ènìyàn mo ilé, èyí tí ó bá dára yẹn ni a ńpè ní pé ó léwà. Bééna ni tí a ńse kí ti enìkan kò má ní igbò, ṣùgbọ́n kí ǹkan kún fún igbó wọ́n á sọ pé èyí tí kò ní igbó ni wọ́n á sọ wípé ó ní ẹwà.

(268) Ẹwà wà nínú oko tí à ńse. Ó wà nínú isu ó jẹ́ wípé ó léwà. Isu míràn wà tí ó se e jẹ́ bẹ́ẹ̀ni tí a lè fi gún iyán. Isu yẹn dára nìyen gbogbo ènìyàn yíò fẹ́ gbìn.

(269) Ẹwà ni a rí lára rẹ̀, 'table' yí tó jẹ́ orísi mẹ́rin tàbí mẹ́fa, èyí tí ó wà ní ibẹ̀ yẹn ó léwà ju elèyí lọ, èyí à wò 'color' (kọ́lọ̀) rẹ̀ ó mú kí ó wù wá jù èyí lo. Irú bàtà yí bàyí, tí ńwọ́n bá sọ pé kí o mú ìkan níbẹ̀ èwo ni o máa mú—ẹwà se pàtàkì.

(270) [Yorùbá not accessible]

(271) Tí wọ́n bá se èyí, tí ó bá dára jù, tàbí kí ó ní ìjàlójú jù èyí lo. Tí wọ́n bá 'polish' rẹ̀ dáradára.

(272) [Yorùbá not accessible]

(273) [Yorùbá not accessible]

(274) Aṣọ míràn wà tí ó dára ó ní ìwà nìyen. Nínú àwọn ǹkan tí à ńlò òmíràn lè dára súgbọ́n kí ó má ní àlòtọ́ wón á sọ pé ó léwà ṣùgbọ́n kò dára.

(275) Sé o mọ̀ wípé nwọ̀n máa ńse àwòrán. Àwòrán ènìyan tí á dàbí ènìyàn ṣùgbọ́n nwọn kò le se ẹ̀mí. . . . Ṣùgbọ́n fí ẹ̀mí yẹn jù wá lọ nítorínà a kò le ríi.

(276) Àlùjànún jẹ́ ẹni tí ó dàbí ẹni pé ó ńse iṣẹ́ ìyanu. Sé o mọ̀ wípé gbogbo ènìyàn kọ́ ni ó mọ ère gbígbẹ́ àwọn tí ó mọ̀ yen máa ńfi inú wòó bàyí gẹ́gẹ́ bí àlùjànún se rí.

(277) Tí ènìyàn bá se ǹkan tí kò bá dára á ó sọ pé kò dára, èyí tí ó bá dára á sọ pé ó ní ó ní ìmọ̀.

(278) [Yorùbá not accessible]

(279) [Yorùbá not accessible]

(280) A—Dídára ni pé bí a bá fi ǹkan sílẹ̀, kí ènìyàn bí mẹ̀wá sọ pé ó dára. Kí ènìyàn bí màrún sọ pé kò dára èyí tí ènìyàn mẹ̀wá yẹn ló lè mú òkè.

B—Ènìyàn mẹ̀wá lẹ̀ purọ́ kènìyàn kan sọ òótọ́.

A—Òótọ́ rẹ̀ kò ní jẹ́.

B—Òótọ́ ti kú lórílẹ̀ èdè wa. Olóòtọ́ ni à ńpè ní ènìyàn búburú.

(281) Èyí tí ojú rẹ̀ bá fani mọ́ra jù, nwọ́n lẹ̀ mú bí aṣọ mẹ́ta sílẹ̀, nwọ́n á
ní èwo ló dára jù, enìkínní á sọ pé èyí ló dára jù, kí èkejì sọ pé
òmíràn ló wù òun jù, èyí tí ojú bá sọ jù ló má ńwu ènìyàn jù ni
a sọ.

(282) [Yorùbá not accessible]

(283) [Yorùbá not accessible]

GLOSSARY
OF YORUBA TERMS

adáhunṣe: an alternative professional title, used by the *oníṣẹ̀g*

àdìn: behavior

àjẹ́: intellectual (conventionally rendered as "witch")

àlùjànún: genius (conventionally rendered as "evil spirit")

àṣẹ: power

àwọn aráyé: immoral persons

babaláwo: conventionally a person who performs *Ifá* divinati

dá/dára: good

dájú: certainty

eléke: a liar

èmí: the self

ènìyàn: person

ènìyàn burúkú: a bad person

ènìyàn rere: a good person

èrí ọkan: the faculty of judgment, including conscience

èrò ọkòn: thought

Èṣù: a deity associated with chance and coincidence

ẹwà: beauty

gbà: to agree or to accept

gbàgbọ́: to "believe"

gbọ́: to hear or to understand

gbọ́fọ̀: to listen

hùwà: to behave

Ifá: an intricate and extensive literary corpus that also provides a basis for divination

ìgbàgbọ́: "belief"

ìmọ̀: "knowledge"

inú: the self

ìpín: destiny

ìṣesí: behavior

ìwà: character

iyè inú: self-consciousness

mọ̀: to "know"

mọ̀ómọ̀: intentional, deliberate

nwádi: getting to the bottom of the matter

ọgbọ́n: wisdom or understanding

ògínrínrínginrìn: insight

ojú inú: insight

ọkàn: heart and/or mind

Olódùmarè/Ọlọ́run: the supreme deity

olóòtọ́ ènìyàn: truthful person

ọmọ aráyé: immoral persons

ọmọlúàbí: person with good moral character

oníṣègùn: masters of medicine, herbalists, "traditional" doctors

òògùn: medicine

òótọ́: true, truth

ọpọlọ: brain and/or intellect

orí inú: destiny

òrìṣà: deity

ó ṣe é ṣe/kò ṣe é ṣe: possible/impossible

ọ̀tá: enemy

papọ̀: when persons who disagreed come to agree and their words therefore "come together"

puró: to lie

rí: to see

ronú: to think

ronúpìwàdà: to think deeply upon something and thereafter change one's behavior

ṣe: to do [something]

sọ̀rọ̀: to speak

sùúrù: patience

wúlò: useful

BIBLIOGRAPHY

(* indicates publications in which *KBW* or its antecedents are discussed)

Abimbola, 'Wande. 1971. "The Yoruba Concept of Human Personality." In *La Notion de personne en Afrique noire,* pp. 73–89. Paris: Centre National de la Recherche Scientifique.

———. 1975. *Sixteen Great Poems of Ifá.* Niamey, Niger: UNESCO.

———. 1976. *Ifá.* Oxford: Oxford University Press.

———. 1977. *Ifá Divination Poetry.* New York: NOK Publishers.

Abimbola, 'Wande, and Barry Hallen. 1993. "Secrecy and Objectivity in the Methodology and Literature of *Ifá* Divination." In *Secrecy: African Art That Conceals and Reveals,* ed. P. Nooter, pp. 213–21. New York: Museum for African Art, and Munich: Prestel.*

Abiodun, Rowland. 1983. "Identity and the Artistic Process in the Yoruba Aesthetic Concept of *Iwa.*" *Journal of Cultures and Ideas* 1, no. 1: 13–30.

———. 1987. "Verbal and Visual Metaphors: Mythic Allusions in Yoruba Ritualistic Art of *Ori.*" *Word and Image* 3, no. 3: 252–70.

———. 1990. "The Future of African Art Studies: An African Perspective." In *African Art Studies: The State of the Discipline,* pp. 63–89. Washington, D.C.: Smithsonian Institution Press.

———. 1994. "Introduction: An African (?) Art History: Promising Theoretical Approaches in Yoruba Studies." In *The Yoruba Artist: New Theoretical Perspectives on African Arts,* ed. R. Abiodun, H. Drewal, and J. Pemberton, pp. 37–47. Washington, D.C.: Smithsonian Institution Press.*

Abiodun, Rowland, Henry J. Drewal, and John Pemberton. 1994. *Yoruba Art and Aesthetics.* Zurich: Center for African Art and the Reitburg Museum.

Abraham, R. C. 1958. *Dictionary of Modern Yoruba.* London: University of London Press.

Abraham, W. E. 1962. *The Mind of Africa.* Chicago: University of Chicago Press.

Adams, Monni. 1989. "African Visual Arts from an Art Historical Perspective." *African Studies Review* 32, no. 2: 55–103.

Adepegba, C. O. 1983. "*Ara:* The Factor of Creativity in Yoruba Art." *Nigerian Field* 48: 53–66.

Adewale, S. A. 1988. *The Religion of the Yoruba: A Phenomenological Analysis.* Ibadan, Nigeria: Department of Religious Studies, University of Ibadan.

Albert, E. 1970. "African Conceptual Systems." In *The African Experience,* ed. J. Paden and E. Soja, pp. 99–107. Evanston: Northwestern University Press.

Allen, Norm, Jr., ed. 1991. *African-American Humanism: An Anthology.* Buffalo, N.Y.: Prometheus Books.

Allison, P. A. 1973. "Collecting Yoruba Art." *African Arts* 6, no. 4: 64–68.

Anderson, E. 1972. "The Concept of Justice and Morality among the Bakuta in the Congo-Brazzaville." *Ethnos* 37: 5–39.

Anyanwu, K. C. 1987. "The Idea of Art in African Thought." In *African Philosophy. Vol. 5: Contemporary Philosophy: A New Survey,* ed. G. Floistad, pp. 235–60. Dordrecht: Martinus Nijhoff Publishers, and Boston: Kluwer Academic Publishing.

Appiah, Kwame Anthony. 1992. *In My Father's House: Africa in the Philosophy of Culture.* Oxford: Oxford University Press.*

———. 1995a. "Why Africa? Why Art?" In *Africa: The Art of a Continent,* ed. Tom Phillips, pp. 21–26. Munich: Prestel.

———, ed. 1995b. *African Philosophy: Selected Readings.* Englewood Cliffs, N.J.: Prentice Hall.

Arenson, J. J. 1974. *Tradition and Change in Yoruba Art.* Sacramento, Calif.: E. B. Crocker Art Gallery.

Armstrong, D. 1973. *Belief, Truth, and Knowledge.* Cambridge: Cambridge University Press.

Armstrong, Robert P. 1971. *The Affecting Presence: An Essay in Humanistic Anthropology.* Urbana: University of Illinois Press.

Austin, J. L. 1961. *Philosophical Papers.* Oxford: Oxford University Press.

———. 1962a. *How to Do Things with Words.* Oxford: Oxford University Press.

———. 1962b. *Sense and Sensibilia.* Oxford: Oxford University Press.

Awolalu, J. O. 1970. "The Yoruba Philosophy of Life." *Presence Africaine* 73: 79–89.

———. 1979. *Yoruba Beliefs and Sacrificial Rites.* London: Longmans.

Ayoade, John A. A. 1984. "Time in Yoruba Thought." In *African Philosophy: An Introduction,* ed. Richard Wright, pp. 93–112. New York: University Press of America.

Banton, Michael, ed. 1966. *Anthropological Approaches to the Study of Religion.* London: Tavistock Publications.

Barber, Karin. 1991. *I Could Speak until Tomorrow: "Oríkì," Women, and the Past in a Yoruba Town.* Washington, D.C.: Smithsonian Institution Press.

———. 1994. "Polyvocality and the Individual Talent: Three Women *Oríkì* Singers in Okuku." In *The Yoruba Artist: New Theoretical Perspectives on African Arts,* ed. R. Abiodun, H. Drewal, and J. Pemberton, pp. 151–60. Washington, D.C.: Smithsonian Institution Press.

———. 1995. "African-Language Literature and Postcolonial Criticism." *Research in African Literatures* (Austin) 26, no. 4: 3–30.

———. 1999. "Quotation in the Constitution of Yoruba Oral Texts." *Research in African Literatures* 30, no. 2: 17–41.

———, ed. 1997. *Readings in African Popular Culture.* Bloomington: International African Institute and Indiana University Press.

Barber, Karin, and P. F. de Moraes Farias. 1989. *Discourse and Its Disguises: The Interpretation of African Oral Texts.* Birmingham University African Studies Series, No. 1. Birmingham: Centre of West African Studies.

Bascom, W. O. 1960. "Yoruba Concepts of the Soul." In *Men and Cultures: Selected Papers of the Fifth International Congress of Anthropology and Ethnological Sciences,* ed. Anthony F. C. Wallace, pp. 401–10. Philadelphia: University of Pennsylvania Press.

———. 1965. "Folklore and Literature in the African World." In *A Survey of Social Research,* ed. Robert A. Lystad, pp. 469–90. New York: Praeger.

———. 1969a. *Ifá Divination: Communication between Gods and Men in West Africa.* Bloomington: Indiana University Press.

———. 1969b. *The Yoruba of Southwestern Nigeria.* New York: Holt, Rinehart and Winston.

———. 1972. "Yoruba Religion and Morality." In *Religions (les) Africaines come source de valeurs de civilisation,* pp. 16–22. Paris: Presence Africaine.

———. 1973. "A Yoruba Master Carver: Duga of Meko." In *The Traditional Artist in African Societies,* ed. W. L. d'Azevedo. Bloomington: Indiana University Press.

———. 1980. *Sixteen Cowries: Yoruba Divination from Africa to the New World.* Bloomington: Indiana University Press.

Beattie, J. H. M. 1966a. *Other Cultures: Aims, Methods and Achievements in Social Anthropology.* London: Routledge and Kegan Paul.

———. 1966b. "Ritual and Social Change." *Man,* n.s., 1, no. 1: 60–74.

———. 1973. "Understanding Traditional African Religion: A Comment on Horton." *Second Order* 2, no. 2 (July): 3–11.

Bedu-Addo, J. T. 1983. "Sense-Experience and Recollection in Plato's *Meno.*" *American Journal of Philology* 104: 228–48.*

———. 1985. "On the Concept of Truth in Akan." In *Philosophy in Africa: Trends and Perspectives,* ed. P. Bodunrin, pp. 68–90. Ife, Nigeria: University of Ife Press.

Beidelman, T. O. 1986. *Moral Imagination in Kaguru Modes of Thought.* Bloomington: Indiana University Press.

Bell, Richard H. 1989. "Narrative in African Philosophy." *Philosophy* 64 (July): 363–79.

———. 1997. "Understanding African Philosophy from a Non-African Point of View: An Exercise in Cross-cultural Philosophy." In *Postcolonial African Philosophy,* ed. E. Eze, pp. 197–220. Cambridge, Mass.: Blackwell.

Bello, A. G. A. 1988. "Review of *Knowledge, Belief and Witchcraft.*" *Journal of African Philosophy and Studies* (Lagos, Nigeria) 1, nos. 1–2: 93–98.

Ben-Amos, Paula. 1989. "African Visual Arts from a Social Perspective." *African Studies Review* 32, no. 2: 1–53.*

Bewaji, J. T. 1994. "Truth and Ethics in African Thought: A Reply to Emmanuel Eze." *Quest* 8, no. 1 (June): 76–89.

Biebuyck, Daniel. 1973. *Lega Culture: Art, Initiation and Moral Philosophy among a Central African People.* Berkeley: University of California Press.

Bird, C. S., and I. Karp, eds. 1980. *Explorations in African Systems of Thought.* Bloomington: Indiana University Press.

Blier, Suzanne. 1988. "Word about Words about Icons: Iconologology and the Study of African Art." *Art Journal* 47 (summer): 75–87.

———. 1990. "African Art Studies at the Crossroads: An American Perspective." In *African Art Studies: The State of the Discipline,* pp. 91–107. Washington, D.C.: Smithsonian Institution Press.

———. 1995. "Enduring Myths of African Art." In *Africa: The Art of a Continent,* ed. Tom Phillips, pp. 26–32. Munich: Prestel.

———. 1998. *The Royal Arts of Africa: The Majesty of Form.* New York: Harry N. Abrams.

Boas, Franz. 1927. *Primitive Art.* Cambridge, Mass.: Harvard University Press.

Boone, Sylvia. 1986. *Radiance from the Waters: Ideals of Feminine Beauty in Mende Art.* New Haven: Yale University Press.

Bodunrin, Peter. 1975. "'Theoretical Entities' and Scientific Explanation." *Second Order* 4, no. 1 (January): 56–65.

———. 1978. "Witchcraft, Magic and ESP: A Defense of Scientific and Philosophical Scepticism." *Second Order* 7, nos. 1–2 (January–July): 36–50. Reprinted in Mosley (1995), pp. 371–85.

———. 1979. "Belief, Truth and Knowledge." *Second Order* 8, nos. 1–2: 28–46.

———. 1981. "The Question of African Philosophy." *Philosophy* 56: 161–79. Reprinted in Wright (1984), pp. 1–24.*

———, ed. 1985. *Philosophy in Africa: Trends and Perspectives.* Ile-Ife, Nigeria: University of Ife Press.

Carroll, L. K. 1967. *Yoruba Religious Carving.* With a foreword by William Fagg. London: Geoffrey Chapman.

———. 1973. "Art in Wood." In *Sources of Yoruba History,* ed. S. O. Biobaku, pp. 165–75. Oxford: Clarendon Press.

Clifford, James. 1988. *The Predicament of Culture: Twentieth-Century Ethnography, Literature, and Art.* Cambridge, Mass.: Harvard University Press.

Clifford, James, and George Marcus. 1986. *Writing Culture: The Poetics and Politics of Ethnography.* Berkeley: University of California Press.

Cole, H. M. 1964. *Yoruba Sculpture: An Interpretation of Style through Form and Meaning.* M. A. thesis, Columbia University.

Concise Oxford Dictionary. 5th ed. Oxford: Clarendon Press.

Connelly, Frances. 1995. *The Sleep of Reason: Primitivism in Modern European Art and Aesthetics, 1725–1907.* University Park: Pennsylvania State University Press.

Cooper, David E. 1975. "Alternative Logic in 'Primitive Thought'." *Man,* n.s., 10: 238–56.

Cordwell, J. 1952. *Some Aesthetic Aspects of Yoruba and Benin Cultures.* Ph.D. dissertation, Department of Anthropology, Northwestern University.

———. 1953. "Naturalism and Stylization in Yoruba Art." *Magazine of Art* 46: 220–25.

Dalfovo, A. T. 1985. *Lugbara Proverbs.* Rome: Comboni Missionaries.

———, et al., eds. 1992. *African Metaphysical Heritage and Contemporary Life in the Foundations of Social Life.* Washington, D.C.: Council for Research and Values in Philosophy.

Davidson, Donald. 1974. "On the Very Idea of a Conceptual Scheme." *Proceedings and Addresses of the American Philosophical Association* 47: 5–20.

De Certeau, Michel. 1986. *Heterologies: Discourse on the Other.* Minneapolis: University of Minnesota Press.

Delano, I. O. 1969. *A Dictionary of Yoruba Monosyllabic Verbs.* 2 vols. University of Ife, Nigeria: Institute of African Studies.

Devitt, M., and K. Sterelny. 1987. *Language and Reality: An Introduction to the Philosophy of Language.* Cambridge, Mass.: MIT Press.

Dewey, John. 1929. *The Quest for Certainty.* New York: Minton, Balch. Reprint, New York: Putnam (Capricorn Books), 1960.

———. 1933. *How We Think: A Restatement of the Relation of Reflective Thinking to the Educative Process.* Boston: Heath. Reprint, New York: Holt, Rinehart and Winston, 1971.

———. 1934. *Art as Experience.* New York: Paragon Press. Reprint, New York: Perigee Books, 1980.

———. 1938. *Logic: The Theory of Inquiry.* New York: H. Holt and Company. Reprint, New York: Holt, Rinehart and Winston, 1966.

———. 1946. "Propositions, Warranted Assertibility and Truth." In *Problems of Men.* New York: Philosophical Library.

A Dictionary of the Yoruba Language (originally the Church Missionary Society [CMS] dictionary). Oxford: Oxford University Press, 1950.

Douglas, Mary. 1966. *Purity and Danger.* New York: Praeger.

Dretske, F. 1988. *Explaining Behavior.* Cambridge, Mass.: MIT Press.

Drewal, Henry J. 1980. *African Artistry: Technique and Aesthetics in Yoruba Sculpture.* Atlanta: High Museum of Art.

Drewal, Henry J., and Margaret Thompson Drewal. 1983. *Gèlèdé: Art and Female Power among the Yoruba.* Bloomington: Indiana University Press.

Drewal, Margaret Thompson. 1988. *Yoruba: Art in Life and Thought.* Victoria, Australia: African Research Institute, Latrobe University.

———. 1990. "African Art Studies Today." In *African Art Studies: The State of the Discipline,* pp. 29–62. Washington, D.C.: Smithsonian Institution Press.

———. 1992. *Yoruba Ritual: Performers, Play, Agency.* Bloomington: Indiana University Press.

Duerr, Hans Peter. 1985. *Dreamtime: Concerning the Boundary between Wilderness and Civilization.* Oxford: Blackwell.

Dummett, Michael. 1993. *The Seas of Language.* Oxford: Clarendon Press.

Dutoit, B. M. 1960. "Some Aspects of the Soul-Concept among the Bantu-Speaking Nguni Tribes of South Africa." *Authors Quarterly* 33: 134–42.

Dutton, Denis. 1995. "Mythologies of Tribal Art." *African Arts* 28, no. 3: 32–43.

Eades, J. S. 1980. *The Yoruba Today.* Cambridge: Cambridge University Press.

Eboussi Boulaga, Fabien. 1997. *La Crise du Muntu: authenticité Africaine et philosophie: essai.* Paris: Presence Africaine.

Ellis, A. B. 1974. *The Yoruba-Speaking Peoples of the Slave Coast of West Africa: Their Religion, Manners, Customs, Laws, Language, Etc.* London: Curzon Press, and Lagos: Pilgrim Books. Reprint, London: Chapman and Hall, 1894.

Emmet, Dorothy. 1972. "Haunted Universes." *Second Order* 1, no. 1 (January): 34–42.

———. 1986. "Foreword." In B. Hallen and J. Olubi Sodipo, *Knowledge, Belief, and Witchcraft,* pp. 1–4. London: Ethnographica Publishers. Reprint, Stanford: Stanford University Press, 1997.*

Encyclopedia of Philosophy. 1967. Edited by Paul Edwards. New York: Macmillan.

Encyclopedia of Philosophy. 1998. Edited by Edward Craig. London: Routledge.

English, Parker, and Nancy Steele Hamme. 1996. "Using Art History and Philosophy to Compare a Traditional and a Contemporary Form of African Moral Thought." *Journal of Social Philosophy* 27, no. 2 (fall): 204–33.

English, Parker, and Kibujjo Kalumba, eds. 1996. *African Philosophy: A Classical Approach.* Upper Saddle River, N.J.: Prentice Hall.*

Erassov, Boris. 1972. "Concepts of 'Cultural Personality' in the Ideologies of the Third World." *Diogenes* 78: 123–40.

Evans-Pritchard, E. E. 1937. *Witchcraft, Oracles and Magic among the Azande.* London: Oxford University Press.

Ewen, C. L'Estrange. 1929. *Witch Hunting and Witch Trials.* New York: Dial Press.

Eze, Emmanuel. 1993. "Truth and Ethics in African Thought." *Quest* 7, no. 1 (June): 4–19.

————, ed. 1997a. *African Philosophy: An Anthology.* Cambridge, Mass.: Blackwell.

————. 1997b. *Postcolonial African Philosophy: A Critical Reader.* Cambridge, Mass.: Blackwell.*

Fabian, Johannes. 1983. *Time and the Other: How Anthropology Makes Its Object.* New York: Columbia University Press.

————. 1986. *Language and Colonial Power.* Cambridge: Cambridge University Press.

————. 1990. "Presence and Representation: The Other and Anthropological Writing." *Critical Inquiry* 16, no. 4: 753–72.

————. 1995. "Ethnographic Misunderstanding and the Perils of Context." *American Anthropologist* 97, no. 1: 41–50.

————, ed. 1990. *History from Below: The Vocabulary of Elisabethville.* Philadelphia: J. Benjamins.

Fadipe, N. A. 1970. "Religion and Morals." *The Sociology of the Yoruba.* Ibadan: Ibadan University Press.

Fagg, W. B. 1951. "De l'art des Yoruba." *L'Art Negre (Presence Africaine,* vols. 10 and 11): 103–35.

Fagg, W. B., and John Pemberton III. 1982. *Yoruba Sculpture of West Africa.* New York: Alfred A. Knopf.

Falola, Toyin. 1998. *Yoruba Gurus: Indigenous Production of Knowledge in Africa.* Trenton, N.J.: Africa World Press.

Fann, K. T., ed. 1969. *Symposium on J. L. Austin.* New York: Humanities Press.

Fashina, Oladipo. 1989. "Frantz Fanon and the Ethical Justification of Anticolonial Violence." *Social Theory and Practice* 15, no. 2: 179–212.

Favret-Saada, Jeanne. 1980. *Deadly Words.* Cambridge: Cambridge University Press.

Fetzer, James, ed. 1991. *Epistemology and Cognition.* Boston: Kluwer Academic Publishers.

Feyerabend, Paul. 1975. *Against Method: Outline of an Anarchistic Theory of Knowledge.* London: New Left Books.

Finnegan, Ruth. 1969. "How to Do Things with Words: Performative Utterances among the Limba of Sierra Leone." *Man,* n.s., 4, no. 1: 537–51.

————. 1970. *Oral Literature in Africa.* London: Clarendon Press.

Firth, R. 1966. "Twins, Birds and Vegetables." *Man,* n.s., 1: 1–17.

Floistad, G., ed. 1987. *African Philosophy.* Contemporary Philosophy, A New Survey, vol. 5. Dordrecht: Martinius Nijhoff.

Forde, Daryll, ed. 1954. *African Worlds: Studies in the Cosmological Ideas and Social Values of African Peoples.* London: International African Institute and Oxford University Press.

Fortes, Meyer. 1973. "On the Concept of the Person among Tallensi." In *La Notion de personne en Afrique noire,* pp. 283–320. Paris: Centre National de la Recherche Scientifique.

Fortes, M., and G. Dieterlen, eds. 1965. *African Systems of Thought.* London: Oxford University Press.

Frake, Charles O. 1969. "The Ethnographic Study of Cognitive Systems." In *Cognitive Anthropology,* ed. Stephen Tyler, pp. 29–41. New York: Holt, Rinehart and Winston.

Gaba, Christian R. 1971. "An African People's (*Anlo*) Concept of the Soul." *Ghana Bulletin of Theology* (Legon) 3, no. 10: 1–8.

Gates, Henry Louis, Jr. 1988. "A Myth of Origins: Esu-Elegbara and the Signifying Monkey." In *The Signifying Monkey: A Theory of African-American Literary Criticism*, pp. 3–43. New York: Oxford University Press.

Gbadegesin, 'Segun. 1984. "Destiny, Personality and the Ultimate Reality of Human Existence: A Yoruba Perspective." *Ultimate Reality and Meaning: Interdisciplinary Studies in the Philosophy of Understanding* 7, no. 3: 173–88.*

———. 1991. *African Philosophy: Traditional Yoruba Philosophy and Contemporary African Realities.* New York: Peter Lang.

Geertz, Clifford. 1973. *The Interpretation of Cultures: Selected Essays.* New York: Basic Books.

Gelfand, Michael. 1965. "The Normal Man: A New Concept of Shona Philosophy." *Nada* 9: 78–93.

Gellner, Ernest. 1959. *Words and Things: An Examination of, and an Attack on, Linguistic Philosophy.* London: Routledge and Kegan Paul.

———. 1970. "Concepts and Society." In *Rationality,* ed. Bryan Wilson, pp. 18–49. Oxford: Blackwell.

———. 1974. *Legitimation of Belief.* Cambridge: Cambridge University Press.

Goldman, A. 1986. *Epistemology and Cognition.* Cambridge: Harvard University Press.

Goody, Jack. 1961. "Religion and Ritual: The Definitional Problem." *British Journal of Sociology* 12: 142–64.

———. 1967. "Review of *Conversations with Ogotemmeli* by M. Griaule." *American Anthropologist* 69, no. 2: 239–41.

———. 1977. "Intellectuals in Pre-literate Societies?" In *The Domestication of the Savage Mind,* pp. 19–35. Cambridge: Cambridge University Press.

———. 1987. *The Interface between the Written and the Oral.* New York: Cambridge University Press.

Goody, Jack, and I. Watt. 1963. "The Consequences of Literacy." In *Literacy in Traditional Societies,* ed. J. Goody, pp. 27–68. Cambridge: Cambridge University Press.

Gordon, Lewis. 1997. "African Philosophy's Search for Identity." In *Her Majesty's Other Children: Sketches of Racism from a Colonial Age,* pp. 139–48. Lanham, Md.: Rowman and Littlefield.

Griaule, Marcel. 1965. *Conversations with Ogotemmeli.* Oxford: Oxford University Press.

Gundaker, Grey, ed. 1998. *Keep Your Head to the Sky: Interpreting African American Home Ground.* Charlottesville: University Press of Virginia.

Gyekye, Kwame. 1975. "Philosophical Relevance of Akan Proverbs." *Second Order* 4, no. 2 (July): 45–53.

———. 1977. "Akan Language and the Materialist Thesis: A Short Essay on the Relation between Philosophy and Language." *Studies in Language* 1, no. 2: 227–34.

———. 1978. "The Akan Concept of a Person." *International Philosophical Quarterly* 18, no. 3: 277–87. Reprinted in Wright (1984), pp. 199–212.

———. 1981. "Philosophical Ideas of the Akans." *Second Order* 10, nos. 1–2 (January-July): 61–79.

———. 1987. *An Essay on African Philosophical Thought: The Akan Conceptual Scheme.* Cambridge: Cambridge University Press. Revised edition, 1995, Philadelphia: Temple University Press.

————. 1988. *The Unexamined Life: Philosophy and the African Experience.* Accra: Ghana Universities Press.

————. 1996. *African Cultural Values: An Introduction.* Philadelphia and Accra, Ghana: Sankofa Publishing Company.

————. 1997. *Tradition and Modernity: Philosophical Reflections on the African Experience.* New York: Oxford University Press.

Haack, Susan. 1993. *Evidence and Inquiry: Towards Reconstruction in Epistemology.* Oxford: Blackwell.*

Habermas, Jürgen. 1987. *The Philosophical Discourse of Modernity: Twelve Lectures.* Cambridge, Mass.: MIT Press.

Hackett, Rosalind. 1996. *Art and Religion in Africa.* New York: Cassell Publishing.

Hacking, Ian. 1973. *Why Does Language Matter to Philosophy?* Cambridge: Cambridge University Press.

Hallen, Barry. 1975. "A Philosopher's Approach to Traditional Culture." *Theoria to Theory* 9, no. 4: 259–72.*

————. 1976. "Phenomenology and the Exposition of African Traditional Thought." *Second Order* 5, no. 2 (July): 45–65. Reprinted in Sumner (1980), pp. 56–80.

————. 1977. "Robin Horton on Critical Philosophy and Traditional Thought." *Second Order* 6, no. 1 (January): 81–92.*

————. 1979. "The [African] Art Historian as Conceptual Analyst." *Journal of Aesthetics and Art Criticism* 37, no. 3: 303–13.*

————. 1981. "The Open Texture of Oral Tradition." *Theoria to Theory* 14, no. 3: 327–32.*

————. 1995a. "Indeterminacy, Ethnophilosophy, Linguistic Philosophy, African Philosophy." *Philosophy* 70, no. 273 (July): 377–93.*

————. 1995b. "'My Mercedes Has Four Legs!' 'Traditional' as an Attribute of African Equestrian 'Culture.'" In *Horsemen of Africa: History, Iconography, Symbolism,* ed. Gigi Pezzoli, pp. 49–64. Milan: Centro Studi Archeologia Africana.*

————. 1995c. "Some Observations about Philosophy, Postmodernism, and Art in African Studies." *African Studies Review* 38, no. 1 (April): 69–80.*

————. 1996a. "Analytic Philosophy and Traditional Thought: A Critique of Robin Horton." In *African Philosophy: A Classical Approach,* ed. P. English and K. M. Kalumba, pp. 216–28. Upper Saddle River, N.J.: Prentice Hall.*

————. 1996b. "Does It Matter Whether Linguistic Philosophy Intersects Ethnophilosophy?" *APA (American Philosophical Association) Newsletter on Philosophy and International Cooperation, APA Newsletters* 96, no. 1 (fall): 136–40.*

————. 1997a. "African Meanings, Western Words." *African Studies Review* 40, no. 1 (April): 1–11.*

————. 1997b. "What's It Mean?: 'Analytic' African Philosophy." *Quest: Philosophical Discussions* 10, no. 2 (December): 67–77.*

————. 1998a. "Academic Philosophy and African Intellectual Liberation." *African Philosophy* 11, no. 2 (November): 93–97.*

————. 1998b. "Moral Epistemology: When Propositions Come Out of Mouths." *International Philosophical Quarterly* 38, no. 2 (June): 187–204.*

————. 2000. "Variations on a Theme: Ritual, Performance, Intellect." In *Insight and Artistry: A Cross-cultural Study of Art and Divination in Central and West Africa,* ed. John Pemberton. Washington, D. C.: Smithsonian Institution Press.

Hallen, Barry, and J. Olubi Sodipo. 1986. *Knowledge, Belief, and Witchcraft: Analytic Experiments in African Philosophy.* London: Ethnographica Publishers. Reprint, with a new foreword by W. V. O. Quine and a new afterword by Barry Hallen, Stanford: Stanford University Press, 1997.*

———. 1994. "The House of the '*Inú*': Keys to the Structure of a Yoruba Theory of the 'Self.'" *Quest: Philosophical Discussions* 8, no. 1: 3–23.*

Hallett, G. 1973. "The Theoretical Content of Language." *Gregorianum* 54, no. 2: 307–36.

Hallpike, C. R. 1979. *The Foundations of Primitive Thought.* Oxford: Oxford University Press.

Harris, Leonard, ed. 1999. *The Cultural Pragmatism of Alain Locke: A Reader on Value Theory, Aesthetics, Community, Culture, Race, and Education.* Lanham, Md.: Rowman and Littlefield.

Hart, W. A. 1972. "The Philosopher's Interest in African Thought: A Synopsis." *Second Order* 1, no. 1: 43–52.

Hegba, M. 1982. "Eloge de l'ethnophilosophie." *Presence Africaine* 123: 20–41.

Hobsbawm, Eric, and Terence Ranger, eds. 1983. *The Invention of Tradition.* Cambridge: Cambridge University Press, 1983.

Hollis, Martin. 1970. "The Limits of Irrationality." In *Rationality,* ed. Bryan Wilson, pp. 214–20. Oxford: Blackwell.

Hollis, Martin, and Steven Lukes, eds. 1982. *Rationality and Relativism.* Oxford: Blackwell.

Horton, Robin. 1960. "A Definition of Religion and Its Uses." *Journal of the Royal Anthropological Institute* 90: 201–226. Reprinted in Horton (1993), pp. 19–49.*

———. 1961. "Destiny and the Unconscious in West Africa." *Africa* 31, no. 2: 110–17.

———. 1963. "The Kalabari *Ekine* Society: A Borderland of Religion and Art." *Africa* 33, no. 2: 94–114.

———. 1965. *Kalabari Sculpture.* Lagos, Nigeria: Department of Antiquities, Federal Republic of Nigeria.

———. 1967. "African Traditional Thought and Western Science." *Africa* 37: 50–71 and 155–87. Reprinted in Horton (1993), pp. 197–258.

———. 1973. "Paradox and Explanation: A Reply to Mr. Skorupski, Parts I and II." *Philosophy of the Social Sciences* 3: 231–56 and 289–312. Reprinted in Horton (1993), pp. 259–300.

———. 1976. "Professor Winch on Safari." *European Journal of Sociology* 17: 157–80. Reprinted in Horton (1993), pp. 138–60.

———. 1978(?). "Traditional Thought and the Emerging African Philosophy Department: A Reply to Dr. Hallen" (unpublished manuscript).*

———. 1982. "Tradition and Modernity Revisited." In *Rationality and Relativism,* ed. M. Hollis and S. Lukes, pp. 201–60. Oxford: Blackwell. Reprinted in Horton (1993), pp. 301–46.*

———. 1983. "Social Psychologies: African and Western." An essay accompanying Meyer Fortes's *Oedipus and Job in West African Religion,* pp. 41–82. Cambridge: Cambridge University Press.*

———. 1993. *Patterns of Thought in Africa and the West: Essays on Magic, Religion and Science.* Cambridge: Cambridge University Press.*

Horton, Robin, and Ruth Finnegan, eds. 1973. *Modes of Thought.* London: Faber and Faber.

Hountondji, Paulin. 1974. "The Myth of Spontaneous Philosophy." *Consequence* 1 (January-June): 11–38.

———. 1983. *African Philosophy: Myth and Reality.* Bloomington: Indiana University Press.

———. 1985. "The Pitfalls of Being Different." *Diogenes* 131 (fall): 46–56.

———. 1990. "Scientific Dependence in Africa Today." *Research in African Literatures* 21, no. 3: 5–15.

———. 1995. "Producing Knowledge in Africa Today." *African Studies Review* 38, no. 3: 1–10.

———. 1996. "Intellectual Responsibility: Implications for Thought and Action Today." *Proceedings and Addresses of the American Philosophical Association* 70, no. 2 (November): 77–92.

Idoniboye, D. E. 1973. "The Concept of 'Spirit' in African Metaphysics." *Second Order* 2, no. 1: 83–89.

Idowu, E. Bolaji. 1962. *Olódùmarè: God in Yoruba Belief.* London: Longman.

Ikenda-Metuh, Ememie. 1982. "Religious Concepts in West African Cosmogonies." *Journal of Religion in Africa* 13, no. 1.

Ikuenobe, Polycarp. 1997. "The Parochial Universalist Conception of 'Philosophy' and 'African Philosophy.'" *Philosophy East and West* 47, no. 2 (April): 189–210.

Irele, Abiola. 1981. *The African Experience in Literature and Ideology.* London: Heinemann. Reprint, Bloomington: Indiana University Press, 1990.

———. 1983. "Introduction." In P. Hountondji, *African Philosophy: Myth and Reality,* pp. 7–30. London: Hutchinson.*

Jackson, M. 1989. *Paths toward a Clearing: Radical Empiricism and Ethnographic Inquiry.* Bloomington: Indiana University Press.*

Jahn, Janheinz. 1961. *Muntu: An Outline of the New African Culture.* New York: Grove Press.

Jameson, Fredric. 1988. *The Ideologies of Theory: Essays 1971–1986. Vol. 2: Syntax and History.* Minneapolis: University of Minnesota Press.

Jarvie, I. C., and J. Agassi. 1970. "The Problem of the Rationality of Magic." In *Rationality,* ed. Bryan Wilson, pp. 172–93. Oxford: Blackwell.

Jennings, Richard C. 1989. "Zande Logic and Western Logic." *British Journal for the Philosophy of Science* 40, no. 2 (June): 275–85.

Johnson, S. 1921. *The History of the Yorubas.* Edited by O. Johnson. London: Routledge.

Kagame, Alexis. 1956. *La Philosophie Bantou-Rwandaise de l'être.* 8 vols. Brussels: Académie Royale des Sciences Coloniales, n.s. 12, no. 1.

Kasfir, Sidney Littlefield. 1984. "One Tribe, One Style? Paradigms in the Historiography of African Art." *History in Africa* 11: 163–93.

———. 1992. "African Art and Authenticity: A Text with a Shadow." *African Arts* 25, no. 2: 40–53. (For an informative and wide disciplinary variety of responses to this issue, and for Kasfir's final comments and responses to them all, see the two "Dialogue" pieces in *African Arts* 25, no. 3: 14–32 and no. 4: 18–30 and 100–103.)

Kayode, J., and A. Adelowo. 1985. "Nigerian Religions." In *Nigerian History and Culture,* ed. Richard Olaniyan. New York: Longman.

Keita, Lancinay. 1977–78. "African Philosophical Systems: A Rational Reconstruction." *Philosophical Forum* 9: 169–89.

———. 1985. "Contemporary African Philosophy: The Search for a Method." *Diogenes* 130 (summer): 105–27.

———. 1993. "Jennings and Zande Logic: A Note." *British Journal for the Philosophy of Science* 44: 151–56.

Kinyongo, J. 1982. "La Philosophie africaine et son histoire." *Etudes Philosophiques* 4: 407–18.

Kirk, Robert. 1986. *Translation Determined.* Oxford: Clarendon Press.

Kirk-Green, Anthony H. 1974. *Mutumin Kirkil: The Concept of the Good Man in Hausa.* Bloomington: African Studies Program, Indiana University.

Knappert, Jan. 1970. "Social and Moral Concepts in Swahili Islamic Literature." *Africa* 40: 125–36.

Koran: The Holy Qur-an. 1962. Text, translation, and commentary by Abdullah Yusuf Ali. Lahore, Pakistan: Ashraf.

Kwame, Safro, ed. 1996. *Readings in African Philosophy: An Akan Collection.* New York: University Press of America.

Laitin, David. 1977. *Politics, Language, and Thought.* Chicago: University of Chicago Press.

———. 1986. *Hegemony and Culture: Politics and Religious Change among the Yoruba.* Chicago: University of Chicago Press.*

Laslett, Peter. 1970. "The Face to Face Society." In *Philosophy, Politics and Society,* ed. P. Laslett, pp. 157–84. Oxford: Blackwell.

Lawal, B. 1974. "Some Aspects of Yoruba Aesthetics." *British Journal of Aesthetics* 143, no. 3: 239–49.

———. 1985. "*Ori:* The Significance of the Head in Yoruba Sculpture." *Journal of Anthropological Research* 41, no. 1: 91–103.

———. 1996. *The Gèlèdé Spectacle: Art, Gender, and Social Harmony in an African Culture.* Seattle: University of Washington Press.

Lawson, E. Thomas, and Robert N. McCauley. 1990. *Rethinking Religion: Connecting Cognition and Culture.* Cambridge: Cambridge University Press.

Lawuyi, Olatunde. 1988. "The Tortoise and the Snail: Animal Identities and Ethical Issues Concerning Political Behavior among the Yoruba of Nigeria." *Second Order,* n.s., 1, no. 2: 29–40.

Legesse, Asmaron. 1973. "Postscript: An Essay in Protest Anthropology." In *Gada: Three Approaches to the Study of African Society,* pp. 272–91. New York: Free Press.

Le Page, R. B., and A. Tabouret-Keller. 1985. *Acts of Identity: Creole-Bases Approaches to Language and Ethnicity.* Cambridge: Cambridge University Press.

Lewis, Ioan. 1973. *The Anthropologist's Muse.* Inaugural Lecture. London: University of London.

Lienhardt, Godfrey. 1967. "Modes of Thought." In *The Institutions of Primitive Society,* ed. E. E. Evans-Pritchard, pp. 95–107. Oxford: Blackwell.

Lord, Albert. 1960. *The Singer of Tales.* Cambridge, Mass.: Atheneum.

Lucas, J. Olumide. 1948. *The Religion of the Yorubas.* New York: Macmillan.

Lukes, Steven. 1970. "Some Problems about Rationality." In *Rationality,* ed. Bryan Wilson, pp. 194–213. Oxford: Blackwell.

———. 1973. "On the Social Determination of Truth." In *Modes of Thought,* ed. R. Horton and R. Finnegan, pp. 230–48. London: Faber and Faber.

MacIntyre, Alasdair. 1967. *A Short History of Ethics.* New York: Macmillan.

———. 1970. "Is Understanding Religion Compatible with Believing?" In *Rationality,* ed. Bryan Wilson, pp. 112–30. Oxford: Blackwell.

Mair, Lucy. 1969. *Witchcraft.* London: Weidenfeld and Nicolson.

Makinde, M. Akin. 1984. "An African Concept of Human Personality: The Yoruba Example." *Ultimate Reality and Meaning* 7, no. 3: 189–200.

——. 1985. "A Philosophical Analysis of the Yoruba Concepts of *Orí* and Human Destiny." *International Studies in Philosophy* 17, no. 1: 53–69.

——. 1988a. "African Culture and Moral Systems: A Philosophical Study." *Second Order*, n.s., 1, no. 2 (July): 1–27.

——. 1988b. *African Philosophy, Culture, and Traditional Medicine.* Athens: Ohio University Center for International Studies.

Marcus, George, ed. 1992. *Rereading Cultural Anthropology.* Durham: Duke University Press.

Marcus, G., and F. Myers, eds. 1995. *The Traffic in Culture: Refiguring Art and Anthropology.* Berkeley: University of California Press.

Marwick, M. G. 1973. "How Real Is the Charmed Circle in African and Western Thought?" *Africa* 1, no. 1: 59–70.

Masolo, D. A. 1994. *African Philosophy in Search of Identity.* Bloomington: Indiana University Press.*

——. 1997. "African Philosophy and the Postcolonial: Some Misleading Abstractions about 'Identity.'" In *Postcolonial African Philosophy*, ed. E. Eze, pp. 283–300. Cambridge, Mass.: Blackwell.*

Mbiti, John S. 1970. *African Religions and Philosophies.* New York: Doubleday.

Metuge, W. M. 1972. "The African Concept of Man." *Pan-Africanist* (Evanston, Ill.) 4: 36–42.

Meyerowitz, Eva L. R. 1951. "Concepts of the Soul among the Akan of the Gold Coast." *Africa* 21, no. 1: 24–31.

Middleton, John. 1970. "The Concept of the Person among the Lugbara of Uganda." In *La Notion de personne en Afrique noire*, pp. 491–506. Paris: Centre National de la Recherche Scientifique.

Milner, G. B. 1969. "Siamese Twins, Birds and the Double Helix." *Man*, n.s., 4: 5–23.

Minkus, Helaine K. 1980. "The Concept of Spirit in Akwapim Akan Philosophy." *Africa* 50, no. 2: 182–92.

——. 1984. "Causal Theory in Akwapim Akan Philosophy." In *African Philosophy: An Introduction*, ed. R. Wright, pp. 113–48. Lanham, Md.: University Press of America.

Momoh, Campbell S. 1985. "African Philosophy . . . Does It Exist?" *Diogenes* 130 (summer): 73–104.*

——, ed. 1989. *The Substance of African Philosophy.* Auchi, Nigeria: African Philosophy Projects' Publications.*

Moser, P., and A. vander Nat, eds. 1995. *Human Knowledge: Classical and Contemporary Approaches.* 2d ed. Oxford: Oxford University Press.

Mosley, Albert, ed. 1995. *African Philosophy: Selected Readings.* Englewood Cliffs, N.J.: Prentice Hall.*

Mudimbe, V. Y. 1987. "Review of *Knowledge, Belief and Witchcraft.*" *Canadian Philosophical Reviews* 7, no. 5: 200–202.*

——. 1988. *The Invention of Africa: Gnosis, Philosophy, and the Order of Knowledge.* Bloomington: Indiana University Press.*

——. 1994a. *The Idea of Africa.* Bloomington: Indiana University Press, and London: James Curry.

——. 1994b. *Parables and Fables.* Madison: University of Wisconsin Press.

——, ed. 1992. *The Surreptitious Speech: Presence Africaine and the Politics of Otherness 1947–1982.* Chicago: University of Chicago Press.*

Mudimbe, V. Y., and K. Anthony Appiah. 1993. "The Impact of African Studies on Philosophy." In *Africa and the Disciplines: The Contributions of Research* *in Africa to the Social Sciences and Humanities,* ed. Robert H.Bates, V. Y. Mudimbe, and Jean O'Barr, pp. 113–38. Chicago: University of Chicago Press.*

Murungi, John. 1980. "Toward an African Conception of Time." *International Philosophical Quarterly* 20: 407–16.

Nagl-Docekal, Herta, and Franz Wimmer. 1992. *Postkoloniales Philosophieren: Afrika.* Vienna: R. Oldenbourg Verlag.

Needham, Rodney. 1972. *Belief, Language, and Experience.* Oxford: Blackwell.

Newton-Smith, W. 1982. "Relativism and the Possibility of Interpretation." In *Rationality and Relativism,* ed. M. Hollis and S. Lukes, pp. 106–22. Oxford: Blackwell.

Ngugi wà Thiong'o. 1985. "The Language of African Literature." *New Left Review* 150: 109–27.

———. 1986. *Decolonising the Mind: The Politics of Language in African Culture.* London: James Curry.

———. 1990. "English: A Language for the World?" *Yale Journal of Criticism* 4, no. 1: 283–93.

———. 1998. *Penpoints, Gunpoints, and Dreams: Towards a Critical Theory of the Arts and the State in Africa.* Oxford: Clarendon Press.

Nzegwu, Nkiru. 1985. "Are Western Aesthetic Theories Relevant for the Understanding of African Art?" In *The Reasons of Art,* ed. P. McCormick, pp. 173–77. Ottawa: University of Ottawa Press.

———. 1999. "The Concept of Modernity in Contemporary African Art." In *The African Diaspora: African Origins and the New World Self-fashionings,* ed. I. Okpewho, Carole Boyce Davis, and Ali Mazrui, pp. 391–427. Bloomington: Indiana University Press.

———, ed. 1998. *Issues in Contemporary African Art.* Binghamton, N.Y.: International Society for the Study of Africa.

———, ed. 1999. *Contemporary Textures: Multidimensionality in Nigerian Art.* Binghamton, N.Y.: International Society for the Study of Africa.

Ojo, G. J. Afolabi. 1966. "The Content of Yoruba Philosophy." In *Yoruba Culture,* pp. 193–235. Ife, Nigeria and London: University of Ife and University of London Press.

Ojuka, A. 1974. "African Thought and the Concept of Essence." *Thought and Practice* (Nairobi) 1, no. 1: 19–26.

Okafor, Fidelis. 1993. "Issues in African Philosophy Re-examined." *International Philosophical Quarterly* 33/1, no. 129 (March): 91–99.*

Oke, Moses. 1995. "Towards an African (Yoruba) Perspective on Empirical Knowledge: A Critique of Hallen and Sodipo." *International Philosophical Quarterly* 35/2, no. 138: (June): 205–16.*

Okeke, C. 1973. "African Concept of Time." *Cahiers Religions Africaines* 7, no. 14: 297–302.

Okolo, Chukwudum. 1989. "The African Person: A Cultural Definition." *Indian Philosophical Quarterly* 16, no. 1: 67–74.

Oladeji, 'Niyi. 1988. "Proverbs as Language Signposts in Yoruba Pragmatic Ethics." *Second Order,* n.s., 1, no. 2: 45–55.

Oladipo, Olusegun. 1992. "The Debate on African Philosophy: A Critical Survey." *Indian Philosophical Quarterly* 19, no. 1: 41–50.

———. 1998a. "Emerging Issues in African Philosophy." *International Philosophical Quarterly* 38/1, no. 149 (March): 67–75.*

———. 1998b. *The Idea of African Philosophy: A Critical Study of the Major Ori-*

entations in Contemporary African Philosophy. Revised edition. Ibadan, Nigeria: Hope Publications.

Oluwole, Sophie. 1978. "On the Existence of Witches." *Second Order* 7, nos. 1–2: 20–35. Reprinted in Mosley (1995), pp. 357–69.

——. 1984–85. "The Rational Basis of Yoruba Ethical Thinking." *Nigerian Journal of Philosophy* 4–5, nos. 1–2: 14–25.

Ong, W. J. 1982. *Orality and Literacy: The Technologizing of the Word.* London: Routledge.

Oruka, H. Odera. 1975. "The Fundamental Principles in the Question of 'African Philosophy,' I." *Second Order* 4, no. 1 (January): 44–55.

——. 1981. "Four Trends in African Philosophy." In *Philosophy in the Present Situation of Africa,* ed. Alwin Diemer, pp. 1–7. Weisbaden: Franz Steiner Verlag.

——. 1990a. "Cultural Fundamentals in Philosophy." *Quest: Philosophical Discussions* 4, no. 2: 20–37.

——. 1997. *Practical Philosophy: In Search of an Ethical Minimum.* Nairobi and Kampala: East African Educational Publishers.*

——, ed. 1990b. *Sage Philosophy: Indigenous Thinkers and the Modern Debate on African Philosophy.* Leiden: E. J. Brill.*

Oruka, H. Odera, and D. A. Masolo, eds. 1983. *Philosophy and Cultures.* Nairobi: Bookwise Publishers.

Osatuyi, O. L. 1985. "*ọfọ̀:* An African Issue in Philosophy." M. A. thesis, University of Ife, Nigeria.

Overing, J. 1987. "Translation as a Creative Process: The Power of the Name." In *Comparative Anthropology,* ed. L. Holy, pp. 70–87. Oxford: Basil Blackwell.

——, ed. 1985. *Reason and Morality.* London: Tavistock Publications.

Owomoyela, Oyekan. 1987. "Africa and the Imperative of Philosophy: A Skeptical Consideration." *African Studies Review* 30, no. 1: 79–100.*

——. 1997. "African Philosophy: The Conditions of Its Possibility." *SAPINA* (Society for African Philosophy in North America) *Bulletin* 10, no. 2: 119–44.

Oyewumi, Oyeronke. 1997. *The Invention of Women: Making an African Sense of Western Gender Discourses.* Minneapolis: University of Minnesota Press.

Parrinder, Geoffrey. 1970. *Witchcraft: European and African.* London: Faber and Faber.

P'Bitek, O. 1970. *African Religions in Western Scholarship.* Nairobi: East African Literature Bureau.

Pearce, Carol. 1992. "African Philosophy and the Sociological Thesis." *Philosophy of the Social Sciences* 22, no. 4 (December): 440–60.

Pecheux, Michel. 1982. *Language, Semantics and Ideology.* New York: St. Martin's Press.

Peek, Philip. 1994. "The Sounds of Silence: Cross-World Communication and the Auditory Arts in African Societies." *American Ethnologist* 21, no. 3: 474–94.

——, ed. 1991. *African Divination Systems: Ways of Knowing.* Bloomington: Indiana University Press.

Peel, J. D. Y. 1969. "Understanding Alien Belief-Systems." *British Journal of Sociology* 20: 69–84.

Pittman, John P., ed. 1997. *African-American Perspectives and Philosophical Traditions.* New York: Routledge.

Polanyi, Michael. 1958. *Personal Knowledge.* London: Routledge and Kegan Paul.

Popper, Karl. 1962. *Conjectures and Refutations: The Growth of Scientific Knowledge.* New York: Basic Books.

Pratt, Vernon. 1972. "Science and Traditional African Religion: A Discussion of Some of Robin Horton's Views." *Second Order* 1, no. 1: 7–20.

Price, H. H. 1969. *Belief.* London: George Allen & Unwin.

Price, Sally. 1989. *Primitive Art in Civilized Places.* Chicago: University of Chicago Press.

Quine, W. V. O. 1960. *Word and Object.* Cambridge, Mass.: MIT Press.

———. 1969. "A Symposium on Austin's Method, II." In *Symposium on J. L. Austin,* ed. K. T. Fann, pp. 86–90. London: Routledge and Kegan Paul.

———. 1970. "On the Reasons for Indeterminacy of Translation." *Journal of Philosophy* 68: 178–83.

———. 1976. "Linguistics and Philosophy." In *The Ways of Paradox and Other Essays,* pp. 56–58. Cambridge, Mass.: Harvard University Press.

———. 1987. "Indeterminacy of Translation Again." *Journal of Philosophy* 84, no. 1 (January): 5–10.

———. 1990a. "Phoneme's Long Shadow." In *Emics and Etics: The Insider/Outsider Debate,* ed. T. Headland, K. Pike, and M. Harris, pp. 164–67. Frontiers of Anthropology, vol. 7. Newbury Park, Calif.: Sage Publications.

———. 1990b. *The Pursuit of Truth.* Cambridge, Mass.: Harvard University Press.

Quine, W. V. O., and J. S. Ullian. 1970. *The Web of Belief.* New York: Random House.

Radin, Paul. 1927. *Primitive Man as Philosopher.* Foreword by John Dewey. New York: D. Appleton.

Ranger, T., and I. Kimambo, eds. 1972. *The Historical Study of African Religion.* London: Heinemann and Berkeley: University of California Press.

Ray, Benjamin. 1973. "Performative Utterances in African Rituals." *History of Religions* 13, no. 1 (Chicago): 16–35.

———. 1976. *African Religions: Symbol, Ritual, and Community.* Englewood Cliffs, N.J.: Prentice Hall.

Research in African Literatures. 1997. Vol. 28, no. 4 (winter).

Rhodes, Colin. 1994. *Primitivism and Modern Art.* World of Art Series. London: Thames and Hudson.

Richards, Audrey I. 1967. "African Systems of Thought: An Anglo-French Dialogue." *Man* 2, no. 2: 286–98.

Riesman, Paul. 1998. *Freedom in Fulani Social Life: An Introspective Ethnography.* Chicago: University of Chicago Press.

Rigby, Peter. 1992. "Practical Ideology and Ideological Practice: On African Episteme and Marxian Problematic—Ilparakuyo Maasai Transformations." In *The Surreptitious Speech: Presence Africaine and the Politics of Otherness 1947–1987,* ed. V. Y. Mudimbe, pp. 257–300. Chicago: University of Chicago Press.*

Rollins, P. 1967. "Solipsism." In *Encyclopedia of Philosophy,* pp. 487–91. London: Macmillan.

Rorty, Richard. 1991a. *Essays on Heidegger and Others.* Cambridge: Cambridge University Press.

———. 1991b. *Objectivity, Relativism, and Truth.* Cambridge: Cambridge University Press.

———, ed. 1967. *The Linguistic Turn.* Chicago: University of Chicago Press. Reprinted in 1992 with two "Retrospective Essays" by Rorty.

Ruch, E. A., and K. C. Anyanwu. 1981. *African Philosophy: An Introduction to the Main Philosophical Trends in Contemporary Africa.* Rome: Catholic Book Agency.

SAPINA (Society for African Philosophy in North America) *Bulletin Special Tenth Anniversary Issue: An African Practice of Philosophy.* 1997. Vol. 10, no. 2.*

Salemohamed, G. 1983. "African Philosophy." *Philosophy* 58: 535–38.

Schildkrout, Enid, and Curtis Keim. 1990. *African Reflections: Art from Northeastern Zaire.* Seattle: University of Washington Press and New York: American Museum of Natural History.

Serequeberhan, T. 1994. *The Hermeneutics of African Philosophy: Horizon and Discourse.* New York: Routledge.

———. 1999. *Our Heritage: The Past in the Present of African-American and African Existence.* Lanham, Md.: Rowman and Littlefield.

———, ed. 1991. *African Philosophy: The Essential Readings.* New York: Paragon House.

Shaw, Thomas M. 1994. *The Fulani Matrix of Beauty and Art in the Djolof Region of Senegal. Vol. 34: African Studies.* Lewiston, N.Y.: Edwin Mellen Press.

Shelton, Austin J. 1968. "Causality in African Thought: Igbo and Others." *Practical Anthropology* (Tarrytown, N.Y.) 15, no. 4: 157–69.

Silberbauer, George. 1991. "Ethics in Small-Scale Societies." In *A Companion to Ethics,* ed. Peter Singer, pp. 14–28. Cambridge: Blackwell.

Skorupski, J. 1967. *Symbol and Theory.* Cambridge: Cambridge University Press.

———. 1973. "Science and Traditional Religious Thought, Parts I–IV." *Philosophy of the Social Sciences* 3: 97–115 and 209–30.

Sodipo. J. O. 1973. "Notes on the Concept of Cause and Chance in Yoruba Traditional Thought." *Second Order* 2, no. 2: 12–20.*

———. 1983. "Philosophy, Science, Technology and Traditional African Thought." In *Philosophy and Cultures,* ed. H. O. Oruka, pp. 36–43. Nairobi: Bookwise.*

———. 1984. "Philosophy in Pre-colonial Africa." In *Teaching and Research in Philosophy: Africa,* pp. 73–80. Paris: UNESCO.*

Sogolo, G. S. 1990. "Options in African Philosophy." *Philosophy* 65: 39–52.

———. 1993. *Foundations of African Philosophy: A Definitive Analysis of Conceptual Issues in African Thought.* Ibadan, Nigeria: University of Ibadan Press.*

Soyinka, 'Wole. 1976. *Myth, Literature and the African World.* Cambridge: Cambridge University Press.

———. 1993. *Art, Dialogue and Outrage: Essays on Literature and Culture.* London: Methuen.

———. 1997. *The Burden of Memory and the Muse of Remission.* Oxford: Oxford University Press.

Stich, Steven. 1983. *From Folk Psychology to Cognitive Science.* Cambridge, Mass.: MIT Press.

———. 1987. "Review of *Knowledge, Belief and Witchcraft. Ethics* 98, no. 1 (October): 203.*

———. 1990. *The Fragmentation of Reason: Preface to a Pragmatic Theory of Cognitive Evaluation.* Cambridge, Mass.: MIT Press.*

———. 1996. *Deconstructing the Mind.* New York: Oxford University Press.

Stoller, Paul. 1997. *Sensuous Scholarship.* Philadelphia: University of Pennsylvania Press.

Strother, Zoe. 1998. *Inventing Masks.* Chicago: University of Chicago Press.

Summers, Montague. 1973. *The History of Witchcraft and Demonology.* London: Routledge and Kegan Paul.

Sumner, Claude. 1974. *Ethiopian Philosophy: Vol. 1: The Book of the Wise Philosophers; Vol. 2–3: The Treatise of Zara Yaeqob and of Walda Heywat; Vol. 4: The Life and Maxims of Skendes.* Addis Ababa: Central Printing Press (vol. 1); Addis Ababa: Commercial Printing Press (vols. 2–4).

———. 1985. *Classical Ethiopian Philosophy.* Addis Ababa: Commercial Printing Press.

———. 1986. *The Source of African Philosophy: The Ethiopian Philosophy of Man.* Stuttgart: F. Steiner Verlag.

———, ed. 1980. *African Philosophy.* Addis Ababa: Chamber Printing House and Addis Ababa University.*

Taiwo, Olufemi. 1993. "Colonialism and Its Aftermath: The Crisis of Knowledge Production." *Callaloo* 16, no. 4: 891–908.

———. 1996. *Legal Naturalism: A Marxist Theory of Law.* Ithaca: Cornell University Press.

Taiwo, O., and O. B. Lawuyi. n.d. "'Ìwà': Towards a Naturalistic Ethics" (unpublished paper).

Talbot, P. Amaury. 1932. *Tribes of the Niger Delta: Their Religions and Customs.* London: Sheldon Press.

———. 1969. *The Peoples of Southern Nigeria: A Sketch of Their History, Ethnology and Languages.* London: Frank Cass. Reprint, London: Oxford University Press and H. Milford, 1926.

Tambiah, Stanley J. 1990. *Magic, Science, Religion, and the Scope of Rationality.* Cambridge: Cambridge University Press.

Tarratt, J. 1977. "Time in Traditional African Thought." *Journal of Religion* (London) 7, no. 2: 117–26.

Tempels, Placide. 1959. *Bantu Philosophy.* Paris: Presence Africaine.

Thompson, Robert Farris. 1971. *Black Gods and Kings: Yoruba Art at UCLA.* Los Angeles: Museum and Laboratories of Ethnic Arts and Technology, University of California.

———. 1973. "Yoruba Artistic Criticism." In *The Traditional Artist in African Societies,* ed. W. L. d'Azevedo, pp. 19–61. Bloomington: Indiana University Press.

———. 1974. *African Art in Motion.* Los Angeles: University of California Press.

———. 1983. *Flash of the Spirit: African and Afro-American Art and Philosophy.* New York: Random House.

Towa, M. 1971. *Essai sur la problématique philosophique dans l'Afrique actuelle.* Yaounde: Cle.

Turner, Victor. 1967. *The Forest of Symbols.* Ithaca: Cornell University Press.

Tyler, Stephen A. 1969. "Introduction." In *Cognitive Anthropology,* ed. S. Tyler, pp. 1–23. New York: Holt, Rinehart and Winston.

———. 1986. "Post-modern Ethnography: From Document of the Occult to Occult Document." In *Writing Culture: The Poetics and Politics of Ethnography,* ed. James Clifford and George Marcus, pp. 123–39. Berkeley: University of California Press.

Udechukwu, Obiora. 1978. "Concept into Form: Religion and Aesthetics in African Art." *Kalu*: 86–94.

Urmsom, J. O. 1969. "A Symposium on Austin's Method II." In *Symposium on J. L. Austin,* ed. K. T. Fann, pp. 76–85. London: Routledge and Kegan Paul.

Uyanne, Frank. 1994. "Truth, Ethics and Divination in Igbo and Yoruba Traditions: A Reply to Emmanuel Eze." *Quest* 8, no. 1 (June): 90–96

Van Damme, Wilfried. 1987. *A Comparative Analysis Concerning Beauty and Ugliness in Sub-Saharan Africa.* Ghent: University of Ghent.

———. 1996. *Beauty in Context: Towards an Anthropological Approach in Aesthetics.* Leiden: E. J. Brill.

Vansina, Jan. 1984. *Art History in Africa: An Introduction to Method.* London: Longman.

Verger, Pierre Fatumbi. 1971. "La Notion de personne et ligne familiale chez les Yoruba." In *La Notion de personne en Afrique noire,* pp. 61–71. Paris: Centre National de la Recherche Scientifique.*

———. 1972. "Automatisme verbal et communication du savoir chez les Yoruba." *L'Homme* 12, no. 2: 5–46.

———. 1995. *"Ewé": The Use of Plants in Yoruba Society.* São Paulo: Odebrecht.

Vogel, Susan Mullin. 1979. "Baule and Yoruba Art Criticism: A Comparison." In *The Visual Arts,* ed. Justine Cordwell, pp. 309–25. The Hague: Mouton.

———. 1980. "Beauty in the Eyes of the Baule: Aesthetics and Cultural Values." *Working Papers in the Traditional Arts,* No. 6. Philadelphia: Institute for the Study of Human Issues.

———. 1988. "Introduction." In *Art/Artifact: Art in Anthropology Collections,* ed. Susan Vogel, pp. 11–17. New York: Center for African Art, and Munich: Prestel.

———. 1997. *Baule: African Art, Western Eyes.* New Haven: Yale University Press.

Warnock, G. J. 1969. "John Langshaw Austin: A Biographical Sketch." In *Symposium on J. L. Austin,* ed. K. T. Fann, pp. 3–21. London: Routledge and Kegan Paul.

Welsh-Asante, Kariamu, ed. 1994. *The African Aesthetic: Keeper of the Traditions.* Westport, Conn.: Praeger.

Werbner, Richard, ed. 1998. *Memory and the Postcolony: African Anthropology and the Critique of Power.* London: Zed Books.

Westcott, J. 1963. "Tradition and the Yoruba Artist." *Athene* 2, no. 1: 9–15.

Whorf, B. L. 1964. *Language, Thought and Reality: Selected Writings of Benjamin Lee Whorf.* Edited by J. B. Carroll. Cambridge, Mass.: MIT Press.

Willoughby, W. C. 1928. "Some Conclusions Concerning the Bantu Conception of the Soul." *Africa* 1, no. 3: 338–47.

Wilson, Bryan R., ed. 1974. *Rationality.* Oxford: Blackwell.

Winch, Peter. 1964. "Understanding a Primitive Society." *American Philosophical Quarterly* 1, no. 4 (October): 307–24. Reprinted in Wilson (1974), pp. 78–111.

Wingo, Ajume. 1998. "African Art and the Aesthetics of Hiding and Revealing." *British Journal of Aesthetics* 38, no. 3 (July): 251–64.

Wiredu, Kwasi. 1972. "On an African Orientation in Philosophy." *Second Order* 1, no. 2: 3–13.

———. 1976. "How Not to Compare African Thought with Western Thought." *Ch'Indaba* 2 (July–December): 4–8. Reprinted in Wright (1984), pp. 149–62; and in Mosley (1995), pp. 159–71.

———. 1980. *Philosophy and an African Culture.* Cambridge: Cambridge University Press.

———. 1983. "Morality and Religion in Akan Thought." In *Philosophy and Cul-*

tures, ed. H. Odera Oruka and D. Masolo, pp. 6–13. Nairobi, Kenya: Bookwise. Reprinted in Allen (1991), pp. 210–22.

———. 1985. "The Concept of Truth in the Akan Language." In *Philosophy in Africa: Trends and Perspectives,* ed. P. Bodunrin, pp. 43–54. Ife, Nigeria: University of Ife Press.

———. 1987. "The Concept of Mind with Particular Reference to the Language and Thought of the Akans." In *African Philosophy. Vol. 5: Contemporary Philosophy, A New Survey,* ed. G. Floistad, pp. 153–80. Dodrecht: Martinus Nijhoff Publishers, and Boston: Kluwer Academic Publishing.

———. 1991. "On Defining African Philosophy." In *African Philosophy: The Essential Readings,* ed. T. Serequeberhan, pp. 82–110. New York: Paragon. Reprinted in Nagl-Docekal and Wimmer (1992), pp. 40–62.*

———. 1992a. "Formulating Modern Thought in African Languages: Some Theoretical Considerations." In *The Surreptitious Speech: Presence Africaine and the Politics of Otherness 1947–1987,* ed. V. Y. Mudimbe, pp. 301–32. Chicago: University of Chicago Press.

———. 1992b. (a) "The Moral Foundations of African Culture" and (b) "The African Concept of Personhood." In *African-American Perspectives on Biomedical Ethics,* ed. H. E. Flack and E. D. Pellegrino. Washington, D.C.: Georgetown University Press.

———. 1992–93. "African Philosophical Tradition: A Case Study of the Akan." *Philosophical Forum* 24, nos. 1–3: 35–62.*

———. 1993. "Canons of Conceptualization." *The Monist* 76, no. 4 (October): 450–76.

———. 1995a. "Are There Cultural Universals?" *The Monist* 78, no. 1 (January): 52–64. (An earlier version of this paper was published in 1990 in *Quest: Philosophical Discussions* 4, no. 2: 5–19.)

———. 1995b. *Conceptual Decolonization in African Philosophy: Four Essays by Kwasi Wiredu.* Introduced and edited by Olusegun Oladipo. Ibadan, Nigeria: Hope Publications.

———. 1995c. "Custom and Morality: A Comparative Analysis of Some African and Western Conceptions of Morals." In *African Philosophy: Selected Readings,* ed. A. Mosley, pp. 389–406. Englewood Cliffs, N.J.: Prentice Hall.

———. 1995d. "Knowledge, Truth and Fallibility." In *The Concept of Knowledge,* ed. I. Kucuradi and R. S. Cohen, pp. 127–48. Boston: Kluwer Academic.

———. 1995e. "Metaphysics in Africa." In *A Companion to Metaphysics,* ed. J. Kim and E. Sosa, pp. 312–15. Oxford: Blackwell.

———. 1996a. *Cultural Universals and Particulars: An African Perspective.* Bloomington: Indiana University Press.*

———. 1996b. "Reply to English and Hamme." *Journal of Social Philosophy* 27, no. 2 (fall): 234–43.

———. 1996c. "Time and African Thought." In *Time and Temporality in Intercultural Perspectives,* ed. D. Tiemersma and A. F. Oosterling. Amsterdam: Rodopi.

———. 1997. "Democracy and Consensus in African Traditional Politics: A Plea for a Non-party Polity." In *Postcolonial African Philosophy,* ed. E. Eze, pp. 303–12. Cambridge, Mass.: Blackwell.

Wiredu, Kwasi, and Kwame Gyekye, eds. 1992. *Person and Community: Ghanaian Philosophical Studies, I.* New York: Council for Research in Values and Philosophy.

Wittgenstein, Ludwig. 1980. *Culture and Value.* Oxford: Blackwell.

Wright, Richard A., ed. 1984. *African Philosophy: An Introduction.* 3d ed. Lanham, Md.: University Press of America.

Yai, Olabiyi. 1977. "Theory and Practice in African Philosophy: The Poverty of Speculative Philosophy." *Second Order* 6, no. 2: 3–20.

———. 1989. "Issues in Oral Poetry: Criticism, Teaching and Translation." In *Discourse and Its Disguises: The Translation of African Oral Texts,* ed. K. Barber and P. F. de Moraes Farias, pp. 59–69. Birmingham University African Studies Series, No. 1. Birmingham: Centre of West African Studies.

———. 1994a. "In Praise of Metonymy: The Concepts of 'Tradition' and 'Creativity' in the Transmission of Yoruba Artistry over Time and Space." In *The Yoruba Artist: New Theoretical Perspectives on African Arts,* ed. R. Abiodun, H. Drewal, and J. Pemberton, pp. 107–15. Washington, D.C.: Smithsonian Institution Press.

———. 1994b. *Yoruba-English/English-Yoruba Concise Dictionary.* New York: Hippocrene Books.

Index

BARRY HALLEN
is a Fellow of the W. E. B. Du Bois Institute for Afro-American Research
at Harvard University and Professor of Philosophy at Morehouse
College. He is coauthor (with J. Olubi Sodipo) of *Knowledge, Belief,
and Witchcraft: Analytic Experiments in African Philosophy.*